GIFT OF

DON R. KENDALL

Elites and the Idea of Equality

A Comparison of Japan, Sweden, and the United States

Sidney Verba

and

Steven Kelman
Gary R. Orren
Ichiro Miyake
Joji Watanuki
Ikuo Kabashima
G. Donald Ferree, Jr.

Harvard University Press
Cambridge, Massachusetts, and London, England
1987

Library of Congress Cataloging in Publication Data

Verba, Sidney.
  Elites and the idea of equality.

  Bibliography: p.
  Includes index.
  1. Elite (Social sciences)—Japan. 2. Elite
(Social sciences)—Sweden. 3. Elite (Social
sciences)—United States. 4. Equality—Japan.
5. Equality—Sweden. 6. Equality—United States.
I. Title.
HN730.Z9E49 1987   305.5′2   87-7432
ISBN 0-674-24685-3 (alk. paper)

Acknowledgments

The research reported in this book spans three continents and numerous years. Many people and institutions in many places helped us in the long process. We are happy to begin by acknowledging that help.

In each of the participating nations one colleague was crucial in developing and implementing the survey on which this book is based. In Japan, we are grateful to Kiyoshi Shima of Musashi University; in Sweden, to Leif Lewin of the University of Uppsala; and in the United States, to Barry Sussman of the *Washington Post*.

A number of others aided in the conduct of the research. In Sweden, Siv Vedung provided research assistance and technical support. Sverker Gustavsson and Olof Petersson were generous with comments on the translation of the questionnaire into Swedish and on other matters. Officials of various Swedish organizations were helpful in arranging the cooperation of leaders in their sectors; these include Åke Bäckman of the Swedish Federation of Small Business; Gunnar Nilsson of the Swedish Federation of Labor; Åke Ortmark of Swedish Television; and Carl-Johan Westholm of the Swedish Federation of Employers. In Japan, we had the assistance of the following in arranging the survey of students: Juichi Aiba, Hiroya Fujisaki, Minoru Miyakawa, Michio Muramatsu, Tsuneji Ozawa, Yoshihiko Sato, Shizuo Senju, Kenjiro Suzuki, Susumu Takahashi, Kei Takiyama, and Mitsuru Uchida. In the United States, we benefited from the able research assistance of Michele Campbell, Michael Dawson, Matthew Dickinson, James Duane, Philip Guentert, Helen Milner, Stephen Shuff, Stuart Smith, and Lars-Gunnar Wigemark. Paul Cole assisted us in managing the coding of the Swedish data.

For financial support to conduct the research we are grateful to the Toyota Foundation, the Swedish National Bank's Tercentenary Fund, the Ford Foundation, and the *Washington Post*. The Toyota Foundation also supported the publication of a book based on the Japanese study: Miyake Ichiro, Watanuki Joji, Shima Kiyoshi, and Kabashima Ikuo, *Byōdō o me-*

guru erīto to taikō-erīto (Elites and counter-elites on equality) (Tokyo: Sobun sha, 1985). The Japan Society for the Promotion of Science provided travel funds. The John F. Kennedy School of Government of Harvard University provided help and stimulation, and Gary Orren is grateful for research support from its Japanese Corporate Associates Program.

The comparative study was conducted under the auspices of the Center for International Affairs at Harvard University. We are indebted to the center and to its directors, Samuel P. Huntington and Raymond Vernon, for providing a supportive environment for research that needed much time and much support.

A version of Chapter 9 first appeared in Samuel P. Huntington and Joseph S. Nye, Jr., eds., *Global Dilemmas* (Cambridge, Mass.: Harvard University Center for International Affairs, and Lanham, Md.: University Press of America, 1985), © The President and Fellows of Harvard College, 1985.

Among those who worked diligently on the manuscript are Takako Kadotani, Reiko Kitayama, Jennifer Olson, Kumiko Sonoda, and Chii Tsuji. Susan Hogan was infinitely patient and competent in getting us into and (more important) out of the word processor. Evelyn Brew held it all together from beginning to end, responding with constant patience and good humor to confusing materials from confused authors.

Our families tolerated our being away—away in other countries, away at the word processor or computer terminal—many times during the process of research and writing. They more than anyone made it possible.

Contents

Tables

Figures

Elites and the Idea
of Equality

Equality and the Welfare State

Equality is everywhere on the agenda. It fuels political conflict wherever people experience a disparity between their condition and that of others and wish that disparity changed. Such disparities are the subject of electoral contests, interest group competition, and political protest. And the disparity can be of many sorts—between classes, between women and men, among racial and ethnic groups. The major role that the modern welfare state plays in allocating benefits puts the issue of equality at the center of politics everywhere.

This book is about the politics of equality. Its subject is the beliefs and ideologies of those leaders most involved in the development and resolution of conflicts about equality. Its scope is broad, covering many kinds of equality and extending across three nations. It is useful to begin with some distinctions to focus our examination of this wide-ranging subject.

Public and Private

Modern democracies are societies with blurred boundaries. The political borders that separate one from another are penetrated by multinational businesses, by the international movement of labor, and by communications media that make them part of a worldwide network of information and opinion. Within nations, as well, boundaries are blurred. The private and the public sectors intertwine so closely that it is often hard to know where one begins and the other ends. Modern welfare states have taken on many responsibilities once left to individuals and families and, in so doing, have extended the regulatory control of the state into the market. At the same time the functioning of the market affects the welfare state. In the 1970s and 1980s many countries found that their economies could not grow fast enough to keep pace with the expanding demands for government programs. Yet such demands for welfare state services resulted in part from a slowdown in economic performance with its consequent unemployment. Faltering economies simultaneously increase the demand for services by the state and decrease the ability of the state to respond.

The loss of a clear boundary between the public and the private sectors makes even more indistinct the already unclear boundary between politics and economics. Politics everywhere affects the economy. The conflicts among political parties for control of governments, the policies enacted by those governments, the bargains negotiated between government and private actors like business and labor, and the bargains struck among private actors at the instigation of the government, all affect the economy. Similarly, economic actors penetrate political life as businesses, labor unions, farmers, consumers, and others try to influence those government policies that are significant for their own economic welfare.

INCOME EQUALITY

The modern welfare state results, therefore, in the interpenetration of the private and the public sectors, of economics and politics. Thus one of the great issues facing all modern democracies—the issue of equality—is affected by both the private and the public sectors, by both economics and politics. Equality means many different things; indeed, it is one of the purposes of this book to look at the various meanings equality has for different groups in different societies. This variety of meanings makes it difficult to explain the relationship between the welfare state and equality. But if we look at one type of equality, equality of income, we can see that the welfare state has a close but ambiguous relationship to it. Even the minimal welfare state—one that provides a floor of support for those most in need—affects the distribution of income by transferring societal resources to the poorest members. And as the welfare state expands its services, government programs have more impact on the distribution of income. Nevertheless, the relation of the welfare state to income redistribution remains an open issue in most societies. No welfare state has reached consensus on the optimal level of income equality or on how much the state should intervene to level income.

Income equality is itself complex and encompasses a number of issues related to equality. One issue is the standard for fair income distribution. A society can use many possible standards to determine the reward for work: income proportionate to effort, to skill required, to investment in training, to market demand for particular activities, to societal need for the activity (however determined), or to the needs of the income earner. A classic distinction is between rewards based on equality of opportunity, where each is left free to use talent, training, and motivation to achieve whatever income level he or she can, and rewards based on equality of condition, where some level of income equality, including but not necessarily implying complete equality, is specified independent of ability and effort. Connected to the issue of the standard for reward is that of the proper role of the government in fostering equality. One may believe that a certain degree of equality is desirable but may not believe that the government should intervene to achieve that standard, perhaps because one is opposed to giving the state too much power.

The issue of income equality defines the outer boundary of the welfare state. Income equality is the main issue of national debates on the welfare state: should a country stop where it is, move forward to greater government intervention toward equality, or retrench and move backward? Yet a commitment to income redistribution does not merely extend the welfare state's activities. A commitment to provide a basic set of social services for those who cannot obtain them through the market or where the market cannot provide them at all differs sharply from a positive commitment to redistribute income so that it is more equal. Income redistribution may be a side effect of welfare provision, because taxes that fall disproportionately on the more affluent are used for social programs that aid the poorer members of society. But the step toward redistribution as an end in itself may represent a discontinuity.[1] The notion that the state committed to income equality as a goal has taken a major step beyond the now traditional commitment of the welfare state to a basic standard of living may be what makes the issue such a divisive one.

Although the issue comes up in a number of modern democracies, each nation is not at the same stage of welfare provision. Instead, states vary in the number and scope of welfare programs and in the degree to which taxes and government transfers have the purpose and/or effect of redistributing income. We study three nations—Japan, Sweden, and the United States—that differ quite a bit in this regard. And within each country various groups disagree as to whether the state should press forward in fostering equality or should retrench. Each nation is debating the boundary of the welfare state, but that boundary has a different location in each nation.

POLITICAL EQUALITY
The role of the state in economic equality is perhaps the single most ubiquitous equality issue; still, it hardly exhausts the subject of equality in modern democracies. As significant is the issue of political equality: the degree to which all citizens have equal access to the government and equal

ability to influence its decisions. Political equality is of course linked to economic equality. Individuals and groups can exercise their political influence to affect economic equality. Their activities may take many forms. The disadvantaged sectors of society may mobilize to elect governments that will redistribute income in their favor. By contrast, the more advantaged sectors of society may employ less mass-based forms of political influence to protect or enhance their economic condition. Conservatives feared and liberals hoped that creating electoral democracies would lead to the election of redistributionist governments. In some nations this has happened; the four decades of Social Democratic rule in Sweden moved that country to the forefront in government-induced income equality. But as often as not, neither liberals' hopes nor conservatives' fears have borne fruit, largely because the advantaged sectors of society have wielded their political influence to prevent such redistributive outcomes.

The ability of the advantaged groups in society to use their political influence to protect and enhance their positions derives from the reciprocal relationship between equality in the economic and the political domains. Political equality can affect economic equality through the use of the government as the instrument to increase or decrease economic equality. But economic equality can affect the equality of political influence: those who are better off economically can use their resources in the political sphere to influence the government in their favor. This is one way in which the potential for mass-based political activity toward redistribution is thwarted, as those with greater resources use participatory opportunities more effectively so as to exert an amount of political influence disproportionate to their numbers. Thus, the democratic struggle over economic equality closely intertwines with the issue of the equality of political influence; it is another example of the way in which the boundary between economics and politics blurs.

IDEAL AND REAL
The relationship between the domains of political and economic equality is made more complex by another relationship found both within each domain and between the two: the relationship between ideals and reality. In each domain there are ideals about fair distribution; but not everyone shares these ideals, and that creates one of the tensions about equality.[2] Different groups adhere to quite different notions of what is fair, and the ideals of a single group may vary across the two domains. The ideal of equality of condition in relation to political influence is more firmly entrenched than is that of equality of condition in economic matters: the

ethic of one-person, one-vote, basic to electoral democracies, gives each citizen an equal voice, neither more nor less than that of any other citizen; in the economic sphere, however, there is no widely held equivalent ideal whereby all receive the same economic benefit. Of course, the ideal of one-person, one-vote does not exhaust the normative views that people have about politics; political inequality is justified in many ways outside of the sphere of voting. And the ideal of political equality embodied in the rigid definition of how many votes an individual has provides a far from accurate description of the reality of political life. Not all individuals are equal when it comes to voting: some never cast their ballots, whereas others, through persuasion, campaign activity, or otherwise, influence many votes. Furthermore, voting does not exhaust the modes of political activity in which people can engage. In these modes the restrictions found in voting rarely apply. We doubt that anyone fully believes political influence to be equal. But the gap between the ideal and the reality remains and produces a constant tension over the issue of political equality.[3]

A similar tension appears in the economic realm. There is no ideal of equality of economic condition parallel to the political ideal, limited though the latter may be. But within nations people strongly disagree about the degree to which incomes ought to be unequal. The gap between ideal and reality fuels demands for political intervention to bring the two into line. Various groups have different perceptions of the gap: some see the income differential as being less than it ought to be, others see it as being more. And this disagreement can spark a political struggle over government policy.

Lastly, the ideals in one domain can affect equality in the other. If inequalities in the economic sphere are legitimate because effort and skill should be rewarded, then using economic influence in the political sphere is also legitimate.[4] But if using differential economic resources in politics subverts desirable political equality, then that ideal becomes an argument for decreased income inequality.[5]

THE ROLE OF THE STATE

We have made several distinctions that will be useful in understanding equality as an issue in modern welfare states: the distinction between economic and political equality; the distinction between ideal and real; and, within the ideal, the distinction between equality of opportunity and equality of condition. Further, we have raised the issue of the role of the government in determining the level of equality in a nation. This role may differ with regard to political and economic equality, because the former domain falls more naturally under the government's auspices. In addition, the real-ideal gap affects the role of the government. Some or all citizens may call on the government to close that gap by bringing social reality into closer alignment with their desires. The crucial issues sometimes turn on the extent to which the government will interfere in the workings of the market to move in the direction of equality of condition. The government can be invoked to enforce equality of opportunity by removing artificial discriminatory barriers to individual advance. Equality of condition, however, requires more positive government intervention. Equality of condition—say in income or some other social good—usually represents a deviation from what would happen if individuals were left free to exploit their own talents and motivations.

The distinctions just spelled out do not, of course, exhaust those one can make within the realm of equality. Almost all societies face equality issues with a special character. These issues arise from the claims of particular groups for redress of disadvantages due to past or present discrimination. In many cases these groups represent categories of individuals identified by ascriptive characteristics such as race or ethnicity. Gender is also such a characteristic. The demands of such groups for equal treatment can be partially understood in terms of the other equality distinctions we have made. These groups seek political and economic equality. They often make claims in terms of a perceived gap between the professed ideals of their society and reality. They sometimes ask for greater guarantees of equality of opportunity through the removal of discriminatory barriers; they sometimes also seek equality of results when past discriminations do not allow full access to equality of opportunity. They seek government intervention to achieve their goals. By so doing, they add a new dimension to the conflict over equality: specifying particular groups whose past deprivation warrants more intensive intervention to achieve equality.

Leaders and Values

This book is about equality in modern democracies, looked at in terms of the distinctions just made. Our study of this vast topic by no means encompasses the many facets of the problem; rather, our aim has been to address some fundamental issues associated with the issue of equality by focusing on the values and beliefs of leaders from various sectors of society in Japan, Sweden, and the United States. The sectors include established economic groups, such as business, labor unions, and farm organizations; groups challenging established hierarchies, such as disadvantaged minority groups and feminist groups; and other institutions, such as political parties, the media, and universities, that take part in or mediate the struggle over equality. Our interest is in how the various groups of leaders view the issues of equality: what positions they take on the issues and, more fundamentally, what they believe the major issues are. As we have pointed out, equality is an amorphous and multidimensional concept. Before we can determine whether various groups want more or less equality, we have to know what they mean by it—whether they have a common concept of equality when they debate the issue.

We focus on leaders because they shape the political struggle over the issue of equality. Hence their values and beliefs are particularly relevant. Philosophers have written much on equality but little in terms of the issues of public policy. Members of the public have views on equality, but their opinions are often poorly articulated and are not always related to policy choices. Leaders actively engaged in the issue conflicts that relate to equality are usually articulate and active advocates for various positions, and one can expect that what they mean by equality will have both coherence and consequences.

We focus on values because we believe that they have an important effect on the reality of equality. Some people look on beliefs and values as irrelevant to the real issues of distribution. The explanation of equality and inequality, according to some, lies in market forces modified by the self-interested behavior of those who use the government to interfere with those forces. Others, usually at the other end of the political spectrum but with similar disdain for values, see values and beliefs as simply the ideological superstructure for the workings of economic forces. We believe that values—fundamental conceptions of what is fair—do not merely reflect one's objective position in the structure of production or a rationalization of market outcomes but in fact have an autonomous impact on the state of equality. These values, further, operate on income inequality in two ways: indirectly through the political system and directly on private sector income decisions. Indirectly, beliefs about the fair disparity between high and low income earners may affect the actual distribution of income if such beliefs can be incorporated into government policy through political means. Beliefs and values can, however, have a direct impact on income if private sector earnings are affected by what those involved in earnings decisions consider to be fair rewards. We shall explore the variations in such values among leaders within and across these three nations to try to show how they have some autonomy of their own and relate to actual income.

Three Nations

The reasons we have chosen to study Japan, Sweden, and the United States are both practical and intellectual. On the one hand, a group of scholars with backgrounds and expertise in the three nations had an opportunity to work jointly on a subject matter of interest to us all. On the other hand, the three nations form a very interesting set relative to the issues of equality. They are similar in many ways: all three are relatively affluent stable democracies: in each, the form of government has the basic support of the populace and includes the necessary features for democratic politics—basic freedom of speech and of the press, freedom of political organization, competitive parties, and periodic elections with universal suffrage; and each government has taken on some obligation toward the economic welfare of its citizenry. But here important variations begin: the three nations present three different patterns in the relationship between political forces and economic equality, patterns that vary in the degree of government intervention to foster equality and the degree to which equality has been achieved.

By most international measures Sweden stands out as the vanguard nation of the welfare state. It is the nation in which government policies play the biggest role in redistributing income. These policies evolved during a four-decade period of rule by a Social Democratic party allied with a strong union movement and hence are a clear example of politically induced moves toward equality. Furthermore, international comparisons of the degree of income distribution suggest that government policies have been successful, because Sweden ranks at or near the top in this regard.

In the same international comparisons the United States is near the bottom of the scale. Its welfare state came late and is less well developed, the redistributive thrust of government policies is relatively weak, and the United States has never had a strong socialist movement to push for redistribution. The resulting low degree of income equality is commensurate with these characteristics.[6] But we emphasize that the origins of differences in policies toward income equality cannot be captured in any limited set of characteristics.

Japan presents a curious combination of the two other nations. A conservative party closely allied to business and traditional sectors of Japanese society has held power for many years. Unlike the United States, Japan has a socialist opposition; but the opposition has not shared in government power. Like the United States, Japan ranks low in welfare state development and in state redistributive intervention. When, however, one compares the three nations in terms of the degree of income equality, one finds Japan closer to Sweden than to the United States. If income distribution is high in Japan, it does not seem to result from public policy—at least not public policy of the sort often considered in the framework of the welfare state.[7]

The differences among the three nations make them particularly relevant to the ongoing debate about the source of cross-national variation in income equality. Some scholars argue that the level of income equality depends on levels of affluence and economic growth that make it easier for certain societies to afford redistribution. In addition, the level of need as determined by age distribution creates pressure for redistribution. Politics, therefore, does not matter.[8] Others, however, argue for the importance of political factors. The main political factors appear to be associated not with the degree of democratic participation per se—although positive effects of voter turnout have been found—but with the degree of left or socialist party control over the government.[9] As a nation with an egalitarian income distribution, with long-term socialist rule coupled with strong unions, Sweden clearly fits the political explanation. Similarly, with no socialist rule and a relatively inegalitarian distribution, the United States also corresponds to the political model. Japan, however, is somewhat of an anomaly.

ECONOMIC EQUALITY

Some examples of economic policy, economic outcomes, and political characteristics will make these differences among the three nations clearer. To begin with, comparative data show a clear distinction among the three nations in the degree of income equality (Table 1.1).[10] The Gini index of income inequality as well as an index of the income difference between the top and bottom quintiles based on Organization for Economic Cooperation and Development (OECD) data put Sweden first or second in degree of income equality among the twelve nations ranked; the United States ranks eighth or ninth, and Japan occupies a middle position but closer to Sweden than to the United States and well to the egalitarian side of the median of the nations ranked.[11]

GOVERNMENT POLICY

Japan may be closer to Sweden than to the United States in degree of income equality, but it is much closer to the United States on measures of governmental redistributive policy. Table 1.2 gives examples of this, comparing the three nations with other advanced industrial democracies. Re-

Table 1.1.   Income equality

	Rank			
Measure	Japan (1969)	Sweden (1972)	United States (1972)	Number of countries ranked
Gini index of posttax income equality	4	1	9	12
Quintile income equality (difference in posttax income of top and bottom quintiles)	5	2	8	12

Source: See note 10 to Chapter 1.

distribution can take place through the tax system or through government transfer payments or both. As Table 1.2 shows, the United States and Japan rank toward the bottom of the modern democracies in the extent to which the tax system is progressive or in the extent of government income transfer expenditures. Whereas Sweden ranks first among seventeen industrialized democracies in the progressivity of taxes, the United States and Japan rank thirteenth and twelfth respectively. Other analyses support these OECD data.[12]

A similar difference among the nations appears in the OECD data on the ranking of the nations in terms of expenditures for social transfers (Table 1.2). Proportionately, Sweden spends three times more on such transfers than do Japan and the United States. Similar data come from the International Labor Organization. During the late 1970s Japan spent 9.7 percent of its Gross Domestic Product on social security programs and the United States spent 13.7 percent. In contrast, the figure for Sweden was 30.5 percent.[13]

Table 1.3 gives a more direct gauge of the impact of government policy on income equality.[14] There we present two measures of the pretax and posttax and pretransfer and posttransfer income distribution in the three nations. The first is the Gini index of inequality before and after taxes and transfers. For pregovernment income Sweden has a high Gini index of inequality, which is then substantially reduced by taxes and transfers. Indeed, Sweden ranks first in terms of the percentage reduction in the Gini index caused by government intervention. In the United States, the inequality index is high before government intervention and remains rela-

Table 1.2.   Government intervention to redistribute income

Measure	Japan	Sweden	United States
Progressivity of tax: ranking among 17 nations, 1975	13	1	12
Government expenditures: income transfer expenditures as percent of GNP	9.9	33.1	10.4

Source: See note 12 to Chapter 1.

tively high after government intervention. In Japan, the Gini index of inequality before intervention is relatively low—Japan ranks thirteenth of thirteen nations in the pre–government intervention level of inequality[15]— and it remains low after intervention. A measure of quintile income distribution yields similar results. In Sweden, the share going to the top quintile falls precipitously after taxes and transfers, whereas that of the bottom quintile goes up even more sharply. In the other two countries the change is much more marginal.[16] Thus, in Sweden government action reduces income inequality but in the United States such action has little effect on income inequality.[17] In Japan, taxes and transfers have as small an effect as in the United States, but in Japan incomes are relatively equal before government intervention,[18] whereas in the United States incomes are relatively unequal before and after intervention. This leaves an unequal distribution relatively unchanged in the United States and an equal distribution relatively unchanged in Japan.[19] The fact that Japan and the United States appear similar in the degree of state redistributionist intervention does not imply that the two nations are similar in terms of all state economic intervention. Actually, the Japanese government has intervened more than the U.S. government, but that intervention has been in terms of indicative planning to foster economic growth and international competitiveness. In terms of welfare state and redistributionist intervention, Japan is probably less active than the United States.

A schematic representation of the three nations in terms of their policies fostering equality and the degree of actual equality in each, might look something like this:

	Egalitarian		Nonegalitarian	
Policy	Sweden ————————————————		U.S. —— Japan ————	
Outcome	Sweden ———— Japan ————		U.S. ————————	

Table 1.3. Government impact on income equality

Measure	Japan		Sweden		United States	
	Before taxes and transfers	After taxes and transfers	Before taxes and transfers	After taxes and transfers	Before taxes and transfers	After taxes and transfers
Gini index						
Pretax, pretransfer	.365		.471		.446	
Posttax, posttransfer	.318		.303		.383	
Percentage change due to taxes and transfers	13.0		36.4		14.1	
Rank in terms of percentage change among 13 nations	10		1		9	
Quintile income share						
Lowest quintile	6.1	7.1	0.1	9.4	2.3	4.2
Top quintile	42.2	41.5	47.2	35.6	47.2	45.5
Difference	36.1	34.4	47.1	26.2	44.9	41.3
Ratio after: before	0.95		0.56		0.92	

Source: See note 14 to Chapter 1.

THE ROLE OF POLITICS

The three nations also differ in significant political ways, especially concerning their expectations about the role of politics in creating economic equality. Before we look at these differences, we should note the political similarities among these nations. They are all open societies in which political participation is legal and tolerated and opposition political parties can exist. All three nations rank high on measures of press freedom.[20] And, most important from our perspective, political rights are universal; no group is formally excluded from political participation on the basis of class, gender, or ethnic background.

The existence of democratic rights, however, may be less important for egalitarian policies than the degree to which such rights are equally used. Democracies vary in the extent of their political equality, that is, in the extent to which disadvantaged groups participate in politics as much as advantaged ones, and herein may lie the key. If political equality leads to economic equality, one should find more political equality in Sweden than in the United States. The obvious difference in policies and in policy outcome between the two countries causes this expectation. What one should find in Japan, however, remains uncertain because of its puzzling combination of less egalitarian policies and egalitarian result.

This brings us to a comparison among the three nations in terms of political equality. Political equality is an ambiguous concept. In a broad sense it refers to the extent to which citizens have relatively widespread influence over governmental decisions with each citizen having more or less the same amount of influence. As we use the term, political equality may be high even if political elites have—as they inevitably do—substantially more influence than the average citizen. Our concern is with the dispersion of influence among the general public, in particular with the extent to which participation is concentrated in the hands of certain segments of society such as the economically better-off.[21] One reason political democracy may not lead to greater economic equality is that some individuals participate more actively. Insofar as those who are more economically advantaged are also more politically active, participatory systems may lead to policy outcomes biased in favor of the affluent. The redistributive consequences that might have emerged from mass political participation by the disadvantaged are muted by systematic bias in the mobilization of influence.[22]

When it comes to the stratification of participation, the United States does differ from both Japan and Sweden. In the Verba, Nie, and Kim seven-nation participation study, Japan ranked (along with Austria) as the nation with the least participatory stratification; the United States stood at the top in terms of stratification. In Japan, an individual's economic position had almost no correlation to the likelihood of that person's being politically active. In the United States, however, the relationship was substantial. Although Sweden was not included in that study, its participatory profile is probably more like Japan's than that of the United States. Figure 1.1, which shows the voting turnout for various occupations, presents some data consistent with this interpretation. The contrast between the United States and the other two nations is striking. In the United States, voting turnout differs sharply across occupations, with those in higher-status (and higher-paid) jobs more likely to vote. In Japan and Sweden, voting turnout is relatively equal across occupations.[23] Thus, in the United States economic and political stratification are more closely linked: differential economic resources are more easily turned into differential political influence. Not only is income more unequally distributed, but the economically advantaged are somewhat more likely to convert economic into political advantage.

This distinction between the United States and the other two nations appears in the relatively weak attempts to limit the impact of economic disparities on political life in the United States. Although it has generally led other nations in enacting laws to foster public participation in the political process, the United States has lagged behind other nations, including Japan and Sweden, in regulating the use of private money for partisan political purposes. Most other democracies have reduced the significance of private funds in elections by providing public funding of elections and by limiting private contributions. Figure 1.2 compares several democracies in terms of the existence of public funding and limitations on private finance.[24] Note that before 1974 only the United States and Switzerland neither provided public funds nor limited private giving. Even after the campaign funding reforms of 1974, the U.S. limits on private finance remained relatively minimal. One can, in fact, argue that the role of private funds in U.S. elections has grown with the development of political action committees and the continued legality of private direct support of candidates. In contrast, both Japan and Sweden limit private financing of campaigns and provide public funding. The differences are real but should not be exaggerated: Japanese campaign financing laws are easily and often bypassed.[25]

But this solution does not hold up. For one thing, Japan lacks the intervening redistributive policies that would link political equality to economic equality. Furthermore, Japan and the United States have neither the

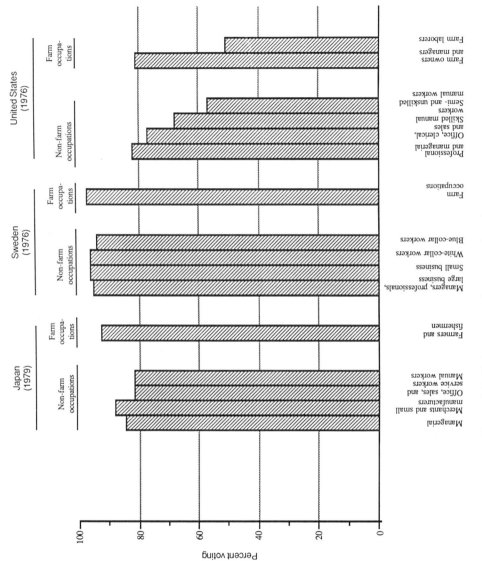

Figure 1.1. Voting turnout by occupation. Source: see note 23 to Chapter 1.

Private finance

	No limits	Limits
None	U.S. (pre-1974) Switzerland	France
Quite limited (usually matching funds or indirect subsidies)		U.S. (post-1974) Canada Ireland Australia
Most or all funding public	Finland Norway Denmark Netherlands	United Kingdom Sweden Italy West Germany Austria Japan

(left axis label: Public finance)

Figure 1.2. Public and private campaign financing in democracies. Source: see note 24 to Chapter 1.

strong socialist parties nor the strong unions that give the disadvantaged the opportunity to affect public policy; Sweden has both.[26] Various categorizations of nations in terms of the strength of socialist parties in the electorate or in government, as well as the strength of unions, find Sweden at or near the top in these respects, the other two nations near the bottom. In sum, Japan and Sweden are similar in egalitarian outcome: income is relatively equally distributed, at least in comparison with the United States. They are also politically similar in the low level of political stratification along economic lines and in the existence of somewhat stronger inhibitions than in the United States against the use of economic resources for politics. Still, those political similarities cannot explain the similarities in income distribution because the nations differ in two crucial ways: in Japan the intervening roles of a strong socialist movement and governmental redistributive policies are missing.

The puzzle of income distribution in Japan has several possible solutions. One has to do with the particular form that political equality takes in Japan. In Sweden, political access of the disadvantaged derives from the mobilizing of the working class through a strong socialist party and strong labor unions. This mobilization, in turn, brings about tax and transfer policies to redistribute income from the more to the less affluent sectors of society. In Japan, such mobilization of the disadvantaged also takes place, resulting in policies that benefit them; but instead of a socialist movement of the working class leading the mobilization, the conservative Liberal Democratic party (LDP) spearheads the movement, and those who are mobilized are agrarian supporters of the LDP. The resulting policies are redistributive. They consist, however, of subsidies for farm products that raise the income of what would otherwise be an economically disadvantaged part of the population.[27] Similarly, the LDP provides economic benefits to small businesses in exchange for electoral support.[28] In this sense government policy is redistributive, but not in the way that tax and transfer policies are in the Scandinavian states.

The Japanese tilt toward the agrarian sector does not fully explain the extent of income equality in Japan. The difference between Japan and the United States extends into the nonfarm segment of society as well. The earnings gap between workers at different levels of industrial enterprises is larger in the United States than in Japan, a difference that cannot easily be traced to Japanese policies toward agriculture.[29] Thus, although government policy plays a significant role in determining the level of income inequality, other factors may be significant. These include the nature of the labor market, the extensiveness and the efficacy of unions, and the rate of economic growth.[30] An additional set of factors, we shall argue, is norms and values about equality.

NORMS AND VALUES

Norms and values about equality form the substance of this book. Can they explain the variations among the three nations in income distribution? As we shall see, there is a congruence between the pattern of attitudes toward equality and the actuality of equality in each nation. This, however, falls far short of an explanation. The causal relationship may go in the other direction with policy determining values, or both values about equality and policies about equality may be the result of other factors. Even if one accepts our position that values are autonomous—that they are not mere superstructure or rationalization of one's economic self-interest—their causal relation to policy would be comprehensible only in the context of a wide range of other political and economic factors. We have presented the variations among the nations so that the reader will have the policy context within which one must understand the values described and analyzed in this book. In the next chapter we will discuss the historical context. Subsequent chapters will, we believe, make apparent the important role that these values—in particular, the configurations created by differences among elite groups within each nation—play in structuring the nature of the conflict over equality in each nation.

In this introduction we have illustrated differences among the three nations by focusing on certain aspects of economic and political equality. In some sense political struggles over economic position are the central conflicts in modern democracies. The relationship between class and politics is at the heart of all Marxist and neo-Marxist analyses of politics and policy as well as most non-Marxist analyses. But the issues of equality go beyond those of economic equality between classes. Among groups defined in noneconomic terms—usually on the basis of ascriptive characteristics such as race, ethnicity, or gender—equality is an issue in all democracies, including the three we study (albeit with differing intensity). In some settings equality conflicts along these lines are much more intense than those along class or economic lines.

Nonetheless, one should not distinguish too sharply between economically based conflicts over equality and conflicts based on, say, race or gender. The claims of disadvantaged minorities and of women are often claims for economic equality, and one can understand such conflicts only in the context of a particular class and economic structure. Yet if one subsumes ascriptive conflict into class and economic categories, one misses some of the more distinctive features of these conflicts over equality that often cut across the economic conflicts in society. In studying values, we will look not only at issues of economic equality but also at these other issues. Indeed, one of our first concerns will be to ask how the leaders we study define the issue of equality—whether they see distinctions between economic equality and equality in other terms.

What Follows

The basic data for this book come from parallel surveys of elites in each of the three nations. The information provides a rich resource for comparative description and analysis. The comparisons will take many forms: across countries, among elite groups within each country, between values and perceptions, and across several domains of equality such as economic, political, and gender. And we will combine these comparisons in various ways. We will compare across nations in terms of the values about equality of parallel groups of elites, a comparison that will reveal significant differences in how much equality similar groups in different countries want. We will also compare across the nations in terms of the similarities and differences among the elite groups within each nation, which will enable us to isolate areas of consensus and disagreement in each nation. We will compare perceptions and values within the several elite groups in each nation to see where the gap between ideal and real is most substantial. And we will compare the gap between perception and value in the domain of economic equality with that in the domain of political equality in order to analyze some fundamental differences between equality conflicts in politics and economics.

The bulk of our data comes from a single time period, the late 1970s when our surveys were conducted. A longitudinal study of elites along the lines of our cross-sectional one, though desirable, was beyond our resources. Our data must be viewed with the caution applied to any cross-sectional study, because values and perceptions may change over time. Nevertheless, we believe that the patterns of values we identify are not ones that change easily. Before turning to the analysis of our data, we look in Chapter 2 at the history of conflicts over equality in each of the nations. There are no historical data parallel in scope and form to our own, but there is abundant evidence of continuity and evolutionary change in basic orientations toward equality.

The circumstances within which equality issues are played out change more rapidly. Economies grow, or stagnate, or develop in other ways that change the relative share of economic benefits received by sectors of society. New groups make claims for equal treatment, but the claims are usually couched in the language of generally accepted norms of equality. Political regimes change and with the change come changes in the priority assigned to the goal of equality, but the new regime still operates within parameters set by common conceptions of equality. After a close look at the attitudes of the elite groups toward equality as they existed at the time of our survey (Chapters 3 through 10), we return in the last chapter to the theme of continuity and change considered historically in Chapter 2. As we shall see, the circumstances within which the debate about equality is pursued have changed in the 1980s. As we shall also see, those changes are being worked out within the framework of certain established values about equality.

2

The Historical Context
of Equality

This book compares a complex phenomenon, equality, across three countries. Chapter 1 summarized our approach to studying equality in Japan, Sweden, and the United States. As all works of comparative research ultimately must, ours uses selection and simplification. We simplify in substance and method: our substantive focus is the beliefs and values of elites in the three nations; our method is the relatively structured questionnaire. These data will reveal some fascinating similarities and differences among the three nations.

Such data run the risk of being inadequately understood when isolated from their contextual background. The beliefs and values we deal with have historical roots and exist in a richer cultural context than our research instruments can explicate. In order systematically to compare these nations, we select for observation and measurement certain aspects of social and political life; hence we inevitably take them out of context. The danger is distortion, because seemingly similar phenomena may have different meanings if looked at within the pattern of meaning of a particular culture. Yet to present that context fully is to present a complete historical and cultural account of each nation—a task for which there are no guidelines for systematic comparison and a task that would, in any case, overwhelm the narrower purpose of our book.

In this chapter we provide a compromise, a condensed and simplified account of the place of equality in the history and culture of each of the nations. For each nation we cover three topics: the historical "meaning" of equality within each nation's political culture, the history of social policy dealing with equality, and the current issues of equality faced in each nation. This contextual material is of necessity schematic and far from complete. To those who know one or more of the nations well, little will be new. But we hope that for those for whom at least one of the nations is unfamiliar, these materials will be a useful introduction. For all readers we hope that this chapter will provide some contextual background against which to understand the comparative data on the beliefs and values of elites. In a sense this issue of satisfying the needs of many different readers parallels a problem we have faced as authors in satisfying ourselves.

Japan

POLITICAL CULTURE

From feudal times until its late-nineteenth-century leap into the ranks of nation-states, Japanese political culture has had two major characteristics: status hierarchy and group conformity.[1] Inculcated through generations, neither value disappeared during the Meiji Restoration, the great dividing line between Japan's feudal past and its modern era. Beginning with the Meiji Restoration in 1868, the Japanese attempted to forge a nation-state capable of withstanding Western imperialism. During a nine-year span the *samurai*, a warrior class who held ruling status in the feudal Tokugawa shogunate, were stripped of their special privileges, signaling a radical change in the power structure of Japan.

Prior to the restoration the status hierarchy principle prevailed in Japanese political culture. Status distinctions, hereditary authority, and warrior rule dominated during this period. Although the emperor symbolized centralized imperial authority, the *shogun, daimyo* (feudal lord), and samurai exercised true power. The *han,* or fief, was the major focus of group loyalty, and the entire political system rested on inherited authority. Every person was located on an ascribed status hierarchy, which left little room for any notion of equality. The Meiji Restoration changed all this; in just one or two generations Japanese society was transformed from one in which status derived from heredity to one in which individual education and personal achievement played the primary roles.[2] The feudal privileges of the samurai status were eliminated step by step between 1869 and 1876. In 1871 the Meiji rulers abolished the outcast status of the *buraku* people.[3] Ostensibly at least the new regime had committed itself to some semblance of equality. Nonetheless, hierarchy remained a key part of Japanese political culture. In 1884 the Meiji rulers created a new Western-style peerage composed of old court nobility, former feudal lords, and those who played a central role in bringing the restoration. Later they also distributed peer status to some of the highest-ranking bureaucrats and military for their distinguished service to the state. Members of this nobility served in a newly created House of Peers, the upper half of a Western-style bicameral parliament, or Diet, established by the 1889 Japanese constitution. This noble class remained an influential part of Japanese politics until it was abolished by the 1947 constitution.

The second feature of Japanese political culture, group conformity, developed as a strong component of agricultural life in Japan, largely because of the cooperation needed to manage the sophisticated irrigation systems crucial to an economy based on rice growing. Group conformity also was strongly reinforced by the Japanese reverence for cohesive family and kinship systems. Within the family the father held absolute authority and transmitted it to the eldest son. The Japanese kinship system, often known as *dōzoku,* was a hierarchy of families based on paternal lineage, headed by the stem family.[4]

Group conformity, like status hierarchy, underwent modification during the Meiji Restoration. At that time village solidarity was linked to a broadened conception of the "family-state" in which the people were seen as an expanded family under the emperor.[5] Thus all Japanese were equal "children of the emperor" (*tennō no sekishi*). Seen in this light, the granting of universal male suffrage in 1925 fitted with the notion of a society in which status distinctions prevailed but all citizens were "equal" under the emperor. Outside the political sphere, business and industrial organizations also followed the principles of hierarchy and group conformity. For example, distinctions between staff and workers were rigid, and discipline to maintain group standards was harsh.[6]

In the effort to create a unified nation-state, the government restructured administrative units after 1871. To link the village to the national government, villages became subunits within prefectures headed by a governor appointed by the central government. Previously the villages had existed as separate, somewhat autonomous entities competing against one another. In typically Japanese style, the government reduced conflict by absorbing competing entities into a larger group.

Competition, however, remained an integral part of Japanese society. It was encouraged among groups within factories as an incentive to spur the nation's rapid industrialization. But it also occurred among bureaucrats and the military. Under the Tokugawa shogunate prior to the Meiji Restoration, administrative power had been vested in the hands of the hereditary samurai. The Meiji rulers incorporated a Western-style legal system and a process of competitive examinations for civil service positions. Status in the bureaucracy came to be based on achievement rather than heredity.

With the groundwork laid for an efficient administrative system, but without any experience with democratic institutions, Japan under the Meiji constitution was ripe for domination by the bureaucracy. During a time of rapid industrialization, the bureaucracy stifled class conflicts through stringent police methods. The persistence of traditional conformist attitudes, the use of conflict-resolving mechanisms such as arbitration, and the strong emphasis on national harmony helped to reduce in Japan the tensions that afflicted other industrializing nations.[7]

The influence of the Japanese bureaucracy undermined the establishment of a representative democratic system despite the establishment of a parliamentary system under the auspices of a written constitution. The prevailing political culture was conducive to carrying out the nation's goals but not to attaining them in a democratic manner that respected minority rights. Takeshi Ishida described prewar Japan this way: "The individual is submerged in a group-oriented society; minority opinions contrary to established group desires are disregarded by a tradition which values group harmony. This process produces a tendency toward national conformism which in turn leads to discrimination against the minority."[8]

Defeat in World War II and the subsequent American occupation provided the impetus to reorient Japanese society toward a more democratic ethos. Since then the Japanese have adopted liberal democratic values as their own. The World War II experience seriously eroded the Japanese emphasis on status hierarchy, and not simply because the occupation forces commanded it. During the war status hierarchy was enforced to a degree quite unreasonable for people as educated as the Japanese. In addition, the destruction of the Japanese economy leveled status differences, as everyone found themselves struggling for food and shelter. After the war various movements founded during the 1920s to seek freedom and equality for disadvantaged groups reorganized.

The postwar Japanese constitution not only contained those rights guaranteed in the U.S. constitution but also specified several more, including the right to unionize and bargain collectively, the equality of the sexes, and the right to equal educational opportunities. Since the war Japanese courts have scrupulously upheld these rights. Although Japanese conservatives attempted in the late 1950s to bring back some of the prewar political principles, they failed to reestablish hierarchical aspects of Japanese political culture. Yet, more than the citizens in other Western democracies, the Japanese accept differing ranks and status as natural and even inevitable.

Even today most groups operate with a system of leaders and followers reminiscent of the traditional family.[9] For example, the Japanese continue to address each other with specific status appelations, such as *kōchō-sensei* (Teacher-Principal) and *shachō-san* (Mr. Company President). They also defer to age, showing greater respect for older people, especially. The enduring legacy of status hierarchy also appears in the exchange of *meishi,* or calling cards. This custom enables new acquaintances to ascertain each other's specific position and group affiliation, thereby establishing the tone for their relationship.[10]

In the postwar era, group conformist norms have centered on the family or business rather than the state. Japanese workers, to a much greater extent than workers in most other countries, see themselves as belonging to a particular company. For example, a Japanese worker may refer to himself as a Mitsubishi Heavy Industrial Man.[11] It is common for Japanese workers to expect to remain with a single company for life.

THE HISTORY OF EQUALITY AS AN ISSUE

The Meiji Restoration brought with it limited gains in political equality. Efforts to improve the lot of the buraku people, for example, contrasted with suppression in the 1880s of the Freedom and People's Rights movement. This group had lobbied for the inclusion in the Meiji constitution of safeguards for human rights, the establishment of popular sovereignty, and the granting of immediate universal suffrage. Instead, the constitution established a Diet with a lower House of Representatives elected popularly whose power was institutionally limited and overshadowed by that of the upper House of Peers. Moreover, the Privy Council (*Sūmitsuin*), which served as an advisory board to the emperor, had a vital say on important matters. The military remained outside the control of the Diet, except for budgetary matters. Because the constitution was considered sacred and could not be revised, any efforts to promote equality through amendments were impossible.

Nevertheless, by the 1920s elected politicians and political parties had increased their power. Cabinet formation began to be based on partisan majority in the House of Representatives, and the lower house assumed stronger control over the military through the budget. The House of Peers was reformed by the appointment of nonnoble members. The establishment in 1925 of universal male suffrage represented a major step toward political equality. Yet even at their zenith of influence during the 1920s the established political parties did not attempt to push political freedom beyond securing voting rights.[12] They held back for two reasons: their eagerness to consolidate their power vis-à-vis the upper house, the Privy

Council, and the military; and their fear of encouraging radical movements, which were already demanding increased political freedom.

One of those movements was organized labor, which started to grow in the 1920s. The *Sōdōmei* (Japanese Federation of Labor Unions) about doubled its membership (to 254,000) between 1923 and 1925. At the same time tenant farmers organized under the banner of a Japanese Farmers Union. The *Zenkoku Suiheisha* (All-Japan Society for Leveling) was formed in 1922 to demand an end to discrimination against the outcast buraku people. Despite a decree by the Meiji rulers proclaiming the end of the outcast status imposed on this group in feudal times, de facto discrimination against the buraku people continued. In 1925 the *Zenkoku Suiheisha* organized more than a thousand protests against discrimination.[13] In 1924 a women's movement, the *Fusen-kakutoku Dōmei* (Federation to Secure Women's Suffrage) was organized. The lower house of the Diet twice passed a law granting women the right to vote in local elections, in 1930 and 1931, but both times the House of Peers rejected it.

The 1920s also witnessed the emergence of several socialist parties. A Social Democratic party, which called for political, economic, and social reforms, had been formed in 1901, but it had been immediately banned by the government.[14] Under the more favorable political climate of the 1920s, with universal male suffrage firmly established, socialist parties could legally form, but the movement was splintered into left, right, and center factions. The Communist party never attained legal status, and all organizations and movements wishing "to change the *kokutai* (national polity) or to end the private property system" became illegal under the Peace Preservation Law of 1925. The legal socialist parties fared poorly at the polls, winning out of a total 464 seats only 8 in 1927, 5 in 1930, and 5 in 1932. In the 1930s all parties lost power to the rising influence of the military, which moved to the fore after the Manchurian incident in 1931 and the assassination of Prime Minister Inukai in 1932. Indeed, despite some electoral gains by the socialist parties in the 1930s, all political parties, labor unions, farmers' unions, and women's associations were forced to dissolve in 1940.

The end of the war marked the collapse of the Japanese military and paved the way for the immediate reestablishment of the prewar Japanese political and social movements. The socialists formed a unified Japanese Socialist party in November 1945, and won 92 seats in the April 1946 general election—far more than its prewar high of 37 seats in 1936. The Socialist program called for full-fledged political freedom, the introduction of socialism, and the eradication of militarism. But the two major prewar parties, both of whom wanted to maintain the emperor and a free-enterprise economy, captured a majority of the lower house, winning 234 of the 464 seats.

In 1947–48 the Socialists, whose 143 seats made them the largest single party in the Diet, formed a coalition with one of the conservative parties. This alliance soon broke down. It was the only time in the postwar period that Japan has not been ruled solely by the conservatives, who in 1955 merged to become the Liberal Democratic party (LDP).

Under the American occupation a variety of measures designed to democratize Japan were set in place: the abolition of the thought police, the legalization of labor unions, the extension of suffrage to women and the elimination of their lower legal status, and far-reaching agrarian reforms including large-scale transfer of land from landlords to tenants. When the occupation forces departed in 1952, two conservative parties, the *Kaishin-tō* and the *Jiyū-tō,* sought to revise all reforms made during the occupation period. In particular, they wanted to increase the emperor's power, to limit labor's rights, to emphasize the family paternal lineage (thus restoring a male-dominated society), and to abolish Article 9 of the 1947 constitution, which forbade the remilitarization of Japan. But they failed to win enough seats in both houses to amend the constitution. Their failure resulted largely from the stronger electoral showing by the Socialists. This party, which reached its peak in 1959 when it won 166 seats in the lower house, drew most of its support from labor unions, women, and youth who opposed a return to prewar principles.

Beginning in 1960, the LDP emphasized the need to maintain economic growth. It added social security and government-sponsored social policy to its agenda and increased agricultural subsidies and public works projects. The party defended these social programs not as redistributionist policies but as means of parceling out bigger slices of an increasing economic pie. Under Prime Minister Kakuei Tanaka in 1972–73 large-scale expansion of social security expenditures took place, as did more public works projects and increased government subsidies. The LDP's allies, business and farm groups, supported these measures until the oil crises and subsequent economic recession of the 1970s. Then business began to oppose further increases in government spending, especially for social security. At the same time the agricultural sector found itself battling to maintain the import restrictions and government subsidies that had protected it during the 1960s and 1970s.

Although sharing the LDP's commitment to economic growth, the opposition parties generally have supported more egalitarian policies. The

Socialists, the largest party in the opposition bloc, have slowly lost electoral ground in recent years. The newly created *Kōmeitō* (Clean Government party) has increased its share of the vote to 10 percent, as has the Communist party. The Democratic Socialists, a moderate socialist group which split from the main Socialist party in 1959, now also commands about 10 percent of the vote.

Like the Japanese political parties, social movements flourished after the war. Once it was legalized by the occupation forces, organized labor rapidly reestablished itself. In the immediate aftermath of the war both white-collar and blue-collar workers, suffering from rampant inflation, food shortages, and a lack of clothing and shelter, feared that their employers might go bankrupt. In response, workers formed "enterprise unions." Composed of all the employees in a single company, these unions demanded and won the abolition of status discrimination between management and laborers, such as different toilets and lunchrooms. They also fought for the extension to blue-collar workers of benefits such as monthly wage payments, twice-a-year bonuses, and retirement allowances for long-term employees, formerly restricted to white-collar workers.[15]

The farm sector also underwent a radical change in the postwar period, following the successful land reforms initiated under the American occupation. The political center of the farming sector shifted from tenant-farmers' unions to agricultural cooperatives. These cooperatives expanded beyond mere agricultural production into the purchase of fertilizer, animal feed, and farm machines, the sale of agricultural products, and the arrangement of financing. This new class of landholding farmers allied itself with the conservative bloc, organizing into political associations to sponsor favored LDP politicians.

The postwar period also saw the reemergence of the buraku liberation movement. In 1946 the *Buraku Kaihō Zenkoku-iinkai* (National Committee for Buraku Liberation) was formed. It allied with the Japanese Socialist party during elections. Although the Buraku's central committee chairman won election to the House of Councilors (which replaced the House of Peers under the 1947 constitution), the buraku liberation movement made little progress during the occupation. Beginning in 1955, however, the movement regained vigor. The liberation committee renamed itself *Buraku Kaihō Dōmei* (Buraku Liberation League) and began to broaden its base of support among the buraku people. It demanded governmental assistance in ending discrimination in education and in improving the districts where the buraku people lived.

The women's movement also expanded during the postwar years, prompted by the extension of suffrage to women in 1945. About 67 percent of eligible women voters went to the polls during the general elections in 1946, and thirty-nine women won seats in the House of Representatives.[16] Since then the League of Women Voters of Japan has played an active role in educating women about politics, in fighting political corruption, and in helping women run for office. This movement has support from women's sections in labor unions and in the Socialist and Communist parties and recently from environmental groups.

Because of the emergence of such political and social movements since World War II, the importance of hierarchy has diminished while the force of group conformity has grown. This change is one reason the disparity between top and bottom wage earners in Japan has shrunk since 1945. In addition, the rise of labor unions has contributed to the relatively equal wage distribution. Japan's enterprise unions may have little political clout but they have helped to set more equal wages within Japanese companies. Their success has affected the model wages that the government bureaucracy establishes as guidelines for private firms. Thus, wage equality comes from the private sector but gains strength from the government's validation.

The Japanese approach to social security also reflects a preference for a mixture of public and private actions. The government has pegged public spending on social security between that of the United States and Western Europe—higher than the former, lower than the latter. But the government expects the private sector to supplement these state efforts. A favorite slogan of Japan's governing party, the LDP, is that Japan should be moving "toward a welfare society full of vitality." By endorsing a welfare society rather than a welfare state, the LDP reflects the view that other social forces (the family, the community, and private companies) must help provide security for older citizens in addition to government efforts.

CURRENT ISSUES OF INEQUALITY

The issue of concentrated property ownership has resurfaced despite the postwar dissolution of the *zaibatsu*, the large landholding families and financial cliques, and the levying of heavy taxes on all property owners. During the recent period of rapid economic growth Japan has witnessed new accumulations of property that have created inequalities and generated a sense of unfairness.[17]

Discrimination against foreigners, especially Koreans, is a continuing problem. Prewar Japan treated Koreans and Taiwanese as citizens coming from colonies. When both colonies gained their independence after the war, those Koreans and Taiwanese who remained in Japan and did not choose to be naturalized became foreign residents. Approximately 670,000 people of Korean origin who have lived in Japan for more than a generation remain Koreans. Because many Japanese laws carry a nationality clause, these Koreans, as well as other foreigners, are excluded from some social security benefits and shut out of governmental jobs including professorships in national and public universities. Koreans also face discrimination in marriage, in education, and in private employment.

The buraku, or, as they are now called, *dōwa* (harmonization) districts, represents another continuing equality issue. Spurred by the buraku liberation movement and public opinion, the Japanese government has taken measures to overcome years of discrimination and administrative neglect in these areas. There are now approximately 4,373 *dōwa* districts comprising 1.1 million people. Despite a 1969 law designed to improve living conditions in these districts, the buraku people's living conditions, job opportunities, and enrollment in higher education remain inferior. In addition, social and even judicial discrimination still exists.

Disputes over gender discrimination also are prevalent in Japan today. Economic growth has caused the number of women employed to double from 1960 to 1980; women now represent one-third of the Japanese work force. Women outnumber men in high-school enrollment, and one-fourth of the undergraduates at four-year universities are women. Despite these gains the average pay of working women in Japan is about half that of men (53.8 percent in 1980).[18] This inequity exists in part because women hold lower-level jobs, have less seniority, work shorter hours, and are more likely than men to be part-time workers. Japanese companies rarely promote women to supervisory and administrative jobs.[19] In 1985, after seven years of debate, the Japanese Diet passed an Equal Employment Bill that encourages employers to end sex discrimination in their hiring, job assignment, and promotion policies.[20]

Despite the enormous increase in higher education and in more equal educational opportunities, as well as the weak correlation between educational level and income in Japan,[21] discrimination by education continues. A student's educational attainment heavily influences what his or her first job will be.[22] Given Japan's system of lifelong employment and seniority-based wages, a worker's first job affects his or her career potential. Therefore, intense competition and prolonged preparation for university entrance exams is the norm. This preparation is expensive, often requiring private tutoring and preparatory classes after school, which of course favors well-to-do families.

Finally, the question of inequality of influence looms large in Japan. Although Japan is a liberal democracy with a high degree of participation and political competition, the LDP, allied with business, the bureaucracy, and farmers, has held power for more than twenty-five years. Groups not allied with this conservative bloc wield much less influence.

Sweden

POLITICAL CULTURE

During the past fifty years Sweden has made probably the strongest effort of any industrialized nation to achieve equality for its citizens. In large measure the unique efforts to achieve equality in Sweden stem from the dominant political role of the Social Democratic party over the past half-century. That dominance itself arises from the interplay of factors in-grained in Swedish political culture. Traditionally, the Swedes have been willing to defer to government authority. Since the middle of the nine-teenth century government commissions acted to promote agreement be-tween contending groups. A third factor is the relative lack of conflict during the period of industrialization. These factors have deep roots in Sweden's hierarchical past.

From 1530 to 1720 Sweden was a European power engaged in wars of expansion. But noble rule in Sweden did not follow the pattern of that in other European nations; most Swedish aristocrats owed their power to the state and their positions to military service. In 1680 King Karl XI confis-cated land held by the nobility, forcing them to exercise power not through landholdings but through bureaucratic privileges.[23] By the early part of the eighteenth century 80 percent of Swedish nobles earned their living as government officials.[24] In effect, the aristocracy become one with rather than hostile to the state. The clergy was also linked to the state through Sweden's national Lutheran church. Clergymen, who were selected and paid by the Crown, often served as chairmen of local councils. Through-out the first third of the nineteenth century the clergy monopolized local education, and they continued to exercise influence over primary educa-tion until the beginning of the twentieth century.[25] Ultimately, however, the monarchy controlled the religious, economic, and political assets of Sweden, deriving ultimate authority for royal prerogative from the belief that "divinity doth touch a king." The Crown was a major landholder, controlling about 35 percent of all farmland in 1700. Peasants working the land paid rent to the king, making him their economic as well as political master.[26]

In the eighteenth and nineteenth centuries the lower classes revolted against this culture. Nevertheless, as in Japan, the cultural patterns that had developed over hundreds of years continued to influence Sweden's political culture during the rise of democratic rule. Indeed, these patterns have carried over into the present. The fact that the Social Democrats assumed power in 1932, shortly after democracy took hold, and remained in power for more than forty years helped maintain the tradition of deference to government. To some extent Swedish citizens were willing to accept the Social Democratic agenda simply because it was a government proposal. Sweden's inegalitarian past made it easier to promote an egalitarian political program.

The challenge to upper-class rule produced political institutions that encouraged conciliatory processes. The adoption of a constitution in 1809, followed by rapid industrialization, strengthened the political power of the landowning peasantry and the middle class. The constitution set up a system where neither the king nor the members of the four estates—nobles, burghers, clergy, and peasants—dominated politically. Laws could be passed only with the approval of both the king and the estates, although the estates had exclusive power to set taxes. The king, however, sat on the highest court, had the power to issue decrees, appointed the cabinet, and dominated both the clergy and the aristocracy. Thus, initially, the king controlled the new constitutional system.

Beginning in the 1830s, however, the king's authority was continually challenged. From the abolition of the estates system in 1866 to the accession of the first cabinet responsible to Parliament in 1905, the parliamentary majority in the lower chamber was almost continuously hostile to the traditional power holders, although the upper chamber remained loyal to the king. At first opposition was concentrated among peasants, but it later spread to the working class and the new Social Democratic party.

In this setting the king and cabinet began establishing government commissions (*utredningar*), with members drawn from cabinet members or bureaucratic officials on one side and legislators on the other. The intent was to promote deference on the part of legislative members toward the nobles in order to get a favorable response to the latter's proposals. The *utredningar* played this role as early as 1823, when a commission was established to discuss currency reform for the 1823 parliamentary meeting.[27]

Similar motives lay behind the appointment in the 1830s of a commission on the tariff. However, the process gradually evolved into one of mutual influence. The change became visible in an 1840s commission appointed to discuss the future of the estates system. The king, who had no strong views and was mainly concerned with reaching a decision acceptable to the higher and lower estates, selected commission members from "among the more moderate in both camps" in the hope that "a compromise under his leadership could be worked out."[28] By the turn of the century the commission institution was an established procedure for formulating new laws, one that remains to this day. This format, with its reliance on face-to-face contact behind closed doors, is particularly suited to promoting agreement on equality issues.

The evolutionary pattern of Swedish industrialization was the final ingredient in its transition from a feudal to an egalitarian society. Sweden did not follow the pattern described by Alexander Gerschenkron and Barrington Moore. These writers have argued that many European governments anxious to modernize intervened actively in the industrialization process. This intervention often made the newly formed industrial groups highly reliant on the state. When the expanding working class demanded the right to vote and other reforms, the government frequently formed "conservative alliances" with the traditional aristocracy and the industrial middle class against the workers—alliances that tended to delay the transition to democracy.[29] Sweden did not follow this "classic" pattern.[30] Its easier industrialization promoted working-class moderation. This, in turn, tempered the reactionary impulses of the established groups toward working-class demands. Also, as in Japan, the absence of deep religious or regional cleavages helped promote national unity.

The relatively moderate character of the Swedish labor movement has contributed to the Social Democrats' success. In many European countries the labor movement was split between Socialists and Communists. In Sweden, despite the existence of a Communist party, most workers, and an even larger proportion of trade-union leaders, have supported reformist rather than revolutionary policies. Furthermore, during the past half-century the Social Democrats have fared relatively well electorally among white-collar workers and their leaders.[31] Such broad-based support would not have been possible if the Social Democrats had demanded the immediate socialization of Swedish industry. Instead, moderation became the norm for the Social Democrats during their collaboration with the middle-class Liberal party in the fight for universal suffrage.

In sum, the long tradition of deference to government authority, the development of institutions that promoted compromise, and the unusual pattern of Swedish industrialization helped shape the special character of Swedish political culture and established an environment receptive to a strong Social Democratic party. These factors also built the foundation for consensus among different elements of Swedish society.

HISTORY OF EQUALITY AS AN ISSUE

The emergence of Sweden as the vanguard of egalitarian-minded nations has actually been swift and dramatic. Sweden was one of the last countries in Western Europe to abolish estates as the basis of parliamentary representation. Even under the new system instituted that year (1866), property requirements limited voting to 21 percent of adult males.[32] Universal male suffrage for the lower chamber of Parliament was introduced in 1909, making Sweden the last of the Scandinavian nations to do so. In addition, until 1919 wealthy citizens had a larger number of votes (up to forty times more) than poorer citizens in elections for the local government body that indirectly elected the upper chamber of Parliament.[33] Both the monarchy and the noble class remained very strong politically almost to the present. And until 1905 the prime minister was chosen by the king instead of a majority in Parliament.[34] Indeed, virtually every prime minister who served before 1905 and every foreign minister who served before 1914 came from the noble class. Nor was the Sweden of a century ago renowned for its economic equality. Although Sweden had a relatively large number of independent, landowning peasants, widespread poverty drove about one-fifth of the peasant population to the United States in the second half of the nineteenth century. Among the European nations only Ireland lost a larger portion of its population through emigration.

Efforts to foster social equality have also been very recent. As the Japanese now do, Swedes once used a stilted and status-conscious form of address toward one another, often referring to everyone but their closest friends by title and in the third person. For example, they would say, "Would Electrician Larsson do this work for me?" Such practices were not eliminated until the so-called Du-reform in the 1960s.[35]

The swift transition from a hierarchical society to one where political efforts to promote equality assumed center stage has occurred with relatively little conflict. Although demands for socialism and radical redistribution of wealth have aroused partisan hostility ever since they began at the end of the nineteenth century, many welfare-state measures have passed with little or no opposition from conservatives. Instead, battles over equality issues in Sweden have historically been fought among the political parties and their close allies. Of the five parties now represented in the Swedish Parliament—Communists, Social Democrats, Liberals, Center party, and Conservatives—the dominant force since 1932 has been the Social Democrats. Although they formed the government from 1932 to 1976 and from 1982 to today, only sporadically did the Social Democrats enjoy an absolute majority. From 1932 to 1939 they were in coalition with the Farmers' Federation (renamed the Center party in 1958); from 1939 to 1945 they were part of an all-party national unity government; and from 1951 to 1957 they were again in coalition with the Farmers' Federation. In addition, during those periods when they governed alone, the Social Democrats had the unofficial support of the small Communist party, which adopted a policy of never causing the Social Democrats to fall.

Since the end of World War II Sweden has had two relatively stable political blocs: the socialist contingent, composed of the Social Democrats and the Communists; and the nonsocialist bloc of Center, Liberals, and Conservatives. The three nonsocialist parties have different historical roots and traditions. The Liberals supported the Social Democrats in the fight for free trade, universal suffrage, and social reform at the turn of the century.[36] The Liberals also defended the political rights of workers, for example opposing conservative efforts in 1889 to institute a gag law similar to Germany's Anti-Socialist law. The Center party joined in coalition with the Social Democrats twice, representing an alliance of workers and peasants, the little people (*småfolket*). Only the Conservatives have consistently opposed the Social Democrats.

Swedish political parties have closely aligned themselves with occupational organizations. Sweden has one of the highest proportions of unionized employees in the world, 85 percent, and separate labor federations represent blue-collar, white-collar, and professional employees. The largest federation, the LO (*Landsorganisationen*), consists of blue-collar unions. Organized by Social Democratic activists, the LO is closely allied with that party, which provides much of its financial support and active members. The fastest-growing labor federation, the TCO (*Tjänstemännens Centralorganisation*), represents white-collar workers. Since the TCO's founding in 1936 almost all of its leaders have been Social Democrats, but its membership splits its vote much as the Swedish population does. The TCO neither endorses nor contributes financially to any party, but it does take stands on specific policy issues. The smallest union federation, SACO (*Sveriges Akadmikers Centralorganisation*), represents professional employees, those whose jobs require at least a college degree. Like the TCO, SACO does not ally itself with any party, but its leaders and its membership tend to support nonsocialist parties.

Swedish employers are also well organized, with a national employer's federation, the SAF (*Svenska arbetsgivareförening*), that for a long time signed collective bargaining agreements directly with the national union federations and several trade associations affiliated in the Federation of Industries (*Industriförbundet*). Neither the SAF nor the Federation of Industries directly endorses political candidates or contributes to any party. Individual firms do, however, contribute large sums to the nonsocialist parties. Farmers are also well organized, although they represent a shrinking portion of the population, now less than 10 percent. An association of farmers' cooperatives formed the RLF, or National Organization of Agriculture (*Riksförbundet landsbygdens folk*), which is closely affiliated with the Center party.

The Social Democrats and the labor unions associated with them have consistently pressed for more equal rewards for their working-class constituency. The Conservatives have steadfastly opposed such equalization and defended traditional privileges. The starkness of this cleavage has been heightened by the virtual absence of other cross-cutting cleavages. Thus Swedish political parties have primarily divided over their stands on issues related to equality.

SPECIFIC POLICY ISSUES OF EQUALITY

In 1880 the lower chamber of the Swedish Parliament approved lowering the property or income requirements for voting, but the upper chamber, with its bias toward wealthy and corporate interests, voted the proposal down.[37] Only when the tariff issue became salient during the late 1880s and the labor movement gained strength did serious agitation for universal suffrage begin. The political battle for universal suffrage pitted the Social Democratic party, formed in 1889, and the Liberal party, formed in 1895, against peasant and conservative parties. By 1900 the Conservatives in Parliament announced that they were willing to accept universal male suffrage but with a weighted voting scale that gave the rich more votes than the poor.[38] A compromise pushed through in 1909 allowed universal male suffrage for the lower chamber but retained a weighted voting system for the upper chamber.[39] Ten years later the weighted voting scheme was abandoned and women were granted the right to vote.

Today Sweden has a dazzling array of social benefit programs.[40] Many are universal and not income related. These include national health insurance, children's allowances (payments to all parents with children), five weeks' annual vacation, and a basic pension. Other benefits are universal but scaled to a person's income: parental leave (time off from work during the year after childbirth), sick pay, unemployment compensation, disability insurance, and supplementary pensions. Some benefits, such as housing allowances and American-style welfare payments, are means tested, going only to those with low incomes. In general, Sweden adopted these laws later than most other European countries.

Two features of early Swedish welfare efforts stand out. First, the Liberals played an active role in alliance with Social Democrats in supporting these measures.[41] Second, the establishment of commissions to investigate these issues proved very successful. For example, Social Democratic inclusion on the 1907 commission studying government-sponsored pensions helped overcome conservative opposition to the proposal, and both sides reached a consensus for a state pension system.[42] By the mid-1920s, however, the pension system and other elements of the emerging welfare state came under attack from the conservatives because of both their expense and their alleged negative effect on people's "psychological health." The Social Democrats, meanwhile, supported an increase in pensions and a move toward financing them through taxation. This was a major issue in the elections of 1924 and 1928, and in 1928 a commission formed with representatives from the major parties began to examine the issue.[43] Six years later the commission, with substantial agreement, recommended that pensions be increased and that some public tax support for the system be introduced.

In the postwar period Sweden became a world leader in the number and generosity of its social welfare measures. Most social welfare programs became law with little partisan disagreement. A 1947 bill establishing children's allowances was passed by Parliament only after a proposal by nonsocialist parties that the size of the allowance be increased for second and third children was defeated.[44] National health insurance passed Parliament unanimously in 1946.[45] But major partisan controversy developed over a proposed governmental supplementary pension based on one's income level. The nonsocialists opposed the plan's socialistic impact; they feared that the huge public funding needed for the program might be used by the government to control investment in the economy.[46]

Efforts to combat unemployment during the Great Depression helped create the political base for forty-five years of Social Democratic rule.[47] During the Depression of the 1930s the Social Democrats fought unemployment through large-scale public-works programs. Some scholars, however, contend that Sweden's success in lifting itself from the Depression resulted largely from rising German demand for Swedish iron and favorable exchange rates rather than from internal pump priming. The Social Democrats carried out these measures in coalition with the Peasant party, which accepted the increased public-works programs in exchange for a tax on margarine. Initially, the measures faced opposition from Conservatives and most Liberals. By the end of the war, however, all the parties supported these efforts.[48]

Postwar governments have continued to intervene in the economy, increasing public-works spending during economic downturns and encouraging firms to put a portion of their profits into tax-free investment funds to be used during recessions. In the 1950s the Social Democrats went further by introducing the so-called active labor market policy, a policy of providing subsidies for workers in declining industries. This policy freed trade unions to pursue a wage-equalization policy and made it easier for laid-off workers to find jobs.[49] Representatives of all Swedish parties endorsed these active labor market policies in a state commission report in 1960.[50]

Despite the existence of a progressive tax system in Sweden, direct equalization—taking a larger proportion of the income of wealthier citizens in order to redistribute income—has not dominated national policy. Instead, the government has emphasized using taxes to finance social programs, an indirect form of equalization. Although Sweden instituted the progressive income tax in 1902, the transition from low-tax to high-tax policies did not take place until the 1930s. This occurred in order to finance the many public-works and welfare programs that had been introduced. The government increased indirect taxes on liquor, coffee, and tobacco, and added surcharges onto the tax rates for income and wealth at higher levels. In 1936 a government commission reviewed the tax system in light of the tax increases of the previous years. The commission, which included all political parties, unanimously ratified the bulk of the tax increases but weakened some of the progressivity of the tax system by lowering the percentage of one's wealth subject to taxation.[51] Since then most of the debate over taxes has focused on the level of taxes rather than their progressivity.

In 1959 a sales tax was introduced for the first time, "the most important tax policy of the postwar era" because "it lay the groundwork for the expansion of the public sector during the 1960s."[52] Increases during the 1960s raised the sales tax to 17 percent by 1970.[53] The Social Democrats supported it, even though a sales tax seems to run contrary to the traditional preference of the left for progressive rather than proportional taxes. The Social Democrats argued that by funding more government programs, the tax would ultimately help low-income groups.[54]

During the Social Democrats' forty-five-year reign Sweden had one of the lowest proportions of state-owned industry in Western Europe despite the fact that the Social Democrats were founded on the principle that the means of production must be put into public hands. Swedish accommodationist institutions and the relative moderation of Swedish workers and employers helped moderate the Social Democrats' demands, although some elements in the party still believe that socialism should be high on the party's agenda.

The Liberal, Conservative, and Center parties are consistent and determined opponents of the socialization of the Swedish economy. Political controversy arises whenever the nonsocialist parties perceive that the Social Democrats are introducing measures that will increase governmental control over investment and production. For example, a postwar program issued in 1944 provoked fierce opposition by calling for increased government control of investments and government participation in an effort to "rationalize" the structure of industry. In the 1948 election the Social Democrats lost support and abandoned most of these proposals.[55]

In 1976 the LO, the blue-collar labor federation, proposed a "wage-earner fund" whereby a company would put a portion of its profits into newly issued shares of stock and transfer these shares into a union-controlled fund. Gradually this fund would achieve majority ownership of major Swedish corporations. The nonsocialists made this far-reaching socialist proposal a major political issue, and it cost the Social Democrats votes in 1976. Opinion polls showed that the proposal received support from only a small minority of Swedish citizens. In 1983 a modest version of the wage-earner fund finally became law, but the nonsocialist parties pledged to abolish the fund should they return to power.[56]

CURRENT ISSUES OF EQUALITY

As in the United States, the late 1960s and early 1970s were a time of political radicalization in Sweden. References to the concept of equality in Social Democratic congresses as well as in editorials rose sharply. A 1969 party program for the Social Democrats deleted a reference in a previous party program that accepted "differences based on differences in effort, ability, responsibility, and initiative."[57] The call for greater equality was the main slogan of the Social Democrats' 1970 election campaign.

Although much of the wakening interest in equality was a response to statistical investigations of the poor in Sweden, most of the measures introduced did not involve new income-transfer or other welfare-type programs. The government did pass a law in 1970 making the tax system more progressive, but the main thrust of the egalitarian efforts was to extend the sweep of government equalization efforts into the workplace through what was called the renewal of working life. This was reflected in the new Law on Co-Determination, which required labor-management negotiations in management decisions at the local level. Laws making it more difficult to fire laborers and increasing occupational safety and health regulations gave the workers greater control over their workplaces. The Liberal and Center parties tended to support these measures; the Conservative party more often opposed them. The number of immigrants arriving in Sweden grew rapidly in the 1960s; by the end of the decade about one-tenth of the population was non-Swedish. Immigrants could come to Sweden only if they had previously arranged jobs. An exception was made for other Scandinavians who, under the provisions of the Nordic free labor market agreement, were allowed easy access. Once in the country, immigrants could stay as long as they wanted and eventually become Swedish citizens. The largest number of immigrants have come from Finland, a poorer country with a very different language that was once dominated politically by Sweden. Significant numbers have come from Yugoslavia, Turkey, and Italy. By the end of the 1970s immigrant issues had not yet received much attention in Sweden's political sphere, despite recurrent accounts of racial tensions and language difficulties among schoolchildren and the beginnings of ethnic concentrations in certain neighborhoods. No political party was identified as being either strongly for or strongly against the immigrants. The immigrants themselves, although obviously poorer than most Swedes, were not well organized and had not made radical demands.

Probably the closest thing in Sweden to an outside group mobilized during the 1960s was young people. Although Sweden largely avoided the violence that disrupted universities in the United States and many Western European countries, many intellectuals and students refused to integrate themselves into the established political system. They gained beachheads among some of the leadership groups, including journalists (in particular, reporters for Sweden's state-owned radio and television networks) and the youth organizations of the Social Democratic and Center parties. Like their counterparts in other countries, these intellectuals adopted a radically proequality ideology, but the specific issues that impassioned them tended to be ones of foreign policy, environmentalism, and antiindustrialism.

Sweden, like other countries, has struggled with economic difficulties since the early 1970s. These difficulties coincided with the rise to power of the nonsocialist bloc in 1976. The welfare state and other equalization measures introduced by the Social Democrats had coexisted with high rates of economic growth that made Sweden one of the most prosperous countries in the world. When economic growth slowed, many major Swedish firms suddenly suffered financial troubles. These economic difficulties were concentrated in industries such as shipbuilding and steel that played a major role in the Swedish economy. Swedish firms outside these industries also experienced sluggish growth and investment.

Slow growth and the high costs of assisting ailing industries created enormous budget deficits. This produced pressures on other budget items, including social spending. The economic difficulties provoked many to question whether social reform efforts had gone too far, especially in terms of the taxes needed to support them. When our survey took place, more than half the Swedish GNP was paid in taxes, with many ordinary workers having marginal income tax rates, including local taxes, of about 50 percent. Opponents argued that high taxes were stifling work effort and entrepreneurship and thus hurting the economy. The hard economic times also revived the debate over whether government programs should be universal or targeted mainly for the poor. Swedish sociologist Walter Korpi has pointed out that in the United States 25 percent of expenditures he classifies as welfare-state benefits go to those with low incomes only, whereas in Sweden this has been true for only 1 to 2 percent of such expenditures.[58] The nonsocialist parties in Sweden have argued that the universal system made people who were paying high taxes dependent on social welfare payments because of their small after-tax income. They supported the idea of restricting the social welfare system to those in need, allowing people to keep a larger portion of what they earn. ("People should be able to live on their salaries," went the slogan.) The Social Democrats have defended the universal benefit arrangement as more advantageous to the poor in the long run than programs aimed only at the poor. Universal benefits, they argue, avoid the creation of a two-class system where wealthy people can purchase a deluxe version of certain services; equality derives as much from capping the rich as from bringing up the poor. Also, universal programs have a potentially broader base of support, which protects them from cuts during hard economic times.[59]

Recently members of SAF, the employers' federation, began advocating radical changes in government policy toward free-market, noninterventionist positions. This new atmosphere, which questioned the political commitment to equalization that had dominated the attention of the Social Democratic government for four decades, developed just when the Social

Democrats were out of power for the first time in the memory of many Swedish adults. Our survey, conducted during those years, therefore took place during a time of transition and testing of Swedish egalitarian policies.

The United States

POLITICAL CULTURE

Since its beginnings the United States has impressed visitors as a nation strongly committed to the ideal of equality. Gunnar Myrdal wrote in the mid-twentieth century of an American "social ethos, a political creed" that embodied among other ideals "the fundamental equality of all men."[60] A half-century before Myrdal, James Bryce observed, "Respect for attainment excites interest, even reverence," but without causing one to act "as if he were made of porcelain and you only of earthenware."[61] Perhaps the most famous of these travelers, Alexis de Tocqueville, writing fifty years before Bryce, observed that the leading characteristic of American life was the "equality of condition."[62]

The ideals of individualism, achievement, dispersed power, equal opportunity, and political equality form the basis of the creed that has steered the American experience for two centuries. The origins of this creed derive from a complex interplay of political and social ideas, free-market capitalism, the circumstances of the nation's founding, its expanding frontier, and the influence of religious dissent.

The American creed is first and foremost political. Americans, perhaps more than others, identify with their country because of its political values and practices rather than its social, geographical, or cultural traits.[63] Although it is difficult to separate the threads of the many ideas loosely woven together to form the fabric of the creed, liberalism and constitutionalism are unquestionably its two major strands.[64] Both ideas have roots that lie deep in the nation's past. Constitutionalism emphasizes rule by law; Americans of the colonial era brought with them the traditions of the British legal code. Liberalism, the notion that the rule of government is based on the rights of the individual, had its origins in the ideals of the Enlightenment and the writings of Locke in particular. But the American Declaration of Independence took these ideas and reformulated them into a concept of political equality. Certain rights, it declared, were God-given, and government existed only to secure them.[65]

The essence of constitutionalism is the restraint of government through law. The essence of liberalism is freedom from governmental control. Together, these two values served to delegitimize hierarchical and authoritarian structures. The continuing American mistrust of concentrated, especially centralized authority testifies to the enduring influence of both ideals.[66] This antiauthority, antipower ethic was buttressed by the founding fathers' view that human nature was inherently evil and that people's dangerous tendencies could be checked only by those of similar nature. The founding fathers designed a republic with a separation of shared powers to fragment authority.

American religious traditions also contribute to dispersed authority. The United States is the only nation dominated by the religious doctrine of Protestant dissent, as embodied in the teachings of such denominations as the Methodists and the Baptists. In general, these religions teach people to follow their conscience, unlike state churches such as the Catholic, Lutheran, and Anglican. This enduring Protestant ethic has reinforced tendencies toward individualism and dispersed power in America.[67]

The conditions under which the United States was founded also nurtured the antiauthoritarian ethic. Unlike Sweden and Japan, the United States had no history of feudalism or monarchy. Citizens had no need to centralize power in order to destroy an existing feudal culture, to challenge the crown, or even to fight large-scale foreign wars—at least for the first 145 years of the country's existence.

In the nineteenth century the development of relatively stable political parties with a mass popular base—the first such parties in the world[68]—pushed suffrage rights faster and further than otherwise might have occurred, even though blacks and women were not permitted to vote until much later.[69] Political equality based on broad suffrage rights with no property qualifications developed in the United States earlier than anywhere else.

This early emphasis on social and political egalitarianism partly explains the relative lack of class-based politics; democracy triumphed before the impact of the industrial revolution and thus before the working class became a powerful force.[70] The early achievement of white male suffrage, the general openness of political institutions, the opportunities for economic mobility, the ethnic diversity and geographic dispersion of the working class, and the prevalence of the liberal-democratic creed hindered the rise of class-conscious workers.[71] Lacking a feudal ethos, the United States lacked as well a basis for socialism.[72] This absence of feudalism permitted the unchallenged spread of liberal-bourgeois values.[73]

Socialism never attracted a solid political following in the United States, and trade unions never gained the strength they have had in Europe.

Instead of a working class and socialistic ethic, the United States developed a distinctly middle-class ethos, a product of the nature of the early settlers—particularly those from the dissenting and separatist religious sects—the abundance of free land, and the opportunities for geographic and social mobility. The many opportunities for landownership and the great expanse of western land helped shield Americans from one another and prevented the rise, except in the plantation South, of agricultural classes.[74] Only when space ran out and America became increasingly urbanized did even the rudiments of class conflict occur.

Immigration has been a fundamental part of American history, especially in the second half of the nineteenth and early twentieth centuries with the massive influx of largely poor immigrants from southern and eastern Europe.[75] These immigrants brought with them an ethic of hierarchy and authority that contrasted in many ways with the prevailing individualistic, antiauthoritarian creed.[76] Although the influx of immigrants surely left its mark on American institutions, especially during the New Deal era, each wave of immigrants abandoned its traditional European ethos and embraced Anglo-Saxon political ideas. Indeed, immigrants have clung tenaciously to the promise of equal opportunity and individual achievement enshrined in the American creed and through their accomplishments have further strengthened these ideas.

The egalitarian ideal has not always squared with the reality. The emphasis on equality of opportunity, combined with a traditional mistrust of government, has discouraged efforts to compensate for economic inequalities that arise in the free-market system.[77] When these economic inequities are converted into political influence for those at the top of the socioeconomic ladder, further inconsistencies emerge between the American ideal—in this case the idea of political equality—and reality.[78]

The United States, both in de Tocqueville's era and today, is a society where fundamental inequalities in economic status are tolerated, even encouraged, as long as they are based on achievement. Efforts to compensate for this perceived imbalance have usually gone far toward equalizing political influence but have done little to correct economic inequities. Undoubtedly, one explanation for Americans' preference for individual effort over government intervention in economic life and their continuing tolerance of substantial economic inequalities is that, although economic stratification remains, economic mobility has been substantial.[79] The very lack of a clearly defined and rigid social structure encourages at once the rhetorical emphasis on equality and the glorifying of economic gain.

HISTORY OF EQUALITY AS AN ISSUE

Equality issues have been at the center of the major upheavals that have erupted on the American scene: the Revolution, the Jacksonian era, the Civil War and Reconstruction, the Populist-Progressive period, the New Deal, and the tumultuous 1960s and 1970s.[80] In each period challenging groups sought both political and economic equality, for themselves and on behalf of others. Inevitably, each battle led to some progress toward egalitarianism on both fronts. In the end, however, each upheaval did relatively little to redress inequalities in the distribution of income and wealth. The enduring and significant result of these historical battles was rather the achievement of greater political equality through the expansion of political rights or the dispersion of political influence. In other words, the principal legacy of the drives for equality in the United States has been a steadily increasing democratization.

The use of the term *revolution* to describe the American War of Independence is misleading. Unlike later revolts along French or Marxist lines, the American Revolution was not rooted in class: merchants, farmers, employers, and workers fought on both the Revolutionary and the Tory sides of the conflict. The war against England brought about not economic, not social, but dramatic political change, backed by new political ideas. Among the many changes were the abolition of legal vestiges of feudalism like entail and quitrents, reform of the penal codes, the enactment of bills of rights, the abolition of slavery in northern states, the separation of church and state, and the break with the Crown. The ideas embodied in these changes were simple but radical: the notion that government derived its legitimate powers from the consent of the governed, a rejection of the institutionalization and legal protection of privilege, and a dedication to the norm of political equality.

Yet for all they promised in political equality to the young nation, these values had few social or economic implications. In the words of Pole, "the American Revolution introduced an egalitarian rhetoric to an unequal society." Economic and social inequalities remained essentially intact. Although slavery was attacked, white servitude was not. Although the United States rejected hereditary rulership, its own gentry retained the power and esteem it had enjoyed for generations, not because of practical strictures on social mobility but because of limited allegiance to true egalitarian values.[81] Even so, for its day American colonial society was economically and socially more equal than its European counterparts.

The election of Andrew Jackson as president in 1832 signaled the second major upheaval in the American political system. A man born in poverty, Jackson represented the rise of the common man to the highest office in the land and the first challenge to eastern political supremacy. Once again, the impulse toward equality took a political direction. The suffrage was extended through the elimination of property requirements in many states. Political parties flourished, political participation increased, and party conventions replaced the system of closed congressional caucuses for presidential nominations. Increasing political equality did not translate into reduced economic inequality, however. The Jacksonian revolution emphasized equality of opportunity but in the laissez-faire economic atmosphere fostered the idea that some people would be better than others at achieving economic progress. In Jackson's words: "Distinctions in society will always exist under every just government. Equality of talent, or of education, or of wealth cannot be produced by human institutions."[82]

The tension between the ideals of political and social equality and the existence of black slavery culminated in the third great upheaval: the Civil War and the subsequent Reconstruction. The Civil War fostered equality by ending slavery, a momentous step in the American effort toward full equality for its citizens. Yet the step was a limited one.

With postwar Reconstruction came the political rights of citizenship and the vote. In the immediate aftermath of the war efforts were made to give the freed blacks equal protection under the law. Congress enacted civil rights legislation rejecting the Supreme Court's racially exclusive definition of citizenship. The fourteenth and fifteenth amendments to the constitution made citizenship race-blind and prohibited state efforts to abridge the right of blacks to vote. Almost immediately, however, efforts to achieve black equality were undercut or dismantled: the Supreme Court, in a series of decisions, eroded the scope of Reconstruction legislation; the institution of literacy tests and poll taxes diluted the fifteenth amendment; and in 1875 Congress passed an emasculated civil rights bill. These actions prevented movement toward social or economic rights. Even black political gains, which eventually proved to be durable, rested on shaky ground.

In the late nineteenth century industrialization transformed America. The quintessential American was no longer the American farmer; he had become the business entrepreneur whose "rugged individualism" the government would preserve with a laissez-faire attitude toward the regulation of commercial activity. As corporate trusts multiplied, the wealth from this new productivity flowed to a small group; an 1893 Census Bureau report estimated that 9 percent of the American families possessed 71 percent of the nation's wealth.[83] These factors spurred the rise of the Populist movement in the 1880s, as farmers and others agitated for economic equality. The Populists' themes were economic as well as political. They felt that they deserved a better fate than victimization at the hand of the new industrialists. Among other things, the Populists advocated a graduated income tax.[84]

As urban politics began to overshadow rural politics, Populism gave way to the Progressive movement around the turn of the century. Progressive reform had a more patrician aura than the Populist platform. The torch of political change in this period of ferment passed from the lower class to the middle class. Better educated and less provincial than the Populists, the Progressives had a Yankee Protestant sense of responsibility for social ills and their solution.

In the American tradition, the Progressives called for more political democracy rather than more economic equality. A number of their reforms genuinely improved and broadened popular control over public affairs. For example, the direct election of senators and the recall made the electoral system more responsive to the public. And granting suffrage to women enlarged the electorate. The Progressives also fought for the adoption of voter registration laws, the referendum, and the direct primary.[85] However, with the notable exception of the adoption in 1912 of a nationwide graduated income tax (the sixteenth constitutional amendment), the Progressives did little to address economic disparities in the United States. In the end, concentrations of power were relocated but not dispersed.

The objective of the New Deal in the 1930s, unlike that of the earlier movements, was not political reform but economic recovery from the Great Depression. Political reform, however, was undeniably one of the New Deal's results. According to William Leuchtenburg, "the New Deal achieved a more just society by recognizing groups which had been largely unrepresented."[86] Thus, Franklin D. Roosevelt's economic programs had significant consequences for the politics of equality. New Deal policies provided some measure of security against severe economic deprivation, but radical redistribution of wealth was neither sought nor achieved. The most significant consequences of the concern for economic equality were political.[87]

Making labor the equal of management was the boldest political stroke of the New Deal. The Wagner Act sought to change "the inequality of bargaining power between employees who did not possess full freedom of association or actual liberty of contract and employers who are organized in the corporate or other forms of ownership association." To do so, it created the National Labor Relations Board and charged it with protecting workers' right to bargain collectively and overseeing the process by which the workers' representatives were chosen. This unprecedented grant of power to an economic group fostered a boom in labor organizing; union membership rose from four million in 1935 to nine million in 1947. The government was now in the equality business without reservation, but the equalization was political. The government provided "countervailing power" to groups too weak to make their own case for social justice.[88]

Another period of political passion brought the rebirth of egalitarianism in the 1960s and 1970s. The Great Society, like the New Deal, had programs that aimed at economic equity but did not radically redistribute wealth. Also like the New Deal, these programs singled out economic groups for special attention—but this time for explicit economic not political assistance. Older social programs such as Social Security did not discriminate by class or race; new measures with economic means tests, like Aid to Families with Dependent Children (AFDC), singled out the poor and thus blacks as particular beneficiaries. This hardly amounted to an equalization of wealth, but consideration of economic equity had entered the mainstream of American political discourse and public policy. The experience of the Great Society neatly illustrates how the political debate in the United States differs from that in Sweden. Liberals in the United States defend group-targeted, means-tested programs as being more egalitarian. In Sweden conservatives favor these policies. The Social Democrats prefer programs with universal benefits to those aimed at the poor, in part because of the difficulty of sustaining political support for such policies.

Political reform with an egalitarian bent bloomed in the 1960s as it had in the other periods of political flux. The reforms included fewer restrictions on voting (the Voting Rights Act of 1965, extension of the vote to eighteen-year-olds), more presidential primaries, delegate quotas by race and gender at Democratic conventions, new campaign finance laws, and freedom-of-information legislation—all aimed to reallocate power from vested political interests. Blacks won greater social and political equality but made less progress against economic inequities. During the seven years after the Voting Rights Act, one million blacks swelled the voting rolls. In the same era the percentage of southern black children attending all-black schools fell from 98 percent to 9 percent. Yet despite real economic gains for black wage earners, blacks made limited headway relative to whites. A continually widening schism developed within the black community between middle-class and lower-class blacks. The small number of black husband-and-wife families made impressive gains on comparable white families; with the growing "feminization of poverty," however, more and more female-headed black families sank into destitution. Increasingly dissatisfied with this situation, women and racial minorities began to demand the use of quotas, affirmative action, and other compensatory programs to remedy past discrimination and close the gap between themselves and more advantaged segments of society. Much of the current equality debate in the United States revolves around these demands.

To the extent that the 1960s are not yet history, it is impossible to judge which of its measures for equality will survive. As in other periods of upheaval, however, the political will probably overshadow the economic. The young were given a political tool, the vote. The use of that tool was guaranteed to blacks, but this step has not translated into direct or dramatic economic gain. The gap in earnings between white males on the one hand and blacks and women on the other persists into the 1980s. These disadvantaged groups have increased their political power; their relative economic improvement is much less obvious.

In the United States as in Sweden political parties have served as the principal arenas for battles over equality issues. Although American parties differ considerably from their counterparts in other countries—in having less rigidly ideological positions and weaker ties to particular social groups—they have traditionally staked out divergent positions on issues of economic equality and, to a lesser extent, on other aspects of equality. The differences between the Democrats and the Republicans are real and crucial. This is especially true for party leaders who differ substantially from one another on equality issues as contrasted with the more centrist views of the American public.[89]

PUBLIC POLICIES DEALING WITH EQUALITY

As the above discussion indicates, the history of public policy directed at equality in the United States shows steady progress toward political democratization but fewer efforts at economic redistribution. It also displays a strong bias toward equality of opportunity rather than equality of result.

The United States has long been one of the most egalitarian of nations in the political realm. At the time of the Revolution, the voting franchise was generally limited to adult white males who owned at least fifty acres of land or who satisfied other standards of property ownership or tax payment. Over the next four decades property and tax requirements gradually disappeared, and by the start of the Civil War universal white manhood suffrage existed. The ratification of the fifteenth amendment in 1870 extended the franchise to black adult males. But as noted above this was a symbolic victory because the southern states where most blacks lived used poll taxes, literacy tests, and other statutory means to disenfranchise blacks. These barriers persisted for almost a century until the civil rights movement in the 1950s and 1960s, together with federal court action and Great Society legislation, destroyed them. The twenty-fourth amendment, passed in 1964, abolished the poll tax; the Voting Rights Act of 1965 barred literacy tests and also provided for federal examiners to register voters in states or counties where more than half the voting-age population had failed to register or vote during the 1964 election. The nineteenth amendment, ratified in 1920, gave women the right to vote and nearly doubled the size of the electorate. Finally, the last major expansion of voting rights came in 1971, when the twenty-sixth amendment lowered the voting age from twenty to eighteen.

In other ways the United States pioneered the expansion of mass political participation: early New England town meetings came closest to the ideal of direct democracy; several American states adopted procedures, like the referendum, initiative, and voter recall, that permitted wider citizen participation in government affairs; in 1913 a constitutional amendment permitted the popular election of senators; and the development of the direct primary gave the public a major voice in selecting candidates.

Efforts aimed at economic equality have been far less successful in the United States. Throughout its history the distribution of wealth in this nation has remained essentially the same. Concentrations of wealth were unequal but stable during the colonial era. During the next century, however, wealth became more unequally distributed over the nation as a whole. This change was most pronounced in the antebellum period, coincident with an increasing wage premium for skilled labor.[90]

The nineteenth-century surge in economic inequality was balanced by three periods of income equalization, the only periods of equalization in American history. The first and most dramatic was the emancipation of the slaves. The second occurred during World War I, when the gap between rich and poor fell sharply, possibly the result of a shortage of unskilled labor, increased product demand, inflation, and greater mobility between classes. The last and most important period of equalization was the income revolution that leveled wealth distribution between the 1920s and the midcentury; inflation and more balanced growth across sectors favored unskilled labor once again. Since World War II government transfers producing a fairly stable distribution have balanced a slight increase in pretax inequality. Overall, as Jeffrey Williamson and Peter Lindert have found, "inequality of wealth today resembles what it was on the eve of the Declaration of Independence."

Many of the most "radical" or at least most aggressive redistributive policies in the United States have actually been dismantled or undermined. Such post–Civil War Reconstruction programs as the Freedmen's Bureau and the Southern Homestead Act, which were designed to pull up blacks economically and socially, failed because of southern obstructionism. The federal income tax has been so altered by loopholes and deductions that it no longer operates as a progressive tax.[91] Many Great Society programs, such as welfare aid, food stamps, and social service block grants, have lost part of their funding in the conservative backlash of the Reagan administration.

The policies that have survived and prospered are broad-based and individualistic, and they promote equal opportunity, not equal results. There is no strong sentiment from any part of the U.S. political spectrum for government-sponsored redistribution of wealth; even the most basic social welfare policies have appeared only recently in the nation's history. In trying to redress economic inequality, Americans seem willing only to place a floor under incomes to eliminate extreme poverty; they refuse to discourage achievement by placing a ceiling on income and wealth. Furthermore, government efforts such as social security and the wide array of education programs usually focus on individuals. Spending for education exceeds that in other nations: the United States ranks first in per capita spending on schooling and first in the percentage of the population that has received higher education. Popular support for education in the United States is long-standing: the first public school in the world opened in Boston in 1635, and as early as 1700 the Carolina legislature passed a law providing for public support of a library in Charleston. Education programs have ranged from the Morrill Act (1862), which provided federal property for land-grant colleges, to the G.I. Bill (1944), which paid education costs for veterans of military service. Support for education harmonizes perfectly with the American ideology. It reflects the American emphasis on both equal opportunity and individual achievement. Education, as Seymour Martin Lipset puts it, is the most equally distributed item in America.[92] But the educational system also has been the main channel for upward mobility. As such, it is a source of economic inequality rather than equality, fostering disparities in income and occupational status.

Ultimately, these inequalities spill over into the political sphere, under-cutting the political equality that American values and policies endorse.[93] Thus, in the United States more than in comparable nations, political ac-tivists come disproportionately from the better educated and the more af-fluent.[94] Also, although the potentially corrosive effect of money in politics is a traditional American concern, the United States poses fewer obstacles to the exploitation of economic resources for political purposes than do other industrial democracies.[95]

In contrast with its early and far-reaching efforts in the field of public education, the United States ranks quite low in the government's commit-ment to policies fostering economic equality. It was not until 1965 that legislation was enacted that established a broad-based system of medical care. Even so, Medicare and Medicaid coverage remains much less exten-sive than medical programs found in other industrialized nations. The United States also ranks low among industrial nations in expenditures for social security, income maintenance, and income-transfer payments. It has yet to pass a family allowance or comprehensive health insurance plan,[96] and it also ranks near the bottom of industrial nations in its use of taxes to reduce inequality.

CURRENT ISSUES OF EQUALITY

Over the past two decades the equality debate shifted from a concern with individual gains and equal opportunity to a focus on group claims and equal results. Group-based claims to equality have always been a counter-point to the dominant proindividual theme. With the rise of the civil rights and feminist movements, however, these group pressures grew quite po-tent. This shift represented, in Theodore White's words, an effort "to transform the traditional credo of American politics, 'equality,' into the credo of 'group equality' . . . what blacks want most is public acceptance of equality, not only on the basis of individual merit, but on the basis of group results and group shares."[97]

President Lyndon Johnson articulated the ideal that guided many of the reforms of the Great Society: "We seek not just freedom but opportu-nity—not just legal equity but human ability—not just equality as a right and a theory but equality as a fact and a result."[98] The tensions reflected in this statement remain unresolved; perhaps the most acute arise from the issue of affirmative action and from compulsory integration policies such as school busing.

As the fiery rhetoric of egalitarianism intensified, as the federal govern-ment affirmed its commitment to equality and launched new policy initiatives, and as the judiciary asserted itself where the bureaucracy was unresponsive to equality claims, an antiegalitarian backlash spread. The concern for and rhetoric of equality were so intense that an entire movement, neoconservativism, sprang up in reaction to what its exponents felt were dangerous excesses.[99] Irving Kristol warned against those who "prize equality more than liberty." His neoconservative colleague Robert Nisbet called the egalitarian fervor "the single greatest threat to liberty and social initiative."[100] Corporate and affluent interests launched an organized and effective counterattack to the egalitarian thrust against the establishment.[101]

The Reagan presidency represented the most significant response to the earlier egalitarianism. The Reagan administration tried to turn back the tide, with some success. As President Reagan said, "the central political error of our time is the view that government and bureaucracy are the primary vehicle for social change."[102] The purpose of the Reagan program, as one sympathetic observer put it, was to restore "incentives in our economy to produce income and wealth and raise the absolute level of income on average . . . and this in turn depends in no small measure on our ability to achieve a degree of control over the exploding growth of transfer-payment programs."[103] Reaganomics meant a scaling down of government-sponsored programs and a greater reliance on market forces to revive a slumping economy.

In the 1980s the rhetoric softened. Despite the more muted discourse, however, equality issues continued to fill the agenda of politics and policy-making. In the 1984 election, for example, issues of equality came to the fore. Theodore White suggested that the underlying plot of the campaign was a "testing . . . of the meaning of the word 'equality' with blacks and women playing the leading roles." The first serious black candidate sought a party's presidential nomination, and the first woman ran on a major party's presidential ticket. The Democrats charged that Reagan was excessively generous to the rich and unfair to the poor; the Republicans countered that the Democrats were captives of special interests. The candidates debated who should shoulder how much of the tax burden.

Economic equality returned to the national agenda in 1985, when Reagan proposed sweeping changes in the federal tax code. Questions of equity quickly dominated the tax-reform debate. Critics claimed that the middle class and residents of states with high taxes would suffer unfairly under the Reagan plan. Group after group defended its special tax privileges. The issue of equality was once again at the center of the American political debate.

Comparative Analysis

In the preceding pages we have described important differences and similarities among the political cultures and historical experiences of Japan, Sweden, and the United States; these are patterns reflected in the public policies pursued in each country. In the United States individualism reigns supreme; the Swedes and especially the Japanese submerge the individual to the group. Equality of opportunity is the dominant norm in the United States; by contrast, the more group-oriented political cultures, especially Sweden, favor the ideal of equality of result. The United States also differs from the other two countries in the nature of its government and public attitudes toward governmental authority: central government authority is relatively weak, and Americans take pride in their antiauthoritarian tradition; Sweden and Japan have stronger central governments and long histories of public deference to established authority.

From its birth U.S. political culture was characterized by strong adherence to liberal-democratic values. Political equality, although initially limited to white property owners, became a key part of the American political creed at an earlier stage than in any other nation. In Japan and Sweden, by contrast, centuries of rule by hereditary elites delayed the transition to political democracy. Sweden did not abolish the system of estates until 1866. The Japanese introduced democratic procedures at about the same time, but democratic values and institutions did not really take root in that country until after World War II.

Even in the modern democratic period the legacy of feudalism has left a strong residue of deference to authority in Japan and Sweden. It may be no coincidence that both countries have been dominated for the past half-century by single parties. By contrast, in the United States since 1940 the Republicans and the Democrats have each won the presidency six times.

The political cultures of Japan and Sweden thus share some important features. Other characteristics of their political and belief systems separate them. Sweden has a strong Socialist party that is closely allied with a powerful organized labor movement. In the United States and Japan, on the other hand, unions are weak. There is no national Socialist party in the United States, and in Japan the power of the Conservative party has relegated the Socialists to permanent opposition status. Support for fairly radical redistribution policies is widespread in Sweden, nearly nonexistent in the United States, and confined to a small group on the left in Japan.

The evolution of democratic rule in Sweden occurred in conjunction with the industrialization of the nation. In Japan, democratic institutions also first emerged during the drive to modernize. Industrialization spawned class-based workers' movements in both nations. In the United States, however, political equality was already enshrined in the constitution before industrialization. Lacking a feudal tradition, the United States had no class-based movement among the workers and thus no strong support for socialism. Both Japan and Sweden developed socialist movements but with differing consequences, in part because the heavy emphasis on group conformity and status hierarchy in Japan as well as government opposition hindered the development of a powerful workers' movement.

In Sweden, the middle class aligned with the workers to demand suffrage rights. This agitation, combined with the evolution of accommodationist mechanisms—the use of government commissions—afforded the Social Democrats a legitimate place within the political system. The workers gained political clout, and trade unions flourished. The Japanese emphasized accommodation as well but within the hierarchy of emperor rule rather than among competing constituencies within the polity. In Japan, the Socialist party was not granted legal status until well into the twentieth century. The military and the bureaucracy resisted civilian control in the 1920s, and by the mid-1930s these two groups held a tight grip on the political system.

The political institutions in each of the three countries have influenced the policy on egalitarian issues. The United States has a republican form of rule with a decentralized governmental apparatus. This fragmented political structure has discouraged the rise of ideologically based political parties more common in both Sweden and Japan. The American party system is a more centrist and moderate one where neither party has extreme ideological leanings. The nature of this system makes it vulnerable to being pulled apart by "new" issues, such as those of race or gender. Sweden's stronger party system has shown itself better suited to incorporating such potentially divisive issues into its traditional partisan rubric.

In the United States and Sweden, the main forces in the twentieth century for more egalitarian-oriented public policy—the New Deal and Social Democracy—were each domestic movements that were driven primarily by internal events. In Japan, however, democratizing reforms, including land reform and the legalization of trade unions, resulted largely from external intervention of the American occupation forces. Yet these imposed policies took root and have held securely, in part because they are compatible with the traditional Japanese commitment to group conformity and cohesion. Moreover, although Japan was set on the road to greater equality by mandated policies, that progress was sustained by impressive economic growth, government subsidies to the farm sector, and gradual wage increases in private enterprises.

This brief historical survey suggests that the United States has less economic equality than Sweden or Japan, at least in part because American cultural values and political structures do not foster it. The history of these three countries demonstrates that there are no necessary or automatic links between political equality and economic equality. The United States has experienced steady movement toward political equality yet relatively little change in the distribution of economic resources. Historically, Japan and Sweden have had less political equality; citizens in both those countries have more willingly accepted hierarchical authority and more readily deferred to the government than the American public has. Yet these traditions of deference and hierarchy have facilitated the creation of the strong government and strong political parties needed to pursue policies that reduce inequality.

Ironically, the strong U.S. commitment to political equality and the strong antipathy to established authority limit the state's ability to "enforce" equality. The U.S. government is weak; it would have trouble launching an ambitious redistributive effort, and few people appear to want it to do so. Americans endorse equality of opportunity, an ideal that fits well with the individualistic, achievement-oriented principles of free-market capitalism. This view is reflected in the strong American commitment to public education. Concern for opportunity instead of condition delayed the introduction of a system of comprehensive health care until the mid-1960s, and even that program was quite modest by European standards. U.S. social welfare policies have generally been means tested and individualistic. The more ambitious egalitarian programs of the Great Society have caused continuing controversy and political battles. The existing income tax system, if slightly progressive, permits the wealthy to avoid being unduly burdened; the United States tolerates considerable income inequality.

The United States also has faced a troubling irony throughout its history: although it encompasses an extraordinary diversity of ethnic, racial, religious, and regional groups—as contrasted with the homogeneity of Japan and Sweden—it has always preferred to address equality issues in highly individualistic terms. Group-based claims do not fare well in the American political system. More than a century after a civil war was fought to establish black equality, the battle over racial equality raged on. Blacks had to mount massive demonstrations to force their grievances onto the political agenda, and a nonelected and nonrepresentative body, the court system, had to address those grievances. Furthermore, ascriptively defined groups like blacks or women have fared better than poor people, whose group-based claims have made the least headway in the U.S. political system.

One would expect to find more support for redistribution in Sweden and Japan, given their less individualistic, more group-oriented beliefs and the greater support for equality of result in these two countries. Their strong central governments also make it possible for them to pursue such policies. As we know, Japan and Sweden have, however, chosen substantially different policy routes in terms of government support of equality.

The difference may lie in politics. In Sweden unions are a way of life, not only for employees, but for management and farm groups as well. The success of the socialist-union alliance has meant a strong effort to achieve equality of result. Social welfare legislation has been extensive, with program eligibility generally not restricted to the poor; most programs provide universal benefits, sometimes scaled to income. These programs include national health insurance, pensions, unemployment and disability payments, and child allowances.

Japan, led by a conservative-business alliance after World War II, has not followed the same path of government-sponsored social welfare as Sweden. The government introduced equality-promoting social welfare measures late in Japan, and these measures have expanded slowly. The substantial expansion and leveling of the social security system did not occur until the 1970s. In the 1980s the governing conservative leaders started to talk about cutting it back, before it had reached full maturity. They called for the creation of a "Japanese-style Welfare Society," emphasizing the welfare functions of family, community, and private enterprise. On the other hand, in postwar Japan wage differentials within companies—whether between executives and lowest-rank workers or between white-collars and blue-collars—have been relatively small in comparison with those in the other industrial nations. This is because of the equalizing activities of enterprise unions, coupled with the lifelong employment and seniority wage system. Various government subsidies and public-works programs have protected workers in agriculture and the rural sector and in other industrial and regional sectors from declines. The "extra social security" welfare measures sponsored both by the government and private corporations have been a hallmark of postwar Japanese society.

Both Japan and Sweden, unlike the United States, have strong governments with close ties to leading economic actors—labor in Sweden, business in Japan. Equality policies in Sweden are supported by widespread egalitarian values and deference to the government, a government that today happens to be Socialist. In Japan, policies in firms, families, and some government efforts support equality outside the public sector, but the government does not use the tax and transfer system for redistribution as in Sweden.

Government efforts to reduce economic inequality in each of these three countries have been hampered in recent years by economic hard times. Conservatives have called for a reduction in the social welfare system. Whether the political pendulum is swinging to the right or the left, equality issues remain at center stage in all three nations. In Chapter 3 we introduce the actors in this drama, the leaders who shape the equality debate.

3

Who Are the Leaders?

Our main purpose is to study beliefs and values about issues of equality in three nations. But whose beliefs and values? We do not assume that any of these nations has a single belief system or homogeneous equality values among its diverse population groups. Indeed, we seek to locate the areas of agreement and disagreement among such groups. To do so, we must select the population groups we want to study.

The standard approach would be to look at a national sample of the population at large and to consider the differences across classes, ethnic groups, and the like. Instead we decided to look at leaders. They are the individuals most involved in disputes over equality, the people who set the agenda of debate and who actively carry on that debate. The groups of leaders we chose ranged across the spectrum of opinion on equality: from those most committed to a hierarchical system to those most committed to an egalitarian one. By this means we hoped to locate the full range of variation in each nation and, in turn, to compare the nations in terms of the degree of consensus or disagreement on equality. The leaders we have selected are not philosophers or scholars who have written on the issue of equality, yet they are actively involved in issues within that broad realm. We may expect from them more carefully considered, more integrated, and more articulate views on equality than one finds in the population at large. And their views have more influence.

But in choosing these leaders we did not identify the elites of the United States, Sweden, and Japan. In the first place, there is no accepted definition of a sample frame for elites. There exist, at least in theory, lists for a variety of universes such as citizens of the United States, or towns in Japan, or companies in Sweden. Drawing a sample from these universes consists of choosing elements from such lists with a known probability. Of what would the list of American leaders or Japanese leaders or Swedish leaders consist? This question has fired controversy in both academic and political circles; no one agrees how such a theoretical list should be drawn up.[1]

Even if one could compile a list of leaders generally acceptable to social scientists, one might not wish simply to draw a random sample from it. In order to examine consensus and disagreement among significant political groups within the three countries, we adopted a more structured approach.

Certain general goals were common to the design for each of the three countries. First, we wanted a sample broad enough to encompass the range of opinion in each nation, yet one with a manageably small number of groups. Second, each group had to be large enough to permit reliable estimates of its characteristics and examination of major internal cleavages. Third, we sought leaders with a wide scope and an institutional base—not informal opinion leaders but individuals who occupy significant positions at the head of organizations. These organizational leaders can be identified and located in a comparable manner from nation to nation. Furthermore, although we cannot be sure they are the real leaders, we can be confident that they represent the views of their sectors better than leaders selected in other ways. The leadership samples vary for each nation because of different organizational structures, different configurations of organizations, and different sources of available organizational lists. The types of leaders, however, are as comparable as possible.

The sampling appendix includes a full description of the criteria used to define and select our samples of leaders as well as information on response rates and sample sizes. The following provides an overview of the leadership sample. To gather a full range of opinion, we looked for leaders in three sectors. The "established" sector comprises groups such as businesses and business organizations, labor unions, and farm organizations that have a legitimate voice in modern industrial society. They structure basic economic conflict. Such groups might tinker with the existing distribution of rewards, but they probably would not alter the character of the system.

We call the second sector "challenging," because groups in this sector are typically disadvantaged within the system. Thus, they are likely to favor greater change in the status quo and to oppose groups that broadly support it. In our three countries advocacy groups for feminists and (where available) ethnic minorities represented the challenging sector. In addition, the Japanese data included certain civic associations, such as environmental and antinuclear groups. Although we cast our net widely in each nation in order to locate the major challenging voices on the equality issue, some challengers fall outside the boundaries defined by the groups in our sample. Our goal was to find major alternative voices—spokespersons for groups whose voices carry some weight in national debates. Our sample of challenging groups draws on the established rather than the fringe leaders. We believe we have captured the major alternative positions extant in each nation; we do not—and could not—capture every voice.

Between the established and the challenging sectors is the "mediating" sector. Neither inherently supportive nor fundamentally challenging of the economic status quo, groups in this sector deal less with tangible resources than with ideas. They include communicators who structure debate and discussion and those actively engaged in politics. The term *mediating* does not imply that these groups are completely neutral or that they are powerless. Established groups may likely see these mediating groups as challenging, whereas those in the challenging sector may well see them as playing an established role supportive of the status quo. The mediating sector consists of political parties, the media, and the intellectual elite. Although one might select other sectors or other groups than the ones we have chosen, these groups enable us to examine consensus and disagreement in a meaningful way. To avoid overidentifying a sector with any particular group, we chose several groups to represent each sector.[2]

As shown in Table 3.1, the groups for each country may overlap extensively, but not completely. Not surprisingly, the greatest overlaps occur in the established sectors. In keeping with the nature of the sampling, we maintain a distinction between local and national business leadership for Sweden.[3] In addition, we break down the labor leadership for Sweden into those representing unions of blue-collar workers (LO), white-collar workers (TCO), and professional workers (SACO).

There is a good deal of prima facie comparability in the mediating sector. Most of the differences have to do with peculiarities of the party systems of these nations. Thus, whereas a simple Republican/Democratic dichotomy suffices for the United States, the multiparty systems of Japan and Sweden require more complex analysis. For Japan, we group the parties into three broad blocks: the governing Liberal Democrats and their allies; the parties of the left; and other parties. For Sweden, a fourfold categorization is necessary. The makeup of the party groups differs as well. In Sweden and Japan, but not in the United States, members of the Parliament enter the sample. Also, because Swedish newspapers tend to have close links with political parties, only television represents the Swed-

Table 3.1.   Scheme of sectors and groups

Groups	Japan	Sweden	United States
Established groups			
Capital	Business	National business	Business
		Local business	
Land	Farm	Farm	Farm
Labor	Labor	Blue-collar union	Labor
		White-collar union	
		Professional union	
Mediating groups			
Ideas	Intellectuals	Professors	Intellectuals
Communication	Media	Television reporters	Media
Politics	LDP and allies	Social Democrats	Republicans
	Left parties	Center	Democrats
	Other parties	Liberals	
		Conservatives	
"From above"	Bureaucrats	N/A	N/A
Challenging groups			
Women	Feminists	Feminists	Feminists
Minorities	Buraku	N/A	Blacks
	Liberation		
	League		
"Protest"	Civic groups	N/A	N/A
Youth	Students	N/A	Students

ish media. Print editors are included in the party groupings. (See the appendix for more details.)

As noted above, we have added to the sample one other group, the Japanese bureaucrats. They do not fit neatly under the rubrics established, although they might, because of their hierarchical position exercising the power of the state, be considered "mediators from above." Rather than trying to fit them into a procrustean set of categories, we have chosen to keep them as an additional group.

The challenging sector shows most strongly the special nature of each of the political systems with which we are dealing. Challengers are found among disadvantaged and excluded groups. Of particular interest to us were groups disadvantaged on the basis of ascriptive characteristics. Only one such characteristic—gender—found parallel expression in all three countries. Sweden's basic homogeneity meant that there was no appropriate challenging group based on other ascriptive characteristics. The civil rights movement in the United States and the Buraku Liberation League in Japan provided examples of challenging groups based on ascriptive characteristics. Finally, in Japan there was a special collection of groups—here dubbed "civic movements," which included antinuclear groups, consumer groups, environmental groups, and the like.

Lastly, in two nations—Japan and the United States—we included future leaders by sampling from the student bodies of elite colleges.

Demographic Composition

The leadership samples are not representative of the populations in general. Compared with the general public, they are older, more likely to be male, more apt to have high levels of education, and more likely to come from middle-class backgrounds. The appendix shows more clearly how much this is the case. Beyond these similarities there is demographic variation among the leadership groups within each nation as well as variation from nation to nation in the characteristics of leaders who occupy parallel positions. Within each country demographic groups otherwise underrepresented appear in the leadership of their own organizations: women in the leadership of feminist organizations, blacks at the head of civil rights organizations in the United States, and representatives of the people of the buraku at the head of their organization in Japan. Although one would expect this, it is a point worth stressing given the relative absence of members of disadvantaged groups elsewhere in the leadership samples. Leadership in private organizations—businesses, unions, voluntary associations—represents a major way in which the political leadership is developed. Insofar as women and members of disadvantaged minorities hold few leadership positions in mainstream organizations, they lose that opportunity. Thus the existence of feminist or minority organizations creates a resource unavailable elsewhere.

The appendix contains data on the demographic characteristics of the various elite groups, indicating some of the variations within and across nations. Where differences among the groups are relevant to our argument, we will refer to them in the text. In the remainder of this chapter we turn to data on the leaders' political resources and political activity. These data reveal that our leaders are influential, active, and different.

Political Resources and Influence

In general, the leaders in our samples are politically well connected. They have access to and control over many political resources; money, skill, and control over the organizational resources are three of the most important. But the resources a group possesses do not reveal how politically influential it is because the group may not deploy its resources for political purposes. We therefore chose a different measure of resources—personal acquaintance with people in political and governmental office. Such acquaintanceship is not the same as the exercise of political influence. Knowing a person in a position of influence— a legislator, a bureaucrat, a journalist—does not guarantee a favorable response to one's request. But it certainly helps.

Table 3.2 depicts for the three countries the percentage of each group reporting that they knew various types of people well enough to contact them if they (the respondents) had a problem.[4] Using the data in Table 3.2, we can compare the elite groups within each nation; we can compare similar groups across the nations; and we can do both while comparing across the various types of people known. These patterns of acquaintanceship are interesting per se but are not our main intellectual concern. Thus, we shall comment briefly on some of the general patterns contained in the table without delving into some of the patterns within nations.

To begin with, these elites have powerful connections. Consider their acquaintanceship with governmental officials. Predictably, party leaders know many legislators. But the leaders of business, labor, and farm organizations also report quite high personal acquaintanceship: three-quarters or more of them say they know a member of the national legislature. The one exception is national business leaders in Sweden, where the figure is 61 percent; but Swedish business is otherwise quite well connected. The data on leaders reporting acquaintanceship with a member of the cabinet are even more striking. To know a member of the legislature is by no means unusual—many ordinary citizens do. But few ordinary citizens would be acquainted with a cabinet member. Yet a remarkable number of leaders of established organizations do—about one-fifth to one-quarter in most cases.

Finally, we note the data on the Swedish prime minister. The proportion of leaders who report personal acquaintanceship is quite high, given that we are asking about one individual at the highest governmental level. Eight percent of the business leaders and eight percent of the professoriate claim such acquaintance. Among farm leaders, however, almost a third

Table 3.2. Political resources: acquaintanceship with particular types of influential people (percent knowing person well enough to contact that individual)

Japan	Diet member	Cabinet minister	Opposition leader	Government official	National journalist	Local journalist	Television reporter
Established groups							
Business	77	28	17	40	45	35	20
Farm	77	19	14	16	13	31	15
Labor	86	9	60	24	42	35	26
Challenging groups							
Feminists	61	5	33	14	44	28	31
Buraku Liberation League	53	4	50	8	16	26	13
Civic movements	57	7	24	7	53	53	36
Others							
Intellectuals	19	4	5	7	25	19	18
Media	59	24	28	32	73	56	72
Liberal Democrats	87	43	20	36	44	56	34
Left parties	81	37	70	41	56	54	41
Center parties	91	25	59	29	40	60	35
Bureaucrats	64	15	12	39	44	35	23
Students	2	a	a	1	4	3	3

Sweden	MP	Cabinet minister	Prime minister	Opposition leader	Opposition figure	Agency head	Major journalist	Local journalist
Established groups								
Business	61	31	8	10	24	36	44	51
Farm	92	68	30	4	29	50	40	74
Blue-collar union	88	23	5	46	54	42	57	66
White-collar union	70	26	6	21	41	40	61	43
Professional union	62	38	5	6	25	50	51	38
Challenging group								
Feminists	59	18	4	2	10	9	24	59
Others								
Professors	54	36	8	15	24	45	58	44

Table 3.2 (continued)

United States	Senate member	House member	Cabinet secretary	Bureau chief	National media	Local media
Established groups						
Business	78	86	27	42	23	81
Farm	61	74	23	29	19	58
Labor	65	76	21	35	24	46
Challenging groups						
Feminists	48	56	8	28	23	74
Blacks	67	78	13	26	27	82
Others						
Intellectuals	28	37	4	17	14	39
Media	72	83	19	40	80	83
Republicans	80	87	41	51	32	86
Democrats	88	95	7	28	40	90
Youth	7	15	1	5	6	28

a. Less than 1 percent.

make such a claim; this figure confirms the importance of party-based connections, because at the time of our survey the prime minister came from the center party, the traditional party of the agrarian sector. Similarly, two-thirds of the farm leaders report acquaintanceship with a cabinet minister. Perhaps better than any other figure, this illustrates the close integration of the various sectors of Swedish society into the decision-making apparatus of the national government. (Data reported below suggest that a similar figure would have been obtained if we had surveyed labor leaders under a Social Democratic regime.)

One deviation from this pattern for established groups is interesting. In Japan labor union leaders are less than half as likely as their counterparts elsewhere to report knowing a legislator and one-third as likely as are Japanese business leaders. The data clearly reflect the position of Japanese labor leaders outside the dominant coalition—business, bureaucracy, and the LDP. The weaker position of Japanese labor must be seen in the context of the position of labor in the other two nations. In both Sweden and the United States we conducted the survey under conservative governments—a Republican administration in the United States and a conservative coalition in Sweden. It is not merely that the party in power in Japan, the LDP, is one that is somewhat distant from labor, but that it has been in power for so long in circumstances that have left labor outside the ruling coalition.[5]

Like leaders of the established groups, leaders of the challenging groups are quite well connected. In general, they do not report levels of acquaintanceship as high as do the established leaders, but they are far from isolated. In this sector the role of legislative representatives appears particularly crucial. More than half of the leaders of the challenging groups are acquainted with a legislator on the national level. By contrast, leaders of challenging groups report levels of acquaintanceship with cabinet ministers well above what we would expect for ordinary citizens but in most cases well below the levels reported by the leaders of the established groups.

This difference between the established and the challenging groups manifests itself in their connections with high bureaucratic officials such as bureau chiefs and agency heads. In general, the challenging groups are less well connected to the upper levels of the bureaucracy than the established groups are. These data suggest that challenging groups know fewer government officials. They have close ties to legislative representatives, often to opposition members, but lack the access to the bureaucratic inner workings of the government that the established groups have.

Although compared to established groups challenging groups are certainly less well off vis-à-vis the bureaucracy than are established groups, they do quite well with the media. Black and feminist leaders in the United States are as well acquainted with journalists as is the American group with the best governmental connections, top business leaders. And in Japan, leaders of civic organizations and feminist groups more frequently report acquaintanceship with media people than do the leaders of the established sectors. (In Sweden, the challenging group of feminists are better connected to local media than are business leaders, but they are relatively poorly connected to the national media.) The media, like legislators, are open to new groups who come from the outside. One would assume that such acquaintanceship is not as useful as that with governmental "insiders," particularly those insiders at the top, but it represents a significant channel of access nevertheless.

In Japan and Sweden, leaders reported their acquaintanceship with parliamentary leaders of the government and of the opposition. This enables us to look for a somewhat richer pattern than can be explored in the United States, where we made no such distinction. Groups in Japan and Sweden tend to know either government leaders or opposition leaders, and the difference can be quite strong. In both countries conservative regimes held at the time of the survey. We find that business leaders are much more likely to know a cabinet minister than his shadow counterpart. By contrast, labor leaders (at least, the blue-collar union leaders in Sweden) are more likely to know an opposition leader than a member of the government. This pattern holds, with varying strength, for leaders of the civic movements, feminists, and especially the Buraku Liberation League in Japan.

Acquaintanceship is a political resource; it opens doors for those who would make some claim on the government and makes it more likely that a letter will be read, a telephone call returned. But leaders must use such channels of communication if they are to be effective. How active, then, are the leaders in our study in the political life of their societies? There are, of course, many ways in which individuals can be active. For the kinds of people in our study, many of the political activities that interest students of mass politics are not particularly relevant. These leaders probably vote, contribute to political campaigns where possible, and certainly discuss political matters. They operate in a world where such activities are common. All would be, by any criterion based on the political behavior of the mass public, political activists. The extent to which they are personally acquainted with public figures makes that clear.

More important, however, these leaders can be politically active in ways rarely found among the general public. We focus on two types of political activity: that directed at a broad audience and that directed at specific government officials. In the former case, a leader tries to convince the public at large or a broad group of his or her position; in the latter, a leader carries his or her argument to a particular office or individual. The former is sometimes called an outsider strategy, the latter an insider one. The two are, of course, not mutually exclusive, but they represent quite different approaches to political influence; they require different resources and they have different consequences. An insider strategy is not easily available to all. It requires close established connections with government officials, and it works most effectively where there is a communality of interest and values between the person using the strategy and the official. It operates quietly and therefore (for reasons we shall spell out more fully in Chapter 8) more effectively. We assume that most groups would most prefer an insider approach. Those groups who do not have an established position may adopt an outsider strategy. Such groups are more in need of allies in the public at large and among other groups to accomplish their purposes.[6]

In Table 3.3 we show the participatory profiles of the various leadership groups. We limit the data to the major established and challenging groups in order to focus the presentation. Also, the political participatory behav-

Table 3.3. Participatory profiles: those engaging in outsider or insider strategies (percent reporting activity "a few times a year")

Japan	Outsider strategy			Insider strategy		
	Made speech	Radio/TV appearance	Wrote article	Spoke to Diet member	Spoke to local official	Spoke to government official
Established groups						
Business	47	9	47	63	64	79
Farm	66	17	23	64	76	84
Labor	78	12	28	81	80	72
Challenging groups						
Feminists	54	23	55	47	50	70
Buraku Liberation						
League	68	2	14	50	79	88
Civic movements	58	27	41	36	63	65

Sweden	Made speech	Radio/TV appearance	Wrote article	Ever contacted MP	Ever contacted agency bureaucrat
Established groups					
Business	69	37	49	39	64
Farm	87	44	67	65	75
Blue-collar union	87	51	65	53	63
White-collar union	87	66	49	49	75
Professional union	86	70	42	47	79
Challenging group					
Feminists	66	28	23	29	41

United States	Made speech	Radio/TV appearance	Wrote article	Wrote to congressman	Spoke to congressman	Spoke to local official
Established groups						
Business	83	49	41	84	86	92
Farm	74	36	61	72	62	83
Labor	81	24	43	82	68	78
Challenging groups						
Feminists	90	60	48	82	57	85
Blacks	92	78	75	69	75	95

ior of professionals such as party officials and (in Japan) government bureaucrats does not compare meaningfully with that of nongovernmental leaders. The activities fall roughly into two categories: those aimed at a broad audience (outsider activity) and those aimed at specific government officials (insider activity). We asked about the frequency of speechmaking at a public meeting, appearances on radio or television, and the frequency of writing articles for publication as examples of the former, and about contacts with government officials as examples of the latter.

The data for so many groups and so many forms of activity do not lend themselves to easy summary, and we cannot comment on all the interesting within-nation patterns that are found. In the broadest sweep the data tell us that the leaders we studied are indeed political activists at a very high level and that the insider/outsider distinction is useful in understanding the strategies used by various groups. Although the particular preferred modes of activity differ from nation to nation and among groups within each nation, almost all groups of leaders report high activity levels in one or more modes. Consider those activities aimed at a broad audience: in the public at large the number of people who make speeches, appear on radio or television, or write articles is very small; among the leadership groups it is substantial. Indeed, for almost every group there is one mode of public activity undertaken by at least half of the members "a few times a year."

These public activities are most common in the United States, where feminist leaders and black leaders are especially active. Of the various public activities, speechmaking is engaged in the most. In Sweden, labor and farm leaders appear to be the most active. In Japan, the leaders report somewhat less activity: the leaders of civic organizations and of feminist groups are more active than other groups; leaders of business groups and of the BLL are somewhat less active.

As for direct contact with government officials, these leaders also show remarkably high levels of activity. To get as close as possible to insider activity within our questionnaire framework, we asked respondents whether they had spoken to particular officials. Anyone can write to a government official; to speak to an official requires greater access. Furthermore, the official must allocate his or her scarcest resource— time—to the leader. We find that at least half of almost every group has had direct contact with one or another of the officials about whom we asked. Direct contacts are somewhat more frequent in the United States than in Japan (with the Swedish figures not directly comparable).[7] The leaders report contacting members of the national legislature somewhat less frequently than they contact the other officials about whom we asked—local officials (in the United States and Japan) and bureaucrats (Japan and Sweden). One pattern is worth noting: the leaders of the Buraku Liberation League in Japan were relatively low in the frequency of public activities—especially radio and television appearances and article writing—but they were the most likely to report contact with a bureaucratic official and near the top in contacting a local official. We believe this reflects the significant role played by the Japanese bureaucracy in relation to disadvantaged groups. (See Chapters 7 and 9 for further discussion.)

The data make clear that our leaders are indeed just that: they are generally well connected with government officials and active in relation to them. They differ somewhat in both the level and the nature of their activity: some groups work more directly with government officials, whereas others take the outside route through the public. But all are active in both modes. These, then, are the leading actors in the controversy about equality. Let us see how they play out their roles.

4

Equality Demands
and the
Political System

The leaders in Japan, Sweden, and the United States, as we have seen, actively shape the debates on political and economic equality in their countries. In this chapter we present an overview of their attitudes on the welfare state and equality, focusing on how groups of leaders differ within each of the nations and across the nations. Here we offer only a preliminary picture; more elaborate analysis of the data will follow. To begin with, we are interested in the answers to several questions. First, where do the various elite groups stand on equality-related issues; do most of the members of a group take an egalitarian or an antiegalitarian position? Second, what are the patterns of intergroup consensus and disagreement and how do they compare across the groups in each of the countries? On some issues we shall find all groups on the same side of the issue and close to one another; these are examples of strong consensus where an issue is in some sense settled—the contrary position is beyond the normal range of political dispute. On other issues we shall find groups sharply polarized on an issue, at the outer ends of the issue continuum. And sometimes all groups cluster around the middle of an attitude scale. In these cases groups support different sides of an issue but their positions are relatively moderate; there is little polarization. And one last interesting pattern is where all groups accept or oppose a particular policy but one set of groups is much stronger in that position than the other. As we shall see, issues of equality and the welfare state produce different patterns, sometimes as one moves from issue to issue within the same nation and sometimes as one moves from nation to nation on the same issue.

Equality issues form the traditional stuff of political conflict, and we chose our leadership groups to represent alternative positions in this conflict. We expect, therefore, to find clear divisions among the leadership groups. The absence of a division would be positive evidence that a consensus exists within a nation on that issue. We should find differences across the nations, especially concerning which issues groups have agreed on. As we have explained in Chapter 2, the three nations differ substantially in terms of the degree to which the welfare state has been institutionalized and the degree to which equality has been achieved. In Sweden welfare-state activities have the broadest scope and have made the greatest contribution to increased equality. Furthermore, Sweden is characterized by a strong Socialist-labor alliance and by deference to government—all of which should lead to citizen acceptance of a strong state role in welfare and income distribution. At the other extreme is the United States with a less well developed welfare state and less income equality. And the weak government and weak labor movement (relative to Sweden) in the United States, coupled with American individualism and reluctance to defer to the government, ought to result in less support for the welfare state and greater ambivalence about the role of the government. Japan lies in between, with weaker welfare-state institutions but with somewhat more equality than one would expect from that fact. The commitment to equality that is connected with the communal rather than individualistic ethos in Japan, coupled with more deference to authority than in the United States, would suggest that the pattern of opinion in Japan should closely resemble that in Sweden. But it does not. The difference may lie in two factors: the absence in Japan of a historically strong Social Democratic party linked to a strong union movement and the presence of a tradition of responsibility for welfare among nongovernmental institutions, in particular families and firms.

One must view the comparative data with great caution. We compare the responses to similar questions asked of the elite samples in each of the three nations. Such comparisons are fraught with uncertainty because of the vagaries of translation, the different meanings that varying contexts can give to a particular question, and the many other familiar problems that beset measurement across cultural borders. Our main concern, however, is not with absolute differences across nations but with the pattern of relations among groups within each nation. This eases the comparative problem somewhat, because groups within each nation are reacting to the same stimulus.

The survey questions took the form of four-point or seven-point scales. The seven-point scales present two alternatives, and respondents place themselves at either end of the scale or somewhere in between. The four-point scales are items with which an individual expresses strong or moderate agreement or disagreement. We will present the mean score for each leadership group on each scale. Not all our leadership groups, however, have clear analogues in all three nations. For current purposes we select five groups in which leaders hold analogous positions: business, labor, farm organizations, and the main left and right parties. The party categories require some choice, but it is fairly evident in each case which parties represent the meaningful political alternatives on the left and the right. In Sweden, we take the Social Democrats for the left and the Conservative party for the right. In Japan, we report the data for the Japanese Socialist party (JSP) and the Liberal Democrats (LDP). And, in the United States, we naturally choose the Democrats and Republicans. Each of these is heterogeneous. On the left, the U.S. Democratic party is a broad umbrella party that professes none of the socialist commitments of the Swedish or Japanese left parties. On the right, the Japanese Liberal Democratic party is a multifactioned, coalitional party quite different from the narrower and smaller Swedish Conservative party. The U.S. Republican party, in turn, is a broad party like the LDP but with fewer clearly defined factions. Despite these differences, each pair of parties sets the boundaries of effective political competition. In this sense the pairs are equivalent. If, for example, the Democratic party does not set the boundary as far left as its Swedish or Japanese counterpart, that is not measurement artifact but the very phenomenon we wish to report.

In this chapter we will look at a variety of attitudes associated with equality and the welfare state—ranging from questions about traditional welfare-state policies to more radical proposals at the outer limits of the welfare state. Traditional welfare proposals have two characteristics: they are already well established and they do not entail substantial direct redistribution. They emphasize support for the disadvantaged rather than substantive equality among citizens. The more radical proposals involve a more direct commitment to redistribution and, deriving from that redistributive impulse, more direct conflict between the haves and the have-nots. Unlike the more traditional welfare state proposals, radical redistribution goes beyond the current policy of welfare states toward substantial equalization—something often on the agenda of socialist parties but rarely attained.

The pattern of the data across all the issues shows the elite groups arrayed in a similar manner in each nation: at one end are leaders of the left party and of labor unions; at the other are business leaders, farm leaders, and leaders of the conservative party. On equality issues the basic left-right cleavage is alive and well—not surprisingly, because these issues gave birth to this split. Beyond this similarity in relative position, however, there are numerous and important variations. To appreciate these, we must look at the several sets of issues separately.

Issues of Equality

TRADITIONAL WELFARE

Two questions asked in each of the three countries tapped attitudes on traditional welfare-state policies involving government provision of benefits to the disadvantaged. The first asked whether respondents believed that "all except the old and the handicapped should have to take care of themselves without social welfare benefits" and the second whether the government "should see to it that everyone has a job." We designed both these questions to see whether people believed that government should take steps to assure some minimum standard of living for people—either through social-welfare benefits or through employment.

Figure 4.1 displays the leaders' responses to these two questions. As expected, we see a pattern in which the left party and labor unions cluster on one side of the figure, with business, farm, and conservative party leaders on the other. The closeness of the clustering on both sides impressed us: labor leaders and the left party, business leaders and the right party are always quite close; farm leaders sometimes move away a bit, but they stay fairly close to the conservative pair.

Despite this similarity, important differences separate the nations. The pattern in the United States stands out: attitudes toward the welfare state create political cleavage in the United States, with the two sides far apart. On the issue of the old and the handicapped, the groups on the left take a clear pro–welfare state position, whereas the more conservative groups are neutral or mildly opposed. On the issue of jobs the Democrats and Republicans stand much farther apart than the Socialists and Liberal Democrats in Japan and the Socialists and Conservatives in Sweden. Moreover, even the supporters in the United States of a government guarantee of jobs are on average less committed to that position than are their counterparts in the other two nations, where one finds virtual unanimity of strong support by leaders of left groups. And the conservative groups in the United States much more strongly oppose a government jobs guarantee program.

The contrast between the United States and Sweden is clear. In Sweden, no group—even the most conservative—takes a position on the negative side of the scale on either variable.[1] For the question about whether all but the old and the handicapped should have to get along without government

All except the old and the handicapped should have to take
care of themselves without social welfare benefits

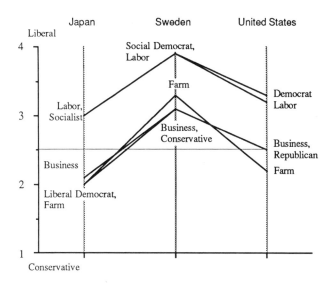

The government should guarantee jobs

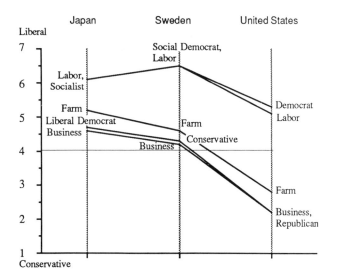

Figure 4.1. Attitudes toward welfare benefits and government-guaranteed jobs:
established groups and parties

assistance, the mean response for every group surveyed lies in the strong pro–welfare state range. Responses to the jobs question are not so lop-sided. Conservative and business leaders give little support on average to the welfare state. (Presenting responses only for Conservative party lead-ers underestimates the breadth of support for the welfare state among the nonleft parties. The Liberal and Center parties are generally allied with the Conservatives against the Social Democrats, but on welfare-state is-sues their leaders are almost as close to the Social Democrats as they are to their Conservative allies.)[2]

The Swedish Conservative and business leaders are far more supportive of the welfare state than their American colleagues. These results presage and dovetail nicely with the data we will present in a later chapter regard-ing views among different leadership groups on fair differences in income among occupations.

The Japanese data are somewhat more ambiguous than those in Sweden and the United States. On the question of job guarantees, the Japanese pattern resembles the Swedish one: all groups indicate support of the wel-fare state. On the question of aid to all but the old and the handicapped, one finds a division similar to that in the United States, with labor and the socialist party on one side and the conservative triad of business, farm organizations, and the LDP on the other. The groups in Japan are, how-ever, somewhat closer to one another on the jobs issue than are the Swed-ish ones: the left-leaning groups are closer to the center and the conservative groups are farther to the left.

The answers to this question resemble other patterns of response in Japan, but the more divided response on the old and handicapped deviates from the general Japanese pattern. The extent of that deviation will be-come evident when we look at other questions about the welfare state, after which we shall return to this issue.[3]

MODERATE REDISTRIBUTION
Two additional questions on the survey explored attitudes toward govern-ment activities to influence the distribution of income in favor of disadvan-taged groups. One question asked whether "the government should work to substantially reduce the income gap between rich and poor" and the other whether "taxing those with high incomes to help the poor" was fair or whether it "punishes the people who have worked hardest."[4] These questions go further than the benefit-provision ones, because they imply lowering the top as well as raising the bottom. And the question on pro-gressive taxation involves not only equalization through the way govern-

ment money is spent but also promotion of greater equality in raising the money that the government is to spend. These questions deal with government programs that take money from the more affluent to distribute to the poor, but they are only moderately redistributionist in that—unlike some questions to which we shall shortly turn—they do not set any clear target for the result of redistribution. Programs of the sort referred to in these questions will permit relatively wide inequalities in income after redistribution. Furthermore, these policies already exist. The leaders responded to them quite differently than they responded with regard to programs that refer to equal results as the outcome.

Figure 4.2 illustrates the pattern of response to these questions. The pattern in each nation generally resembles that found for the welfare state in Figure 4.1. In Sweden and Japan, the range of response lies between strong support on the part of Socialists and union leaders and center positions of the more conservative groups. Polarization is somewhat greater in Sweden than in Japan. The left groups in Sweden stand near the extreme proredistribution end of the scale, indicating near unanimity in strong support for the proposition; the comparable Japanese groups are more moderate. And the conservative groups in Japan support the proposition somewhat more than the conservative groups in Sweden. In Japan, leaders of farm organizations and of the LDP clearly fall on the proredistribution side of the scale, whereas business leaders are close to the midpoint of the scale. Farmers have benefited from a policy of income gap reduction in Japan, a policy advocated by the LDP. In Sweden, the conservative groups are arrayed farther toward the conservative end. Most important, however, leadership groups in both countries show little strong opposition to the government's involvement in some redistribution; the positions range from strong support to moderate acceptance or neutrality.

The data for the United States differ in two ways. First, leaders hold generally more conservative opinions than those in the other two countries; leaders of unions and of the Democratic party are only moderately favorable to redistributive policies. Second, there is more disagreement in the United States; whereas in Sweden and Japan such government intervention is accepted or viewed neutrally, in the United States conservative groups are arrayed on the negative side of the issue scales.

Of the four issues covered in Figures 4.1 and 4.2, the Swedish conservative groups come out on the negative side only with regard to taxing the rich to aid the poor. On this issue Swedish business and Conservative party leaders are somewhat negative, like conservative groups in the United States. This position reflects a break in the Swedish supportive

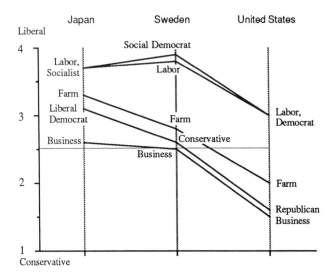

The government should work to substantially reduce income gap

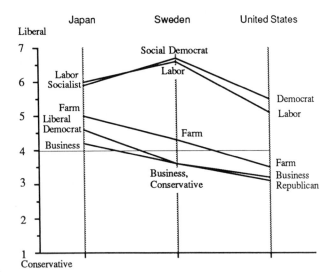

It is fair to tax the rich to help the poor

Figure 4.2. Attitudes toward government measures to equalize income: established groups and parties

consensus on the welfare state and indicates a belief that the welfare state, especially as expressed in steeply progressive tax rates, has gone too far in a redistributive direction (see Chapter 7).

In sum, the questions on the current welfare state—a welfare state devoted to employment and welfare measures to help those in need and to the use of state power to transfer some income from the more to the less affluent—show a favorable consensus in Sweden and Japan. There is more apparent consensus in Japan, with groups closer to one another. In Sweden, the consensus in favor is weakened by a fairly wide distance between the left and the right groups with the former staunch supporters of the welfare state items and the latter nearly neutral. In the United States, the left and the right groups are generally more conservative and they are arrayed on opposite sides of the issue.

Two features of the Japanese response deserve special notice. The first is the response to the question about the old and the handicapped. The response is anomalous, both compared with the response in the United States and Sweden and compared with the other responses to moderate welfare-state questions in Japan. In the other two countries, this question elicited the most proegalitarian response of any of the four—left groups were farther left and conservative groups were more divided. In Japan, exactly the opposite holds true. The Socialists and union leaders only mildly oppose the statement that "all except the old and handicapped should have to take care of themselves without social welfare benefits." Both groups have responses to the right of their counterparts in the United States, the only traditional welfare-state question for which this is the case. Similarly, Liberal Democrats and business leaders take more conservative positions than their counterparts in the United States. Furthermore, the pattern of response in Japan to this question differs from that to the questions on jobs, income gap reduction, and taxing the rich. In those cases we found consensus in favor of welfare-state policies, at least compared with the other nations.

The explanation for the response to the old and handicapped question appears to be a view traditionally widespread in Japanese society that public welfare is a last-resort means of providing for citizens when other, more indirect means fail. As Ezra Vogel puts it: "One of the tenets of the Japanese approach to welfare in the broad sense is that there should be economic employment opportunities for everyone and that those who work and exert themselves for their organizations should be appropriately looked after. The government's policy of distributing wealth throughout the society is not based on public welfare but on fine calibrations of wages, taxes, budget redistribution to poorer prefectures, and subsidized rice price paid to farmers . . . In short, the Japanese have been able to provide for the well-being of their population without requiring many except the very old and infirm to become economically dependent on the state, and they have done it in such a way as to reinforce their communitarian ideals."[5] From this perspective it is interesting to note that the leaders of labor and the JSP do support broader social welfare programs.

Another feature of the Japanese responses was that the Liberal Democratic leaders are consistently less conservative, and by a fair amount, than business leaders. In all three countries business leaders display greater conservatism than leaders of the conservative party, but these differences in general are very small. In Japan they are fairly large. Liberal Democratic leaders tend to take positions midway between business leaders and farm leaders, whereas the conservative party leaders in the United States and Sweden are much closer to business than to farm leaders. This difference reflects the importance of farmers as a constituency of the Liberal Democratic party. It also bears witness to the catchall nature of the LDP, which covers a wide spectrum of factions and ideologies.

RADICAL REDISTRIBUTION

A welfare state is not an egalitarian state. A nation may make a strong commitment to major welfare-state policies in health care, pensions, and manpower policy yet permit varying levels of income equality. In the United States, the New Deal introduced many welfare-state policies but had little impact on income equality; in Sweden, traditional welfare-state measures have been accompanied by greater income equality; and in Japan, we find the latter without the former. Just as the extent of equality is somewhat separate from the extent of traditional welfare-state programs, so attitudes on the two subjects may differ. Consensus on one subject does not imply consensus on the other. We asked several questions about more radical measures to redistribute income in order to compare the answers with the more moderate welfare-state measures. One inquired whether the government should put a top limit on income; another asked respondents which is a fair economic system: one in which "all people would earn about the same" or one in which "people with more ability would earn higher salaries." Both items contrast equality of results, where a clear limitation is placed on inequalities deriving from differential talent or effort, with equality of opportunity, where individual differences in effort or talent are given free rein to produce inegalitarian outcomes.

Figure 4.3 reports the results to these questions. In all countries we find

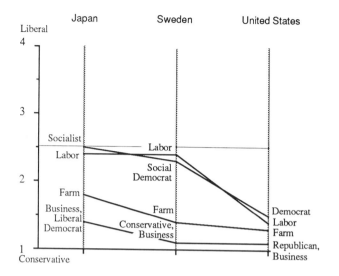

There should be a top limit on income

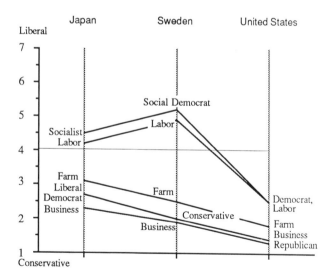

In a fair economic system, people would earn about the same

Figure 4.3. Attitudes toward radical redistribution: established groups and
          parties

a shift to the right in the replies. Conservative groups oppose such radical redistribution more than moderate welfare state proposals; left groups show less support for these radical measures. The American data show this most clearly. The welfare state divides the American left from the American right, but both groups express strong, almost total, opposition to a top limit placed on high incomes and to the idea that everyone should earn about the same. Left leaders are more egalitarian than right leaders, as is the usual pattern, but the distance between the most left and most right positions is smaller than that for any other question in any of the three countries. The leaders show more unanimity here than on almost anything else in our survey. The data reflect a strong and consistent pattern that will appear again and again in our work: the rejection by all American leadership groups—including those farthest to the left—of radical redistribution and any policy directed toward equality of results.[6]

In the other two nations one finds a mirror image of the responses about moderate welfare-state measures: the conservative groups strongly oppose radical redistribution; the left groups take positions ranging from mild opposition to mild support, hovering around the neutral point of the scale. On these radical redistributionist proposals, just as with the moderate welfare-state proposals, we found greater polarization in Sweden than in Japan. Swedish conservative groups are more conservative than their Japanese counterparts, whereas the left groups in Sweden—at least on the issue of equal earnings—are to the left of their Japanese counterparts.

CONFLICT

Because redistribution takes from some to give to others, it inevitably causes conflict. Thus accepting such policies implies a belief in a conflictual model rather than a harmonious model of politics. Responses to two items dealing with general views on the capitalist system show this. We asked respondents whether they thought that the capitalist system was fair to workers and whether they believed that the interests of employers and employees were basically opposed. Figure 4.4 illustrates the answers to these questions. The responses parallel those about radical redistribution, as we might expect because the questions about radical redistribution deal with a highly conflictual issue. In the United States no group takes the position that capitalism is unfair to workers or that there is an inevitable conflict of interest between workers and management; even leaders of the Democratic party and unions reject those propositions, albeit by a small margin. By contrast, in Sweden these issues polarize the leaders. This is hardly surprising because the cleavage over socialism has been a major

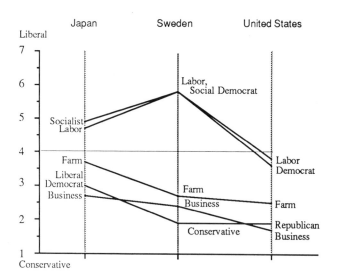

Private enterprise is fair to workers

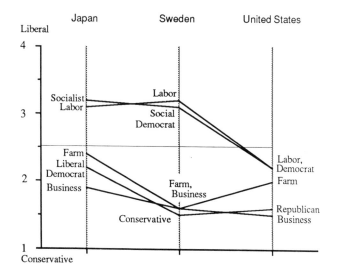

The interests of employers and employees are, by their very nature, basically opposed

Figure 4.4. Perceptions of equity for workers in private enterprise: established groups and parties

feature of political conflict in Sweden. The pattern in Japan resembles that in Sweden: groups support both sides of the issue but, as is characteristic of the Japanese data, with less polarization. The United States and the other two nations differ on the left: American labor leaders and Democratic party leaders do not see the world in terms of class conflict as do their counterparts in Japan and Sweden, and this is consistent with their policy positions on redistribution.

Summary: Three Patterns

The data presented thus far provide an overview of the nature and location of the debate about equality and the welfare state in each of the nations. Figure 4.5 summarizes the three patterns by indicating the spread of positions on the various issues. As pointed out above, the debate takes a similar form in each nation: labor and the left party on one side of the issue and business, farm groups, and the right party on the other. But the continuum is differently located from nation to nation. In Japan and Sweden, all groups accept the welfare state, but radical redistribution and socialism are controversial. In the United States, all groups oppose radical redistribution and socialism, whereas the welfare state is controversial. Labor and Democrats in the United States are less likely than business and Republicans to oppose radical redistribution, but the former do oppose such notions. Business and conservatives in Japan and Sweden are less likely than labor and the Socialists to favor the welfare state, but the former do favor it. In general, Japanese and Swedish leaders hold opinions to the left of American leaders. On issues of economic equality the American political spectrum is truncated on the left; no American group occupies the position of the left groups in Japan or Sweden. At the same time, Japan and Sweden are truncated on the right; no group there occupies the position of the conservative groups in the United States.

The anomalous views of two groups are noteworthy—the opposition by American labor (and its political allies) to radical redistribution and the support by Swedish business (and their political allies) for the welfare state. The views go against what at first appears to be the narrow self-interest of the group in question. The American consensus against radical redistribution thus depends on the views of American labor, and Swedish consensus for the welfare state depends on Swedish business. In Japan one finds a more muted anomaly among Japanese businessmen who give moderate support to the welfare state. The mainspring of consensus in Japan, however, appears to be that the two sides, wherever they are on the

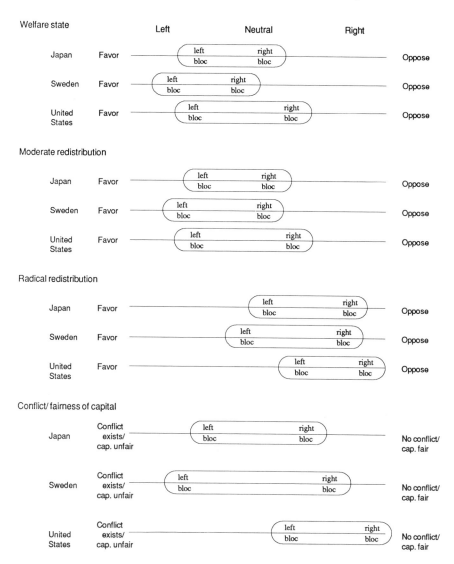

Figure 4.5. Ranges of opinion on equality issues

continuum, are closer to each other than in the other two nations. The failure of America, virtually alone among industrial countries, to develop a mass-based socialist movement—often referred to as American exceptionalism—has received much attention from historians, sociologists, and American socialist intellectuals.[7] Our data suggest that one ought to examine a Swedish and, to a lesser extent, a Japanese exceptionalism as well, not among workers but among business leaders and conservatives.

The varying location of the political debate in these three nations matches our expectations that nations differ in the institutional structure within which the ideological debate takes place among contending groups. The United States, with no active socialist party or socialist-oriented unions, still debates the welfare state, and no group presses for more radical redistribution. In Japan and, more so, in Sweden groups on the left would consider—if not enthusiastically support—such radical moves. The data also are consistent with the commitments to individualism that we find in the three nations. Leaders in the United States show the greatest commitment to individual provision for social welfare; their commitment reflects scepticism about the welfare state and rejection of government involvement to create income equality. In Japan and Sweden, where leaders demonstrate greater commitment to community than to individualism and a greater deference to the state, we also find greater acceptance of a positive government role. But in Japan this acceptance of the state is more qualified; the Japanese leaders believe that welfare—particularly of the old and those who cannot fend for themselves—should not be the prime responsibility of the government.

Challenging Groups

Thus far we have illustrated the positions of some of the main contenders over equality issues—the main parties on the left and the right as well as their union and business allies. Because they are the main political antagonists, they set the parameters of the debate on equality. Yet they may draw the boundaries too narrowly for some groups challenging the current distribution of positions in their society. More radical egalitarian groups may outflank the established groups on the left if they find the parties unresponsive. Indeed, a significant feature of the political debate in any nation is the extent to which new demands, such as those for new levels of equality, are encompassed by the political parties (the left party being the obvious candidate) rather than being the province of groups outside the main party contest.

The positions on equality of such challenging groups interest us. We have sought comparability across nations by looking for groups that have a significant political role and that speak for important disadvantaged segments of the population. As we discussed in the previous chapter, the nations differ in the extent to which such groups and movements exist. In each nation we looked to leaders of feminist groups as well as to leaders of groups disadvantaged on the basis of some ascriptive characteristic such as race or other status acquired at birth. In the United States, these were leaders of black civil rights organizations and in Japan, the leaders of the Buraku Liberation League (BLL); there are no parallel groups in Sweden. In Japan we also included leaders of various extraparliamentary citizens' groups—environmental, consumer, antinuclear, and other groups who challenge the system from outside of the dominant coalition of groups.

The views of these challenging groups are plotted in Figure 4.6. We present data for three of the items discussed above (the other items show a similar pattern). We also include and connect with solid lines the positions of the main left and right parties to help locate the new groups. In the United States and Japan the black civil rights leaders and leaders of the BLL outflank the left political party. In relation to equal income in Japan and in relation to the fairness of capitalism in the United States, these challenging groups move far to the left. In the United States, feminist groups also are to the left of the Democratic leaders, except on the issue of jobs; in Japan, feminists are a bit on the conservative side of the JSP. Indeed, in the United States the black and feminist challenging groups maintain that the system is unfair, a position that neither labor nor Democratic leaders adopt. But the two challenging groups do not on balance see the interests of employers and employees as basically opposed, and they join with labor and Democratic leaders in opposing radical income redistribution, both on the issue of a generally equal income (illustrated on Figure 4.6) and on the issue of a top limit on income.

The civic groups in Japan vary in their location on the scale relative to the other groups, but they tend to be close to the JSP and feminists. They do not present a radical alternative comparable to the Buraku Liberation League, but they unequivocally stand with the left groups and the JSP to challenge the positions of the LDP and its coalition.

In Sweden, however, no ascriptive groups challenge the system from the outside. The feminists are relatively conservative, located closer to the Conservative party leaders than to the leaders of the Social Democratic party. One can argue that we might have found more extreme advocates of equality if we had in Sweden representatives of some ascriptive group more comparable to the civil rights groups or the BLL. But such groups did not exist.[8]

In sum, we find that the main political parties in Sweden are farther apart than their Japanese and American counterparts. Moreover, only in

The government should see to it that everyone has a job

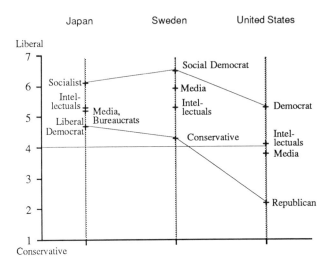

In a fair economic system, people would earn about the same

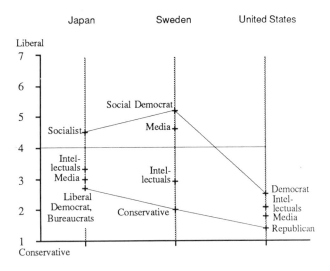

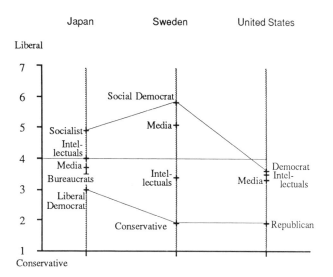

Figure 4.6. Attitudes toward equality issues: challenging groups and main political parties

Sweden do the main equality contenders take positions within those boundaries. As we shall see, this reflects the fact that the Swedish party system has more fully incorporated the issue of equality than has the party system in the other two nations.

Mediating Groups

Lastly, we report in Figure 4.7 the positions of the mediating groups on these issues.[9] A few generalizations are possible across the countries. The mean response of the intellectuals and media leaders never occurs to the left of that of leaders of the left party in that country. This applies even to the relation of intellectual and media leaders to Democratic party leaders in the United States. Our data, then, do not confirm the belief that media and intellectual leaders are alienated outsiders on the left.

The pattern of responses for these groups in the United States has a number of interesting features. Only in this country do both media and intellectual leaders take positions closer to the left groups than to the right. Furthermore, intellectual and media leaders tend to stand farther to the left on questions involving radical redistribution and the fairness of capitalism than on the traditional welfare-state questions.

The government should see to it that everyone has a job

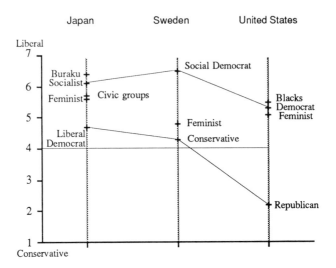

In a fair economic system, people would earn about the same

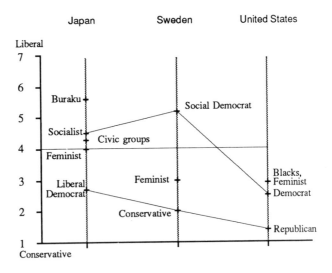

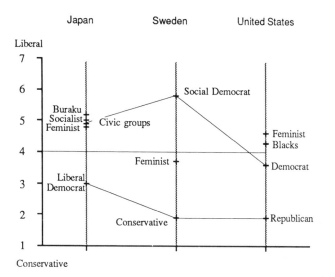

Figure 4.7. Attitudes toward equality issues: mediating groups and main political parties

In Sweden, however, intellectual leaders are relatively conservative and media leaders relatively left compared with those in the other two countries. The mean response of the television and radio journalists is closer to the mean response of Social Democrats than is the response of media leaders in the other countries to that of their left parties. Unlike in the United States and Japan, where intellectuals take positions to the left of the media, in Sweden intellectuals stand to the right of the media. In part, this may be an artifact of our sample. The sample of intellectuals in Sweden included only university professors, but Swedish nonacademic intellectuals are generally assumed to be to the left of university professors. Nonetheless, the phenomenon is real. Swedish professors, like high civil servants in both Japan and Sweden, have close ties to traditional elite groups of church and state. By contrast, American professors are to a greater degree outsiders.[10] Fewer professors are leaders of political protests in Sweden than in America. As for television and radio journalists, the results are in line with the general impression in Sweden that television and radio are slanted to the left. Many have a similar impression about American television, although our evidence shows little such bias on the part of media leaders.

Finally, it should be noted that in no case do the mediating groups fall outside of the boundaries of the political dispute when there is consensus among the contending groups. Thus, in the United States the various mediating groups join the other groups in rejecting radical income distribution, whereas in Sweden they join all other groups in approving the traditional welfare state.

In this chapter we have seen how the positions of established, challenging, and mediating groups on issues of equality relate to one another. How do the leaders of these groups view and define equality? We will answer this question in the next chapter.

5

The Dimensions
of Equality

In the previous chapter we considered the attitudes of our respondents toward issues of economic equality and the welfare state. The data reveal patterns of consensus and cleavage across the various leadership groups; the patterns vary according to the equality issue. In particular, there appears to be a clear distinction between attitudes toward traditional welfare-state programs and more radical redistributive programs. But equality, like other social concepts such as liberty and democracy, has many meanings. Indeed, as Douglas Rae has made clear, one should talk not of equality but of equalities. Noneconomic equality, for example, between men and women or between other ascriptive groups, has recently sparked intense public debates. The first task, therefore, is to clarify the meaning of equality.

The alternative uses of words like *democracy* and *equality* often reflect the political and ideological maneuverings of groups who want to identify themselves with these issues. "True" democracy may mean a free press, mass-based political parties, worker control of enterprises, subservience to the leading role for the Communist party, or a sharing of work in the household. Which is the "true" meaning depends upon one's institutional, ideological, and national location. The same is true for equality; the term is honorific, and many people want to demonstrate their commitment to it. That often means showing that my equality, not yours, is the true equality. An advocate of affirmative action in the United States claims that only through such programs can the nation achieve true equality. The opponents of affirmative action also claim to support equality. Each side has given the word a different meaning.

This semantic complexity does not merely reflect attempts to stake out persuasive political positions. The domain of equality is inherently complex. The idea that two equal things are identical works far better in the abstract world of mathematics than in the real world of social life. To determine whether two entities are equal, one must precisely define and empirically study them. Neither task is straightforward. Any conception of equality must include a designation of what good or value is to be equal, for what units, and by which criteria.[1] Individuals can be more or less equal in relation to many goods or values—for example, economic goods, political power or influence, social respect, and security. One may think of such equality in relation to individuals or to groups. Thus if every group has an equal share, the members of different groups may have different individual shares. This will happen if the groups are of unequal size even if the members of each group have the same shares. If groups have shares proportional to their size, individual shares may still differ within some or all groups. Furthermore, one must define the nature of the groups involved. Lastly, one may have different standards for evaluating a just level of equality: equality of opportunity versus equality of results; complete identity in possession of some good versus possession proportionate to some other characteristic such as need. The analytical distinctions fill the philosophical literature.

We are interested, however, in how our respondents, who are sophisticated participants in the struggles over equality but not philosophers, organize the issue in their own minds. In the real political world issues of equality do not emerge in neat analytical form. Any equality issue encompasses many dimensions and represents many analytical distinctions. The issue of government-mandated quotas in institutions of higher education for people of a disadvantaged ethnic background is many issues at once. It is about a particular valued good (education), the standards for access to that good (membership in a group rather than individual achievement), the equality criterion (opportunity or results), equality for a particular group in relation to the rest of society (the chosen disadvantaged group rather than some other disadvantaged group), as well as the extent to which the government ought to intervene to create conditions of equality. An individual's position on such an issue will depend on a complex summing across all those aspects. And each person may assign different weights to these aspects: for some the issue may be educational access, to be judged in terms of whether the policy satisfies the individual's notion of proper educational standards; for others the appropriateness of quotas and their implication of equality of circumstance for disadvantaged groups; for still others evaluation of the particular group; and for a final group the proper role of government. And these are only a few of the potential dimensions within which the issue can be evaluated. Furthermore, some people will evaluate the issue in terms of a number of dimensions simultaneously; for others a single dimension will dominate.

Thus individuals and groups may differ in two ways on matters of equality: where they stand on an issue and how they define it. Two groups might agree that the main issue in the example above is that of quotas, with one in favor and the other opposed. Or they might disagree about the relevant dimension, one thinking the issue to be equality for a particular group, the other believing the issue to be university admission standards. In the latter case the groups may, indeed, be talking different languages.

Therefore, we must consider how the leaders in our samples conceive the issue of equality. Several questions are involved. First, do the attitudes of our respondents have a well-defined and consistent conceptual structure? Many studies have shown that political attitudes in mass publics are inconsistent.[2] We ought to expect, however, a more consistent pattern of interrelationship among attitudes for elite groups such as those we are studying.[3] Assuming that we find a structured set of attitudes among our respondents, we must address a second question: what are the dimensions that organize the issue domain of equality? A third question, closely related to the second, asks how much the various leadership groups share that structure of attitudes: do the various groups conceptualize equality using the same dimensions?

If we identify a shared set of equality dimensions, we will have a tool that allows us to compare more efficiently the positions of the leadership groups with one another. This comparison will have several advantages over a comparison of the responses of the various groups to specific questions. The meaning of the answer to any individual question is always unclear because of the nuances that each question embodies. These nuances are particularly relevant when comparing questions asked in several languages and in different countries. The issues with which questions deal will differ substantially from nation to nation even if they are ostensibly on the same subject. And the "same" question is inevitably different when translated from one language to another. In any case, our main interest is not in the substantive issues embodied in individual questions; instead, we are concerned with the more general views that respondents have on matters of equality, views that will guide their response to future issues. In considering the more general and abstract dimensions of equality, we move away from the current issue debate in these nations to a position from which we can reach a broader and less contingent understanding. Our first task is to locate similar general dimensions of equality in each nation. After that we will be able to place each leader and each group of leaders on those dimensions relative to other leaders within that nation. These relative positions within each nation then become the basis of a comparison among the nations that is more cross-nationally valid than a direct comparison across national borders of specific attitudes on specific issues.

The Structure of Attitudes

In our survey we asked a number of questions about attitudes within the broad domain of equality. Many of the individual items were similar across the three nations. In the previous chapter we presented data on many of those similar items that dealt with economic equality and the role of the welfare state. We also asked questions about equality for men and women, as well as equality for traditionally disadvantaged minorities. Other questions addressed the causes of various kinds of equality and government programs relating to equality. In many cases the questions are similar from nation to nation, in a few quite different. Questions on specific minority groups naturally differ from nation to nation because the groups and their circumstances differ. In Japan, we asked about the buraku people as well as about Korean and other immigrant groups; in Sweden, about immigrants and guest workers; in the United States, about blacks.

Furthermore, the individual questions are multidimensional: they deal with many equality issues at once. The multidimensional question about quotas in universities, for example, involves a particular disadvantaged group, educational opportunities, the role of government, and standards of fairness. Most other questions tap multiple aspects of equality issues: attitudes toward government intervention in relation to equality, toward particular disadvantaged categories based on economic, ethnic, or gender characteristics, toward alternative criteria for equality. The multiple meaning embodied in each item allows us to determine the underlying dimensions in which respondents think about equality. We do this by extracting from the responses to the individual questions on equality the common elements on which the answers cluster together. A question about government-mandated job quotas for a minority might be categorized by a respondent as a question about quotas, about government intervention to produce more equality, about programs related to employment, about the particular minority, or about some combination of these issues. By seeing how answers to that question covary or go together with answers to other questions, we can identify the dominant dimension that characterizes that issue for a set of individuals. If, for instance, the answers to the question about job quotas covary with answers to other questions about the same minority—even though the other questions deal with different issues—we would have good evidence that the respondents' primary concern in answering all those questions is their attitudes toward that minority. Or the answers to that question might be more closely related to questions about government-mandated quotas for groups other than the one that was the subject of the first question. In that case we could assume that the main issue for respondents was quotas rather than the treatment of any particular group.

In our study factor analysis seemed to be the appropriate technique for discovering what clustering of questions existed in the data. Factor analysis is a statistical technique that takes the interrelationship among a set of variables and derives estimates of "underlying" variables that can account for those relationships. The underlying variables whose content is inferred from the pattern of relationship of the individual variables to the hypothesized underlying ones can be thought of as the most significant dimensions in the set of variables. A useful technique, factor analysis also provides a means to create summary scales for further analysis—if we find that there are indeed meaningful clusters of issues.

This mode of analysis takes advantage of the otherwise problematic fact that the questions we ask are multidimensional and makes a virtue of the necessity of asking different questions (different both in language and in substance) across the nations. The multiplicity of dimensions within each question allows us to link it to other questions. The basis on which sets of questions cluster together provides evidence of what the most significant dimensions are. Because the sets of questions are heterogeneous across the nations, when we find similar dimensions we have more compelling evidence that the dimensions are in fact the basis by which individuals group specific issues and not an artifact of the particular questions we choose to ask.

Factor analysis is, of necessity, more suggestive than definitive. What comes out of such an analysis depends on what goes into it. Dimensions can emerge only if variables tapping those dimensions are included; underlying dimensions are estimated from observed variables. If we do not ask questions that have reference to a particular dimension, we will of course not find it. Nevertheless, because our questions cover a range of the major policy issues associated with equality in each of the nations, our results are likely to tap many of the major distinctions within that domain of issues.

In each of the nations approximately twenty-five questions about equality were entered into a factor analysis.[4] In Japan and Sweden, five factors were extracted; in the United States, six. In Table 5.1 we list the variables

Table 5.1. Dimensions of equality: rotated structure

Japan (5 factors)	Welfare state	Alien	Buraku	Gender	Radical redistribution
			Factors[a]		
Government should reduce income gap	.47				
Government should guarantee jobs	.54				
Fault of system poor are poor	.45				
Fair to tax rich to help poor	.54				
Laws favor the rich	.48				
Aliens should have political rights		.59			
Koreans may reject repatriation		.49			
Status of foreigners' school		.43			
Aliens may have welfare benefits		.69			
Equal rights to foreign professors		.64			
All expenses to aid buraku			.67		
Discrimination keeps buraku living standard down			.55		
Favor Dōwa (harmonization) education			.72		
Laws discriminate against buraku			.44		
Government should help get jobs for buraku			.67		
Female workers are reliable				.59	
Women are discriminated against				.59	
Women should stay home				.52	
All should receive equal pay					.34
Top limit on income					.42
Equality of result preferable					.38
Quotas for female employment					.49
Quotas for aged employment	.33				

that went into the factor analysis in each nation, as well as the factor loadings over .30 on each of the factors extracted.[5] The factor analysis is fairly clean; most variables load primarily on only one factor. Furthermore, the pattern of variables that load on a particular factor usually has a strong common element, making substantive identification of the factors fairly straightforward.

Four factors containing a similar set of variables appear in each of the nations. One appears as the first factor in each country. On this factor load

Table 5.1 (continued)

Sweden (5 factors)	Welfare State	Socialism/ radical redistribution	Cut back social reform	Gender	Immigrants
Government should reduce income gap	.79				
Government should guarantee jobs	.51				
Fair to tax rich to help poor	.61				
Aid none but old or handicapped	.33				
Support union wage policy	.65				
Equality gone too far	.40				
Top limit on income		.61			
All should receive equal pay		.67			
Equality of result preferable		.41			
Fault of system poor are poor		.42			
Capitalism not fair		.68			
Laws favor the rich		.74			
Interests of workers/employers opposed		.69			
Quotas for jobs for women		.43			
Abolish elementary-school grades		.58			
Decrease, not increase, welfare		.33	.46		
Too easy to get on welfare			.43		
Jobs for Swedes ahead of immigrants			.39		
Wives with working husbands should not be laid off first				.59	
Women should stay home				.63	
More budget money for immigrants	.34				.41
System discriminates against immigrants					.36

(continued)

a variety of questions having to do with the government responsibility for citizen welfare—for jobs or for a decent income—as well as items dealing with the fairness of the market system and the causes of poverty. Prominent among the common items on this dimension are questions dealing with the obligation of the government to reduce the income gap between

Table 5.1 (continued)

United States (6 factors)	Welfare state	Gender	Radical redistri-bution	Quota	Causes of inequality	Race
Government should reduce income gap	.61					
Government should guarantee jobs	.56					
Fault of system poor are poor	.45					
Capitalism not fair	.55					
Laws favor the rich	.56					
Fair to tax rich to help poor	.41					.32
Female workers are reliable		.41				
Wives with working husbands should not be laid off first		.68				
ERA should be passed		.48				
Women are discriminated against		.40			.38	
Women should stay home		.61				
Top limit on income			.44			
All should receive equal pay			.53			
Equality of result preferable			.72			
Quotas for female employment				.83		
Quotas for employment of blacks				.92		
Favor busing				.33		.32
Integration should be speeded				.33		.30
System discriminates against blacks					.71	
Government should help blacks get jobs						.37
Integrate housing						.41
Government should provide welfare						.42

a. Loadings shown are all those above .30.

rich and poor and with the fairness of taxing the rich to help the poor. We have labeled this a welfare-state factor because it deals with the responsibility of the government to intervene to modify the consequences of the market for individual welfare.

In each nation there is a redistribution factor dealing with government policies in relation to economic equality. This differs from the previous factor in that the variables associated with it are tied to more radical redistributive policies. In each of the three nations three similar questions load primarily on this factor. One deals with a top limit on income set by the government, one with the desirability of equal income despite differences in ability, and the third with preference for equality of results over equality of opportunity. Each of these items poses a distinct choice between equality of opportunity and equality of condition. To favor a top ceiling on income imposed by the government is to favor a limitation on the ability of the individual to earn as much as his or her talent and effort will allow. Similarly a preference for equal income despite differences in ability represents commitment to equality of condition and a rejection of equality of opportunity. Other items fall on this factor as well. In Japan and Sweden, a question dealing with job quotas for women—also a radical redistributive item that poses a choice between equality of condition and opportunity—falls on that factor. In Sweden, several additional items fall on this dimension. One clearly taps the condition-opportunity dimension: the question about abolishing grades in elementary schools. The rest deal with such issues as the fairness of the capitalist system and the existence of class conflict between workers and employers. We cannot be certain why these items appear on this dimension in contrast to the pattern elsewhere. We find it interesting, however, that several items that fall on the radical redistribution dimension in Sweden appear on the welfare-state dimension in Japan and the United States. These are items that deal with the fairness of the capitalist system: do laws favor the rich, is poverty the fault of the system or of the individual, and, in the United States, is capitalism fair to workers?

This linkage of the items on the fairness of the market system with the issue of redistribution rather than with the welfare state is what one would expect in a society with a well-established welfare state that is supported by a strong consensus across all leadership groups. Whether or not one considers the market system to be fair, one supports the basic guarantees of the welfare state. Differences about whether the market system is a fair allocative mechanism imply differences over more radical remedies. Those who consider the market unfair and poverty the fault of the system wish to see the government more active in actually leveling income; those who have a more sanguine view of the market see no need for such redistributive measures.

What is most significant, however, is that the distinction between welfare state and redistribution appears so uniformly in all three nations. It indicates that the leaders in all three countries organize their views of equality using the distinction between the welfare state's basic social services and more radical income-redistribution programs. In each nation there is also a clear factor dealing with questions of equality between men and women. The key items deal with stereotypes of women (that they are unreliable workers), with traditional attitudes toward gender roles (that women belong at home), and with beliefs about the extent of discrimination against women. In addition, questions about the Equal Rights Amendment (ERA) in the United States and about employment policies toward women fall on that factor. Again the factor analysis gives us evidence that the gender aspect of an equality issue gives it a distinctive quality. The attitudes that individuals have on gender issues tend to cluster.

One gender-related item does not fall on the same factor as the others. This is the question about job quotas for women in relation to employment. In Sweden and Japan, it loads on the redistributive factor. In the United States, the question on quotas for women loads on a separate factor with a similar question about racial quotas as well as with two other items that deal with strong governmental intervention on racial matters—speeding integration and busing. This shows how the multidimensional nature of any individual policy issue can—when entered into an analysis of the sort we have conducted—reveal the dominant dimensions of the equality issue. Gender issues do form a set by themselves; in that sense the male-female dimension is an organizing principle for equality attitudes. But the issue of quotas for women functions more as an issue of equality of condition—of government intervention to create substantive equality—than an issue of gender equality.

In addition, in each of the nations a factor or factors refers to equality in relation to particular disadvantaged minority groups: in Sweden, questions about immigrants form a separate factor; in Japan, questions about buraku people and questions about non-Japanese residents such as Koreans each produce a factor; and in the United States, questions dealing with equality between whites and blacks generate a factor.

Lastly, there are additional factors unique to a particular nation: one in Sweden and two in the United States. In Sweden, several items that refer to the desire to cut back on the welfare state load on a separate factor. Although the welfare state is well institutionalized in Sweden, recent critics have attacked it as excessive in its coverage and in the demands it places on the economy. Some of that sentiment appears in this clustering of questions. Also found on this dimension is a question dealing with job preferences for Swedes over immigrants. (Why this variable does not appear on the immigrant factor is unclear.)

In the United States, two additional factors emerged. One, already mentioned, contains very strong loadings for two items dealing with quotas for blacks and for women, as well as weaker loadings for two items dealing with strong government intervention to foster racial equality—speeding integration and busing. The factor is extremely interesting because it contains items on gender equality and racial equality that do not fall on the gender or the racial factors. Instead, the strong relationship between these two items makes clear that the issue of quotas overrides the other factors. Respondents appear to organize their attitudes around the issue of quotas when it is raised with other issues. Moreover, the quite controversial issue of busing—also representing strong governmental intervention to achieve equality of results—falls on the same factor. Although respondents organize many issues in terms of their relation to race or gender, they evaluate certain approaches to racial or gender equality in terms of the approach rather than the nature of the affected group. Lastly, two items dealing with the perceived causes of inequality for women and blacks—whether the "system" or the individual is to blame—load on a separate factor.

In general, then, the equality variables do seem to have a meaningful structure. This structure has a good deal of similarity both across the three nations and among the groups within the three nations. In each nation we find a distinction between issues of distribution through governmental welfare programs and redistribution leading to more radical income leveling. Separate factors are organized around gender equality and equality for disadvantaged minorities. And the issue of job quotas stands out; questions on quotas for women cluster with redistributive questions rather than with other questions on male-female differences. None of this implies that across the several nations the leaders take similar positions or that within the several nations the various leadership groups are similar. In fact, we have seen differences on these issues both within and among the nations. What the analysis actually implies is a similarity in some of the major dimensions of equality. We were also interested in the extent to which the structure we find for the full set of leadership groups in each nation is shared among the groups. It would make little sense to compare the positions of the various groups on these factors, if the factors did not adequately describe the salient dimensions for one or more of the groups. To guard against this contingency, we replicated the factor analysis just described within each of the leadership groups in each nation. Although there are some variations—usually revolving around the particular dimension most salient to the group under consideration—the basic pattern holds across groups within each nation.

Group Differences in Attitude

One of the purposes of our dimensional analysis of equality attitudes was to simplify the structure of such attitudes so that we might more effectively compare the groups. To do so, we constructed scales based on the factors found in each nation. The scales were constructed so that each would have a mean of zero and a standard deviation of one. Negative scores indicate attitudes that deviate from the average for all leaders in an egalitarian direction, positive scores indicate positions of a more inegalitarian sort. The standardization allows us to make some very useful comparisons among the groups, yet prevents us from making others. Because the average score a group receives on any of the scales is relative to the positions of all other individuals, we cannot say in any absolute sense how far to the left or right the position of a group is. If we had selected other groups to go into our analysis, the location of a particular group would change. Nor can we say in an absolute sense if a group is farther to the left on one issue than on another. We can, however, locate the average position of each group relative to each other group on each issue scale. Furthermore, we can locate those instances where groups have positions that are particularly distinct from those of the other groups with which they are being compared. In sum, our technique identifies a number of underlying dimensions of equality attitudes in each nation, most of which are quite similar from nation to nation. It also allows us to array each leadership group from left to right relative to the positions of all other groups sampled in their country.

Figure 5.1 illustrates the positions of the various leadership groups on the equality scales in each of the three nations. Although we have reduced the dozens of questions in each nation to a limited set of dimensions, it remains a daunting task to describe the positions of so many groups on so many dimensions. We shall confine ourselves to some general considerations of the positions of the various groups seen in comparative perspective. First, certain groups tend to appear on the left or right on all scales, and these groups are similar across the nations. Second, in all nations there is a polarity between labor and the left parties on the left side of the scales and business and the conservative parties on the right. We see this polarity most clearly on the basic economic issues associated with the welfare state dimension. In each of the nations an additional set of groups also appears on the left—often farther to the left than labor or the left parties, particularly regarding noneconomic issues. In Japan, the farthest left position on all dimensions but the welfare-state dimension belongs to

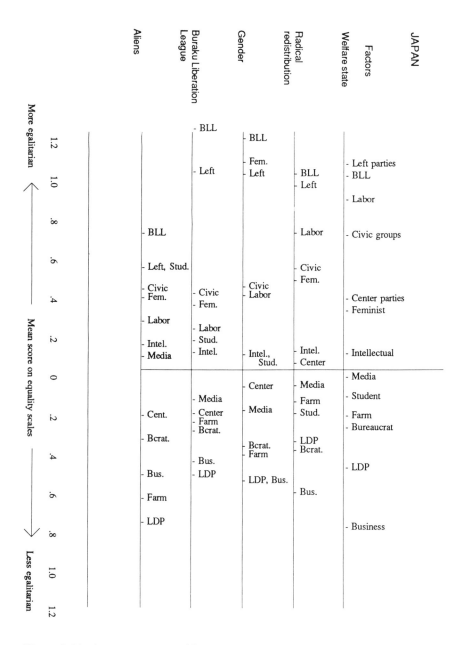

Figure 5.1A. Average group positions on attitude scales in Japan

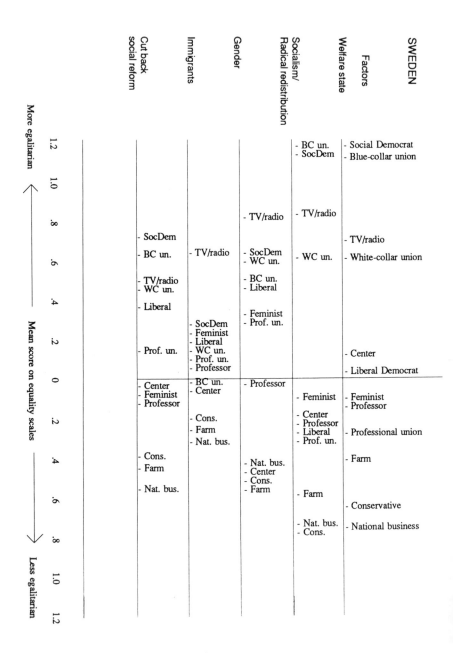

Figure 5.1B. Average group positions on attitude scales in Sweden

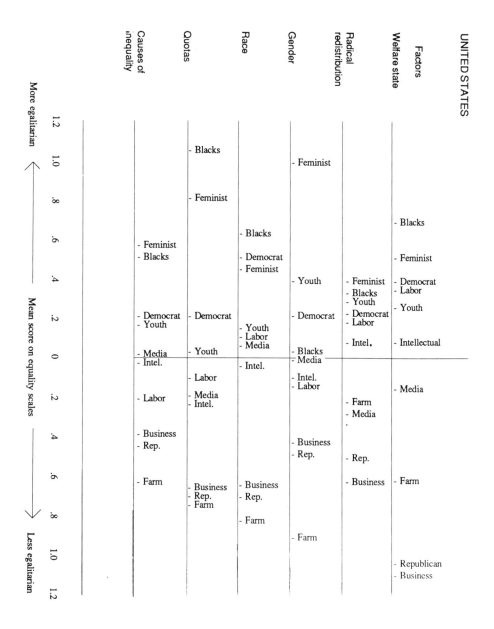

Figure 5.1C. Average group positions on attitude scales in the United States

the leaders of the Buraku Liberation League. In Sweden, TV and radio personnel take positions on the far left; they are beyond the blue-collar union leaders and the Social Democratic leaders on noneconomic issues. And in the United States, black and feminist leaders outflank labor and the Democratic leaders. Which groups appear on the far left depends in part on the groups included in our sample. We had no representatives of disadvantaged minority groups in Sweden, largely because the best candidates for such a category were the foreign workers who have little organized leadership. In the United States and Japan, the far left is occupied by the representatives of such a group, joined by feminist leaders in the United States. In Sweden, the most left group, electronic media personnel, is quite different, reflecting a well-defined ideological bent of those who work for the state-controlled electronic media.

The right side of the scale also has a distinctive set of groups in each nation: the leaders of the conservative party (the Japanese LDP, the American Republican party, and the Swedish Conservative party), business leaders, and leaders of farm organizations. And the center has a similar population across the nations: in each of the nations intellectuals tend to fall toward the center of the attitude scale as do media people (with the exception of the electronic media in Sweden), middle parties, and youth.

This general similarity across the nations and across the issue scales would suggest that although equality has many subdimensions, it also has at its core a general underlying dimension. If one is an egalitarian in one way, one will be an egalitarian in other ways. Such a connection across equality domains, if it exists, is not necessarily dictated by the logic of the situation. A belief that incomes ought to be distributed in a more egalitarian manner has no necessary link to a belief that women should have equal access to the workplace.

The similarity among the equality dimensions is incomplete. There are groups whose positions on the scales of equality differ from dimension to dimension. Most important, however, is that this variation is quite similar across the nations. The main variation across equality dimensions occurs in the positions of the labor unions and farm organizations. (We found the variation quite clearly in the position of Sweden's LO, the blue-collar workers' union.) Labor and farm organizations stand farther to the left on economic than on noneconomic matters. Labor is usually in the egalitarian vanguard in the economic sphere but quite ambivalent toward equality for women and minorities. Farm leaders have a similarly differentiated position, more to the left on economic than on noneconomic issues, but their positions on both economic and noneconomic matters are farther to the right than those of labor. On economic matters they take positions near the middle, much farther left than business and the conservative parties; on noneconomic ones, however, they tend to anchor the right side of the scale.

In Japan, on the left side of the scale, labor union leaders are quite left on the welfare state and less left on redistribution. They move to the middle—outflanked by civic groups, feminists, the left parties, the BLL, and sometimes youth—on issues of equality for women, for buraku people, and for aliens. On the right, farmers are in the three most conservative groups when it comes to the noneconomic equality issues, but they are closer to the center on the economic issues. A similar pattern appears in Sweden: the leaders of LO anchor the left with the Social Democratic leaders on the economic dimensions but move toward the center on the other issues. Furthermore, although the LO is the left-most union group on economic issues, white-collar unionists are more liberal on gender and immigrant issues and professional unionists are more liberal on immigrant issues. On the right, farm leaders are as conservative or more conservative than business and Conservative party leaders on noneconomic issues but much more centrist on economic ones. In the United States a similar relocation takes place for labor and farm leaders. American labor is particularly varied in its positions: it is quite solidly to the left on economic issues but only slightly to the left of the midpoint of the scale (roughly at the mean of all groups) on the race issue and to the right of the midpoint on the issues of gender equality, quotas, and the causes of inequality for women and blacks. Farm leaders show the same pattern of conservatism on noneconomic matters, being to the right of business and Republican leaders on the gender, race, and causes of equality dimensions but toward the middle on economics.

The parallels across the nations are clear. When it comes to economic issues, labor leaders and, to a lesser extent, farm leaders represent groups that consider themselves disadvantaged and prefer more equality. When it comes to noneconomic issues, these groups represent more traditional values and take less egalitarian positions. It is particularly interesting that in Sweden the disjunct pattern appears most clearly in the union representing blue-collar rather than white-collar or professional workers. The traditional, economically based left may be most severely challenged by claims for equality on other than an economic, working-class basis.

These data demonstrate that the multidimensionality of the equality issue has consequences. The differential array of groups from issue to issue should affect the coalitions that can be formed across the several equality issues as well as the intensity of support that various groups will give to different positions. Egalitarian groups do not necessarily have interests or values in common. They may, indeed, sometimes find themselves in sharp conflict because they are committed to different forms of equality.

The position of leaders of ascriptively based minority groups in relation to their "own" equality issue show some interesting similarities and differences. Leaders of black organizations and of the Buraku Liberation League represent radical (in relation to the other groups) claimants for equality for their groups. The variation among feminist leaders, however, is greater. In the United States, they are isolated, far to the left of other groups. In Japan, the feminists are outflanked, even on the gender issue, by the BLL leaders; they take positions quite close to the left party leaders. In Sweden, the feminist leaders are moderate on that set of issues, being outflanked by a number of other groups. This variation reflects some fundamental differences among the feminist groups across the nations in terms of how they relate to other equality-oriented groups in society. We shall return to this in a later chapter when we look more closely at the issue of gender equality.

Lastly, we can consider the position of the political parties on the various equality scales. They are arrayed from left to right in the order one would expect them. We are more interested in their relationship with the other leadership groups with whom they tend to be allied. In each nation the conservative party stands close to business and farm leaders on almost all dimensions. In the United States Republican leaders are between business and farm leaders on all dimensions but in each case closer to business (with exception of the quotas dimension, where all three groups are in an essentially identical position). Indeed, the business-Republican similarity of position across the range of issue scales is the closest pairing of any party with any support group that we find in our data. The relationship of the Conservative leaders in Sweden to business leaders is similarly close. The Conservatives are significantly closer to business than to farm leaders on the basic economic issues, but they are a bit closer to farm leaders on some of the social issues. As with the Republican and the Conservative leaders in the United States and Sweden, the leaders of the Liberal Democratic party in Japan take positions between but close to the business and the farm elites.

On the left we find the Social Democrats, the left opposition parties, and the Democratic leaders surrounded by their support groups. The Social Democratic leaders are never far from their key support in the LO. In Japan and the United States, in contrast, the left parties are fairly distant from labor on the noneconomic dimensions. When a particular challenging group outflanks all other groups, one finds the left parties squarely between the mainstream and the particular group. The best examples of this are the positions of BLL leaders in Japan on the buraku dimension and of U.S. feminists and black leaders on the gender and race issues respectively. The complexities of maintaining party support on the left are clearly reflected.

In sum, there is a relatively definitive structure to equality attitudes in each of the nations. Furthermore, that structure is quite similar across the nations. The distinction between welfare-state policies and policies of a more radical redistributionist sort appears in all three nations. So does a distinction between economic equality and equality based on gender or ascriptive minority status. There are other, more complex similarities across the nations. Labor and farm organizations differ in their positions on economic and noneconomic matters, being farther to the left on the former than on the latter. The position of labor is generally to the left of the farm organizations on both types of equality issues, but the same disjunction between the economic and the noneconomic exists.

6

The Inequality
of Income

Unequal income is a feature of all societies. Some individuals earn more than other individuals and some occupations generate more income than others. Some radically egalitarian social systems have existed, but in most cases these have been small utopian communities. Nations—even those that espouse egalitarianism—have hierarchical income structures. Several general explanations have been put forward for the inequality of earnings, ranging from differences among individuals in talent and effort, to the functional necessity of differential rewards to motivate individuals to do more difficult or responsible tasks, to the illegitimate appropriation by capitalists of the product of the workers.

The ubiquity of income differentiation does not imply similarity across nations in the degree of inequality. Societies—even the three we study that share common features such as relative affluence, democratic government, and (more or less) private ownership—manifest significant variation in the degree to which income is equally distributed. These variations pose an even more interesting explanatory task and the explanations have been numerous. Some are economic, focusing on the structure of the economy, the nature of the supply and demand for labor, the level of affluence of the society, its rate of growth, and the like.[1] Others focus on aspects of politics ranging from the degree of democracy to the extent of political participation to the strength and electoral success of socialist parties.[2] And some attribute cross-national variations to cultural factors such as the degree to which equality is valued in a society.[3]

One should be careful about making the all-too-common assumption that "market forces" operate prior to "political forces," which are seen as being imposed afterward. Market arrangements are established and enforced by the political process in the first place, as should be apparent from any examination of countries where the market plays only a small role or where the government is unable to enforce contracts or protect property holders from theft or violence. Without government intervention, the world is more likely to look Hobbesian rather than a free market of voluntary exchanges. Furthermore, even within the context of a market economy, many specific rules governing individual behavior give the market specific content—is one allowed to use one's property in the form of a stereo player to play loud music at three in the morning, is one allowed to use one's property in the form of a paper mill to dump noxious gases into the air? The government decisions that allow sway to the market in the first place and set up rules for the behavior of market participants affect the distribution of income and wealth. Such decisions are inevitable—the decision to allow markets to operate is a political act as much as is the decision not to allow them—and they are strongly influenced by the values people hold.[4]

It is not our purpose to try to provide an answer to the question as to which explanation for cross-national income differentiation is most potent. Rather we use our data on attitudes toward inequality to demonstrate, we believe, that the last set of factors—the norms and values that people have about equality—are, if not determinative, certainly most relevant. Earnings, being more precisely measurable than attitudes toward other forms of equality, also allow a more precise understanding of *how much* inequality leaders in the three nations desire.

Two basic questions about income inequality must be considered: How much inequality is there? How much inequality should there be? Neither question is simple. The empirical question of the amount of inequality has no unambiguous answer. There are many ways of measuring income differentiation, and the mode of measurement chosen has an impact on the amount of inequality discovered. The normative question of how much inequality there ought to be has an even less definitive answer. Philosophical views range widely as to what is the appropriate basis for determining the income of an occupation—skill, effort, social value, need, and so forth. Furthermore, the two questions—the empirical and the normative—are related to each other. Because there is no agreed measure of the amount of income inequality, the answer to the empirical question is likely to be influenced by one's values. Those who favor more equality are likely to perceive greater inequality than are those who believe that the status quo is acceptable or who favor greater income differentiation. In all societies, this suggests, the debate about income equality will involve at the same time questions of perception and questions of value.

We want to pursue the normative debate about the proper level of equality of income and relate it to the perceptions that individuals have as to actual income differences. It is not our purpose to explain the origins of income differentiation or to estimate its consequences. But our analysis of what is perceived as a proper income gap is not unrelated to those issues. The values people have relating to income differentiation are, we argue, both consequence and cause—at least in part—of the actual situation. As we shall see, the views that individuals have on this issue are clearly affected by the experience to which they have been exposed; in turn, it is fairly clear that the policies pursued in a society in relation to income reflect to some extent the values that its citizenry has on the subject. Our concern with values regarding income equality implies a position on the cause of income differentiation: we assume that differences across nations in the degree of income inequality do not proceed solely from such economic factors as differential rates of growth across sectors in the economy but also are influenced by governmental policies, which in turn derive from social forces and the political values held by the members of the society.

Furthermore, even if income differentials were determined solely by the private sector, the values that certain individuals have relative to a fair income would have an effect on income differentiation. For instance, the salaries of executives of major corporations are not set by market forces alone but by the executives themselves in the light of what they consider to be a proper earnings level. Similarly, views among workers about what constitutes fair wages and fair wage differentials affect the structure of wages, because a perception of unfairness can cause workers to fail to supply their labor or lead to poor productivity among those already employed on a job.[5]

We compare our three nations in terms of the perceptions and values of leaders on what is and what ought to be the income disparity among occupational groups. The comparison is particularly apt. Although the nations differ in the extent of current income differentiation, they are similar in that they are engaged in an ongoing debate as to whether income differentiation is at an appropriate level. In Sweden, a nation with one of the most egalitarian income distributions of modern societies, some argue that there is still too much inequality. Conversely, in the United States, with one of the more inegalitarian distributions, there are those who consider the income distribution too egalitarian. Clearly, such matters are not settled.

The debate takes place in different settings. The three nations differ in the degree to which the government intervenes to foster income equality and in the degree of actual income inequality. In Sweden, a long period of Social Democratic rule resulted in a wide range of social policies and a tax system that are quite redistributive. In Japan and the United States, there has been less governmental commitment to income leveling. Neither the Japanese Liberal Democratic party, which has long been in power, nor the American Democratic or Republican parties have shown great interest in policies that substantially redistribute income. Yet Japan and the United States differ substantially in the degree of income inequality, with the Japanese level closer to that in Sweden than that in the United States. In Sweden and the United States, thus, there is a rough congruence between governmental policy and the degree of income inequality. In Japan, although government policy is less egalitarian, the result is more egalitarian.

As was pointed out in Chapter 4, there are substantial differences among and within the nations in the extent to which leaders are committed to income equality. We can obtain a clearer view of what they consider an appropriate level of inequality by looking at what they consider appropriate earnings for various occupations. But before so doing, it is useful to examine one component of the views discussed earlier: the attitudes of leaders toward the radically redistributive idea of equal income despite differences in ability. Leaders were asked to choose between two definitions of a fair economic system—one in which all people would earn about the same and one in which earnings would be commensurate with ability. Figure 6.1, which plots the responses of the various leadership groups, shows substantial divergence both among the nations and within the nations. In each nation there is a difference between left-liberal and conservative groups on this issue, with left-liberal groups more in favor of income equality, but the more interesting finding is the difference among the nations as to the range of that difference. In the United States, all groups are on the conservative side of the scale, rejecting—to a greater or lesser degree—the rough equality of earnings that is posed as one end of the issue scale. In Sweden, by contrast, the issue is more open. Two groups—leaders of the Social Democratic party and leaders of LO, the blue-collar union—take positions on the equal-shares side of the scale. Their opponents' views on income equality, however, are as negative as those of the more conservative groups in the United States. The result is a much wider polarization on that issue in Sweden. In Japan, the pattern is roughly in between these two nations: one group, the leaders of the Buraku Liberation League, take a quite radical position on the issue, others fall on the midpoint of the scale, and the conservative groups fall roughly where their counterparts in other nations fall. In sum, there is rough consensus against income equality in the United States, a policy difference of not inconsequential magnitude in Sweden, and a more mixed picture in

In a fair economic system, people would earn about the same.

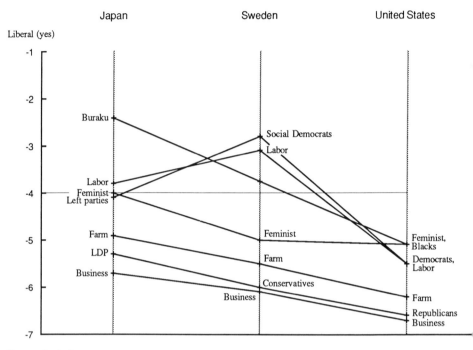

Figure 6.1. Attitudes toward a fair income distribution: established and challenging groups

Japan, where one group stands out in favor of radical equality and others oppose it or are relatively neutral.

The data on the criteria for a fair income distribution illustrate the way in which leaders view the issue within the context of income distribution in their respective nations. Republicans in the United States and Conservatives in Sweden agree that a fair economic system should reward ability; in this sense they agree on the criterion for fair income determination. The nations, however, differ substantially in terms of the degree to which income distribution is in fact equal; and, as we shall shortly see, the leadership groups differ from nation to nation as to how much income inequality they believe to be compatible with fairness. Thus the agreement between the conservative party leaders in Sweden and in the United States masks substantial differences in their views on *how much* additional reward should be given to those with greater ability.

As we have seen, equality is a term with many diverse meanings. There is, therefore, no ready criterion of what is equality of income. One conception links earnings to the nature of work or of the worker—earnings would be equal if two people doing the same or comparable work received the same pay or if workers with identical skill and effort were paid the same. Under this definition the same pay for quite different work would be considered unequal. We use a simpler concept as a benchmark for comparison with what our leaders consider to be a just distribution: pay is equal if it is simply numerically equal. In a sense, we are using as a baseline the full equality that Isaiah Berlin argues is the natural starting point for discussions of equality.[6] Full equality is clearly unrealistic, however, and, as we shall see, almost no one favors it. To understand the debate about income equality, it may be useful to look at this issue for a moment.

Isaiah Berlin has argued that equality is the state most accept as just. If a group is given a cake to divide, the "natural" division is into equal portions; unequal portions have to be explained. But variations in income do not derive from divisions of a cake that has been given to a group but a cake that one or more members of the group have baked or bought—that is, from the work and productivity of some. This, of course, is the basis of the justification for unequal incomes; they represent rewards for differential skill and effort. Deviations from that inequality may require justification. Those who would argue for an equality of condition in relation to income greater than that which would be produced by a system of equality of opportunity that rewards talent and effort are faced with two arguments in favor of the latter: the argument of efficiency and the argument of desert.[7]

The efficiency argument is that to pay each person the same no matter what the contribution to social production would reduce incentives to produce and thus hurt all. Few would argue and few societies offer evidence for the proposition that economic incentives are unnecessary for productivity. Even relatively radical egalitarians would accept some version of Rawls's difference principle whereby inequalities are justified if they increase the absolute welfare of the worst off.[8] The desert argument goes beyond issues of efficiency: it argues that it is unjust to reward equally individuals whose efforts and skills differ. The argument on effort is not very controversial; few think it fair to give equal income to those who work hard and those who prefer leisure to work. The skill or talent side of the question is more controversial. One may argue, as Rawls does, that one's talents are unearned and therefore not particularly worthy of extra rewards.[9]

The philosophical argument is complex and beyond the direct scope of our concern. What is relevant is that one need not be oblivious to the necessity of incentives or opposed to differential rewards for differential effort and talent in order to question a particular level of income inequality.[10] That some income difference is justified by both efficiency and desert does not imply the degree of that difference. The differences of opinion among leaders discussed in this chapter should be seen in that light.

The measurement of income is by no means an easy and settled matter. There are alternative definitions of what ought to be considered to be income—whether, for instance, government transfers, income in kind, and various subsidies should be so considered. Alternative units can be used for comparing incomes—individuals, families, and so forth—and there are choices as to the time frame: income may be considered across an individual's lifetime or one may use a shorter time span.

Our approach begs some of these questions but in a manner that we believe is not inappropriate. Because we compare what leaders believe to be a fair income distribution with what they perceive to be the current distribution in their nations, we had to use the same measurement technique to obtain both perceptions of income and values about income across all the leadership groups.

In our surveys we asked the respondents about a series of occupations, ranging from some of the highest paid to some at the bottom of the earnings hierarchy. For each occupation we asked the respondents what they believed someone in that occupation earned and what someone in such an occupation ought to earn. The occupations about which we asked varied in actual earnings, the skills needed to engage in them, and their prestige. We also chose occupations from the private and the public sectors. The data allow us to make a number of comparisons, singly and in combination: between what is perceived and what is thought fair for an occupation, among occupations in what is or in what ought to be; and these comparisons can be made among leaders within each nation and across the nations.

There remain, however, a number of points to note about this measurement of attitudes on income. We ask about *earnings* for particular occupations, not about wealth. It is possible that one would get quite different responses if one considered the distribution of wealth. The latter is more highly skewed in most societies than is income, and individuals may have different views as to what is just in relation to various forms of unearned income. We were interested, however, in rewards for work. For our purposes the differences in earnings from particular occupations seemed a useful measure of how much differentiation people thought was appropriate among individuals.

One issue in measuring income differentiation is how to handle the impact on earnings of governmental intervention through taxes and transfers. In the United States and Japan we asked about income before taxes and transfers; in Sweden we asked about income both before and after government intervention. In the first two countries, we could ask about pretax income because the distribution of income before and after governmental intervention is relatively similar; this allowed us to simplify the task presented to our respondents, who, we found, tended to think of income as pretax income and could respond easily to our questions. Because it would make little difference, we asked the simpler question about pretax income. In Sweden, it was not possible to avoid the issue of pretax and posttax and transfer income. As indicated in Chapter 1, Sweden ranks first among modern democracies in the extent to which the tax and transfer system is redistributive. Therefore, we asked about respondents' perceptions and values in relation to posttax and posttransfer income. We also asked about perceptions of income before governmental intervention via taxes and transfers. This allows us to analyze, in Sweden at least, the views that respondents have as to the impact of the tax and transfer system on income inequality.[11]

Although the comparison between Sweden, on the one hand, and Japan and the United States, on the other, will be between estimates based on income after government intervention in the Swedish case and before intervention in the other two cases, this should not have, we believe, much impact on the validity of the comparison. Our ultimate goal is to compare what people believe income is and ought to be. In Japan and the United States, where the distribution of earnings before and after government intervention is similar, the question about earnings before taxes and transfers ought to be adequate. In Sweden, we tap more directly the subject of the real income that individuals have at their disposal. Of course, the pretax and transfer income in all three nations represents income before government intervention only in the narrow sense that it is income before taxes are subtracted and transfers are added in. The income is earned under a particular governmental system in anticipation of the subtractions and additions. In the absence of such anticipation, income before government intervention might look quite different.

We asked about similar occupations in each country: the chief executive in one of the major corporations, a cabinet minister, a professor, a school teacher, a doctor, a policeman, a skilled worker in an automobile factory, and so forth. In each case we tried to provide job descriptions and other contextual information about the occupation—where the individual was employed and the length of time in the job—so that respondents had a clear notion of what the job entailed. It is important that fairly fine distinctions were made in terms of the occupations about which we asked, because broad occupational categories can be quite heterogeneous in terms of earnings.[12]

In several instances we chose somewhat different occupations to serve as functional equivalents: in the United States and Japan, we asked about a famous sports star; in Sweden, about a prominent popular singer. In each nation we asked about a skilled artisan with whom the public comes into contact, although the specific occupations differed (a carpenter in Japan, a plumber in the United States, and a television repairman in Sweden). We do not claim that the occupations are identical in function and prestige in each of the nations; our goal was merely to have comparable sets in each nation that covered the full range of positions on the occupational hierarchy in terms of income, prestige, and the like. In particular, we wanted to include occupations at the top of that hierarchy as well as occupations at the bottom so that we could gauge the income gap that respondents considered to be legitimate between the top and the bottom earners.

The task turned out to be one that respondents could and were willing to handle. Most gave us the estimates that we asked for, and few indicated that they had any trouble so doing. The estimates made by our respondents as to the earnings of those in the various occupations appear to be fairly accurate. Table 6.1 shows these estimates and compares them with objective data (from census and other sources) about occupations similar to those about which we asked.[13] There are some misperceptions, such as the overrating of the income of doctors in Japan and the United States, but most of the estimates are close to the actual data. In almost all cases the ranking of the occupations by our respondents corresponds to that yielded by the real world data.

In Sweden, we have the added complexity of having asked our respondents what they believe the various occupations earn before and after taxes and transfers. The estimates that they make are quite close to the actual pretax income of most of the occupations about which we asked and to the actual disposable income after government intervention. Furthermore, the Swedish respondents appear to have quite accurate views on the magnitude of the impact of government intervention—via taxes and transfers—on income.[14]

Table 6.2 presents data on what our leadership samples perceive income to be and what they would consider to be fair. Despite the fact that they represent averages across a wide range of groups, the data make some quite interesting points. In the United States and Japan, respondents want to reduce the income of the top earning occupations. In the United States, respondents would cut the incomes of executives, sports stars, and doctors by fairly substantial amounts, and they would make a deep cut as well in the earnings of plumbers. In Japan, the incomes of doctors, executives, sports stars, and cabinet ministers would be cut, with the first three of the occupations receiving the largest reductions. Japan differs from the United States in that doctors occupy a particularly salient position in the former country: they are perceived to have the highest earnings as well as the earnings that are most out of line.[15] In both countries those perceived to have the highest incomes are perceived to have earnings well above that which would be fair. In addition, there is an inclination in both countries to raise the incomes of those in occupations at the lower end of the income scale by at least some modest amount.

Sweden offers a contrast in that there is less of an inclination to cut income. The star popular singer is the only one whose income would be cut; for other occupations, including that of top business executive, respondents believe that earnings should increase, in most cases, by about 10 to 20 percent. Unlike in the other two nations, in Sweden the general inclination appears to be to raise all incomes rather than to lower the top ones and raise those at the bottom.

The data are at first glance puzzling, because one would have expected greater support for redistribution in Sweden. Instead it is in Japan and the United States that we find a stronger inclination to reduce the income of those at the top and raise the income of those at the bottom. However, another contrast in the data, the much narrower range of earnings in Sweden than in the other two nations, offers a solution to the puzzle. In both perceived earnings and desired earnings, the difference between the highest income-producing occupation and the lowest is much less in Sweden than in Japan and in the United States. In Sweden the ratio of the income of the top to bottom earner is about 3:1; it is about 30:1 in the other two cases. The Swedes appear not to want more redistribution because it has already gone so far.

The data in Table 6.2 are based on an average of all leaders—a dubious summary of heterogeneous groups. To pursue this matter more effectively we must disaggregate the data into the separate leadership groups. Because we are comparing a number of leadership groups in three nations, it is desirable to have some summary measures. For our purposes, three measures are useful: the relationship between what an occupation is perceived to earn and what is thought to be fair earnings for it, between the

Table 6.1.   Respondent estimates and objective measures of yearly earnings. Units are 10,000 yen for Japan, dollars for United States, and crowns for Sweden

Country and occupation	Estimates by respondents	Objective measures
Japan		
Doctor	4,655	2,700
Top executive	4,280	5,650
Airline captain	1,309	1,250
Professor	910	783
Carpenter	510	500
Auto worker	328	344
Schoolteacher	271	269
Policeman	244	205
Bank teller	227	162
Unskilled manual worker	144	136
United States		
Top executive	206,218	230,000–333,000[a]
Star basketball center	159,287	325,000[b]
Doctor	86,263	53,900
Cabinet secretary	50,404	60,000
Aeronautical engineer	26,706	24,600
Professor	21,098	24,400
Plumber	20,009	13,800
Auto worker	12,598	12,600
Policeman	12,345	12,500
Elementary-school teacher	10,699	12,100
Bank teller	9,480	8,300
Elevator operator	7,154	8,400

Country and occupation	Pretax		Posttax	
	Estimates by respondents	Objective measures	Estimates by respondents	Objective measures
Sweden				
Executive in large corporation	319,133	150,000–200,000	103,597	65,500–73,000
General practitioner (M.D.)	211,431	200,000	85,647	73,000
Member of Parliament	169,724	140,000	72,027	62,000
University professor	144,493	144,000	65,795	64,600
Graduate engineer	116,903	120,000	57,246	61,000

Table 6.1 (continued)

Sweden	Pretax		Posttax	
	Estimates by respondents	Objective measures	Estimates by respondents	Objective measures
Television repairman (own business)[c]	79,904	100,000	47,120	62,000
Home builder	75,237	64,500	44,723	44,250
Bank teller[d]	70,142	84,000	42,721	53,000
Policeman[e]	61,436	76,890	39,536	50,445
Elementary-school teacher[f]	61,132	67,400	39,143	45,700
Auto worker	59,648	62,500	38,807	43,250
Supermarket cashier	46,600	58,200	32,683	40,740
Dishwasher[g]	41,315	52,000	30,423	39,000

Source: See note 13 to Chapter 6.
a. The larger figure includes bonuses.
b. Data for NBA basketball star, not necessarily center.
c. This is a rough estimate. Independent small businesses vary greatly in terms of income.
d. Estimate given for *promoted* bank teller.
e. Same with or without five years' experience.
f. Same income regardless of experience.
g. This category does not exist in official statistics. An equivalent, "kitchen worker," has been used.

perceived earnings of two occupations, and between the fair earnings of two occupations. These relationships indicate whether the respondent considers the current earnings for a particular occupation to be fair as well as the respondent's views as to what the difference is and ought to be among occupations at various places on the income hierarchy. For this purpose, we calculate simple income ratios: between what an occupation is perceived to earn and ought to earn, between the perceptions of pairs of occupations, and between what is thought to be fair for two occupations. In each case the measures are ratios of means.[16] The ratios can be interpreted as follows. If all members of a group want to keep the earnings of an occupation at the level at which they, as individuals, perceive it to be, the resulting ratio would be 1. If the group members on average want to raise an occupation's earnings by 50 percent, the ratio would be 1.50; it would be 2 if they want to double earnings, 3 if they want to triple earnings. If they want to halve earnings, the ratio would be 0.50; if they want to cut them to a third of their current figure, the ratio would be 0.33.[17]

Table 6.3 illustrates the ratio between "is" and "ought" as it applies to

Table 6.2.   Perceived and fair annual earnings. Units are 10,000 yen for Japan, dollars for United States, and crowns for Sweden

	Yearly earnings		
Country and occupation	Perceived	Fair	Difference
Japan			
Doctor	4,655	1,907	− 2,748
Top executive	4,280	2,742	− 1,538
Athlete	3,211	2,042	− 1,169
Cabinet minister	2,488	2,065	− 423
Captain	1,309	1,185	− 124
Professor	910	1,077	167
Carpenter	510	558	48
Auto worker	328	382	54
Schoolteacher	271	318	47
Policeman	244	292	48
Bank teller	227	243	16
Unskilled manual worker	144	175	31
United States			
Top executive	206,218	123,757	− 82,461
Star basketball center	159,287	61,039	− 98,248
Doctor	86,263	69,746	− 25,517
Cabinet secretary	50,404	53,490	3,086
Engineer	26,706	26,284	− 422
Professor	21,098	23,889	2,791
Plumber	20,009	16,311	− 3,698
Auto worker	12,598	12,463	− 135
Policeman	12,345	14,929	2,584
Teacher	10,699	13,250	2,551
Bank teller	9,480	10,883	1,403
Elevator operator	7,154	8,362	1,208
Sweden (after taxes)			
Rock star	103,945	83,246	− 20,699
Top executive	103,597	115,748	12,151
Doctor	85,647	86,373	726
Cabinet secretary	72,027	88,729	16,702
Professor	65,795	75,516	9,721
Engineer	57,246	64,493	7,247
Television repairman	47,120	49,617	2,497
Construction worker	44,723	48,566	3,843

Table 6.2 (continued)

Sweden (after taxes)	Yearly earnings		Difference
	Perceived	Fair	
Bank teller	42,721	47,539	4,818
Policeman	39,536	46,392	6,856
Teacher	39,143	44,688	5,545
Supermarket clerk	32,683	39,124	6,441
Dishwasher	30,423	37,234	6,811

top business executives and lowest wage earners (a beginning unskilled manual worker in Japan, an elevator operator in the United States, and a dishwasher in Sweden). It shows for each of the leadership groups the mean logged income it perceives for each occupation, what it believes that income ought to be, and the ratio of the two. The data for the low-paying occupation indicate that almost all leadership groups in all of the nations would raise its income somewhat; the one exception is the group of business leaders in the United States, who would lower the elevator operator's income by a small amount. In each nation, furthermore, one finds a variation among leadership groups: leaders of the left parties—the Social Democrats in Sweden, the left opposition parties in Japan, and the Democratic party in the United States—would raise the income of the low-paying occupation more than would the leaders of parties to the right, and labor would raise incomes more than business. Leaders of other left movements also would raise income.

The data also give some evidence of greater egalitarian commitment in Sweden than in the other two nations. Swedish Social Democrats and Swedish labor leaders (at least, the leaders of LO, the major blue-collar union) would raise the earnings of the low-paying occupation somewhat more than would their counterparts in Japan and the United States—with their U.S. counterparts lagging the farthest behind. But the differences are not great, and the labor leaders in Japan and the United States represent a wider range of categories of workers than do the blue-collar union leaders in Sweden. In fact, if we take the full range of union leaders in Sweden, we do not find them particularly considerate of the low-paying occupation. Indeed, the evidence in the first part of Table 6.3 suggests quite a bit of similarity across the nations.

Greater differences appear with respect to attitudes toward the earnings

Table 6.3 Perceived and fair annual income, by groups (logged data). Units are 10,000 yen for Japan, dollars for United States, and crowns for Sweden

Country and leadership group	Earns[a]	Ought to earn	Ought/is ratio	Earns	Ought to earn	Ought/is ratio
Japan		Young manual worker			Top executive	
Business	131	137	1.1	3,138	3,141	1.0
Farm	135	145	1.1	2,512	2,043	0.8
Labor	129	175	1.4	3,099	1,561	0.5
Bureaucrats	141	153	1.1	2,764	2,348	0.9
Intellectuals	142	168	1.2	2,468	1,751	0.7
Media	143	168	1.2	3,214	2,658	0.8
Liberal Democrats	128	139	1.1	2,108	1,768	0.8
Center parties	127	162	1.3	3,076	1,441	0.5
Left parties	123	148	1.2	2,664	1,685	0.6
Civic groups	135	178	1.3	2,938	1,139	0.4
Feminists	128	161	1.3	2,794	1,537	0.6
Buraku Liberation League	127	172	1.4	2,468	755	0.3
Students	141	175	1.2	2,780	1,706	0.6
United States		Elevator operator			Executive	
Business	7,137	6,990	1.0	199,295	187,314	0.9
Farm	7,096	7,643	1.1	138,325	87,855	0.6
Labor	6,959	8,627	1.3	173,907	90,612	0.5
Intellectuals	7,101	8,261	1.2	189,151	94,741	0.5
Media	7,124	7,861	1.1	179,410	107,322	0.6
Republicans	6,969	7,201	1.0	164,776	130,223	0.8
Democrats	7,008	8,209	1.2	181,754	99,484	0.6
Blacks	6,739	8,121	1.2	130,074	79,761	0.6
Feminists	6,197	8,527	1.4	172,128	69,650	0.4
Youth	6,794	8,026	1.2	152,168	70,615	0.5
Sweden		Dishwasher			Executive	
National business	30,913	32,772	1.1	93,456	140,037	1.5
Local business	31,367	34,137	1.1	82,207	120,708	1.5
Farm	30,508	35,125	1.2	85,527	112,598	1.3
Blue-collar union	28,539	40,692	1.4	118,559	83,452	0.7
White-collar union	29,638	37,814	1.3	101,594	92,371	0.9
Professional union	31,886	35,723	1.1	91,753	116,567	1.3
Media	29,510	41,241	1.4	94,217	78,316	0.8

Table 6.3 (continued)

Sweden	Earns[a]	Ought to earn	Ought/is ratio	Earns	Ought to earn	Ought/is ratio
		Dishwasher			Executive	
Professors	29,386	34,166	1.2	93,086	99,601	1.1
Women	28,874	34,676	1.2	89,356	98,925	1.1
Social Democrats	28,792	42,260	1.5	118,988	86,963	0.7
Center	29,879	36,287	1.2	83,066	86,805	1.0
Liberals	29,556	35,120	1.2	87,265	94,307	1.1
Conservatives	30,716	33,651	1.1	79,909	117,893	1.5

Source: See note 16 to Chapter 6.
a. Earnings after taxes, in Sweden only.

of top executives. Here we find a clear contrast between Sweden and the other two nations. American and Japanese business leaders consider executive income to be fair and they would leave it as it is (given the sample of business leaders, many of them are talking about their own income); but all other leadership groups would cut executive income. The range of income cuts is quite large across the various leadership groups in Japan and the United States, from groups that would reduce executive income to about 80 percent of what it is perceived to be (Republicans in the United States; LDP leaders, bureaucrats, and media people in Japan) to groups that would cut it to about half or less of its actual level (labor and challenging groups in both countries, the Japanese opposition parties and the U.S. Democratic party, and intellectuals in the United States). Indeed, the pattern both in terms of which groups want large cuts in executive earnings and the actual amounts of the desired reductions is quite similar in the two nations. Labor leaders in both nations would cut executive earnings in half, and the Democratic party and the left opposition leaders would treat them similarly. Some of the challenging groups—feminists in the United States, leaders of civic organizations and of the Buraku Liberation League in Japan—would reduce them even more. Black leaders in the United States are somewhat less inclined to cut executive earnings than are other challenging group leaders in the two nations, a difference that seems to be based largely on black leaders' relatively low estimate of what executives in fact earn.

In Sweden, the pattern is quite different. Only a few groups would reduce executive earnings from what they are perceived to be: the leaders of the LO (the blue-collar union), the Social Democratic leaders, and, to a lesser extent, white-collar union leaders and media people. The amount that the Social Democrats and the LO leaders would cut executive income is, however, substantially less than that for parallel groups in Japan and the United States. For instance, leaders of the labor unions in Japan and in the United States would reduce executive incomes to about half of current perceived levels, whereas leaders of the Swedish LO would cut them to about 70 percent. An even sharper contrast with Japan and the United States is the fact that twice as many Swedish groups would raise executive earnings as would cut them. In the case of business leaders themselves and leaders of the Conservative party, the proposed increase is substantial.

The data in Table 6.3 offer an interesting contrast between Sweden and the other two nations, a contrast not quite consistent with what one would expect, given the difference between the first nation and the other two in terms of actual income differentiation: in Japan and the United States we appear to find a greater redistributive impulse than in Sweden. In the former two countries, almost all respondent groups would raise the earnings of those in the lowest-paid occupation and lower the incomes of executives. There is some variation across groups in terms of the amount they would raise or lower earnings, but the pattern is the same in both places. In Sweden, on the other hand, there seems to be a general feeling that both occupations are earning less than they ought to be. In Japan and the United States, the desired income adjustments would lead to a more egalitarian distribution: the top would be lowered, the bottom moved up. In Sweden, they would have less of an egalitarian result with both the bottom and top incomes going up somewhat.

To conclude, however, that Swedish leaders are less egalitarian in their views of income than are the leaders in Japan and the United States would be to misread the data and, at the same time, to miss the major contrast between Sweden and the other two countries that appears in Table 6.3: the gap between top and bottom earnings in the latter two countries is substantially greater than that in Sweden. Note the earnings that people perceive for the low-paying occupation in each country and compare them with what is perceived for the executive category: as noted above, in Sweden, the ratio is about 3:1; the ratio is about 30:1 in the other two nations.[18] This difference is, of course, crucial to the puzzle. To pursue it further, we consider the relationship among occupations, rather than individual occupations.

The Income Gap

Thus far we have looked at individual occupations. This aspect of our study deals only indirectly with the extent to which our respondents perceive and desire income inequality. We can get a better grasp of this matter if we consider the income gap among occupations that our respondents would consider legitimate. How much more income should be derived from one occupation than from another? To answer this question we present attitudes on pairs of occupations. In each country we consider attitudes toward the appropriate income for an executive and for an automobile worker. We also elicit views on income differences between a top executive and an unskilled worker in Japan, an elevator operator in the United States, and a dishwasher in Sweden. The comparison pairs are particularly useful. In the executive/auto worker pair we have a comparison between the top executive in a major industry and a skilled factory worker in such an industry. In the executive/unskilled worker pairings the comparison is between a top earner and someone near the bottom of the earnings hierarchy. The ratio of the perceived income of the top earner to that of the worker in the low-paying occupation should tell us how wide the gap in earnings between the top and bottom is perceived to be; the ratio between the fair incomes for each occupation should indicate how wide a gap between the two ends of the income hierarchy is thought fair.[19]

These ratios, reported in Table 6.4, reveal some striking differences among the countries. Sweden stands out from the other nations in that the income gap is perceived to be much smaller: the executive is seen to earn about two to three times as much as a skilled automobile worker. In Japan, the leadership groups see executives' earnings as seven to ten times greater, and in the United States, executives are perceived to earn ten to fifteen times as much. The lineup of the nations—Sweden perceived to have the most egalitarian distribution of income, followed by Japan and then the United States—is the same as that produced by actual income data. A similar difference exists for the top-earner/bottom-earner comparison: in Sweden, the top earner is seen to make three to four times what the bottom earner makes; in Japan, the perceived ratio ranges from 16:1 to 24:1; in the United States, the ratio ranges from 19:1 to 28:1.[20]

In the light of these perceived differences, the income differences that are considered fair gain their meaning. In the United States and Japan, almost all groups want to see some reduction in the income gap between the top earner and the skilled or unskilled worker—that is, the ratios as to what is fair are smaller than the ratios of perceived income. The only exception is found among business leaders in the United States who believe that the executive/auto worker difference should be somewhat larger than it is. From this perspective one can say that there is a consensus in both countries that the disparity in earnings between those at the top and those at the bottom is too large.

Table 6.4.   Perceived and fair income ratios, by groups (logged data)

Country and leadership group	Perceived income	Fair income	Perceived income	Fair income
	Executive vs. auto worker		Executive vs. young manual worker	
Japan				
Business	9.1	8.6	23.9	22.9
Farm	7.4	5.7	18.6	14.0
Labor	10.1	4.1	24.0	8.9
Bureaucrats	7.9	6.8	19.6	15.3
Intellectuals	7.2	4.4	17.4	10.4
Media	9.4	6.9	22.5	15.8
Liberal Democrats	7.1	5.4	16.5	12.8
Center parties	9.1	4.9	21.7	11.4
Left parties	10.3	3.7	24.2	8.9
Civic movements	10.0	3.3	21.7	6.4
Feminist movements	9.0	4.2	21.9	9.5
Buraku Liberation League	9.0	2.2	19.4	4.4
Students	11.0	5.5	19.7	9.8
	Executive vs. auto worker		Executive vs. elevator operator	
United States				
Business	15.1	15.6	27.9	26.9
Farm	11.1	7.9	19.4	11.7
Labor	14.8	7.2	24.9	10.6
Intellectuals	15.1	7.9	26.6	11.4
Media	14.1	8.7	25.1	13.6
Republicans	13.2	11.3	23.6	18.0
Democrats	15.4	8.2	26.0	12.1
Blacks	10.8	6.4	19.1	9.7
Feminists	15.2	5.7	27.5	8.2
Youth	13.4	6.0	22.6	8.9
	Executive vs. auto worker		Executive vs. dishwasher	
Sweden				
National business	2.4	3.5	3.0	4.2
Local business	2.1	2.9	2.6	3.5
Farm	2.2	2.7	2.9	3.2
Blue-collar union	3.2	1.9	4.1	2.0
White-collar union	2.6	2.1	3.4	2.4
Professional union	2.3	2.7	2.9	3.2
Media	2.4	1.7	3.2	1.9

Table 6.4 (continued)

Sweden	Perceived income	Fair income	Perceived income	Fair income
	Executive vs. auto worker		Executive vs. dishwasher	
Professors	2.4	2.4	3.2	2.9
Women	2.3	2.3	3.1	2.8
Social Democrats	3.2	1.9	4.1	2.1
Center	2.2	2.1	2.8	2.4
Liberals	2.2	2.2	3.0	2.7
Conservatives	2.1	2.9	2.6	3.5

Source: See note 16 to Chapter 6.

However, this consensus needs qualification. A closer look at the data in Japan and the United States shows a wide variation across leadership groups in the extent to which they perceive an income gap that is larger than that which they would consider to be fair. Although business leaders in both countries would reduce the top/bottom gap (and business in Japan would also reduce the executive/auto worker gap), the reduction they desire is quite marginal. They would leave the income gap essentially as it is. Other groups also would change the ratios little: the conservative parties (the LDP and the Republicans) and farm leaders in both countries as well as bureaucrats in Japan. The desired income disparity reduction is, as we would expect, greater among union leaders in the two countries as well as among challenging groups. Union leaders would reduce the income gap for each of the pairs of occupations to about one-half or less of what they perceive it to be, as would the leaders of the Democratic party in the United States and the left opposition in Japan. The challenging groups go a good deal further. In the United States, for instance, feminist leaders believe that a fair income gap would be about one-third of that which they believe is the case. In Japan, leaders of civic associations take a similar position, and leaders of the Buraku Liberation League desire an even greater reduction. Thus we see an across-the-board commitment to some income disparity reduction in both Japan and the United States, but the extent of that reduction varies so much that one cannot easily talk of consensus on this matter.

Nevertheless, there is consensus of sorts in the fact that no leadership groups would reduce the income disparity completely. All groups in Japan

and the United States accept the legitimacy of an income differential between the business executive and the skilled or unskilled worker. In the
United States, most accept a fairly substantial gap. Even the most radical
groups—feminist and black leaders—consider a wide income disparity to
be legitimate: these two groups think that a fair ratio of executive to unskilled worker earnings is between 8:1 and 10:1. In the United States,
thus, there is a rather mixed commitment to equality. Some groups consider the income gap between top and bottom earners to be much too
large; they would reduce the gap substantially, but they still consider it
appropriate that there be a considerable gap. The system produces inequities, they seem to be saying, but complete income leveling is not the
proper response to this situation.

In Japan, there is a similar acceptance of an income disparity between
the top earner and the two other occupations with which the top earner is
compared. There is a tendency, however, to favor a somewhat narrower
income gap, especially in relation to the executive/auto worker difference.
All Japanese groups favor an income ratio much smaller than that considered fair by their counterparts in the United States. Business and labor
leaders in Japan, for instance, favor ratios slightly more than half as large
as those favored by business and labor leaders in the United States. What
is considered a fair income gap between the executive and the unskilled
worker in the two countries is not as clearly distinct because of the special
characterization of the unskilled worker in Japan as a new, young worker;
but even for this comparison there is a tendency for Japanese groups to
favor a narrower gap. And whereas the most egalitarian of the American
groups would consider a gap of between 8:1 and 10:1 to be fair, the more
egalitarian Japanese groups—the Civic Movement leaders as well as the
Buraku Liberation League leaders—would prefer income ratios between
top and bottom substantially less than those proposed by any of the groups
in the United States. The buraku leaders, for instance, consider a ratio of
4.4:1 between the top earner and the bottom earner to be fair. That is still
not strict equality, but it is far from the ratio of 22.9:1 that Japanese business considers appropriate, farther still from the 26.9:1 ratio favored by
American business, and even quite distant from the 9.7:1 ratio favored by
black leaders in the United States. Leaders in both countries, then, desire
some reduction in income disparity, but—especially in the United
States—all groups consider some (often large) income gap between top
and bottom to be fair.

In Sweden, we find a substantially different picture. There is less consensus that the earnings gap between executives and those lower in the

income hierarchy is too large; many groups think that it is fair or is, indeed, not large enough. Consider first the executive/auto worker gap. Several groups—business leaders, farm leaders, leaders of professional unions, and leaders of the Conservative party—believe that this earnings gap should be larger than it is. The leaders of the blue-collar and white-collar unions as well as the Social Democratic party leaders take an opposite position: they think the gap is too wide and should be narrowed. Other groups think the income gap is roughly appropriate. This is in fairly sharp contrast to Japan and the United States where, with almost no exception, the leadership groups believe that the income gap between the two occupations is larger than it ought to be.

The contrast between Sweden and the other two countries is seen even more clearly if we look at the income gap between the executive and the unskilled worker at the bottom of the earnings hierarchy. Here we find a similar pattern of disagreement in Sweden. Business, farm, professional union, and Conservative leaders believe that the income gap is not as great as it ought to be. Leaders of the other two unions, the Social Democratic party, women's organizations, and the media think that the gap is too large. Others think the disparity is about right. Again this is in contrast with the United States and Japan where all groups would reduce, sometimes substantially, the disparity in income between those at the top and those at the bottom of the hierarchy.

From this perspective one sees more of an egalitarian push in Japan and the United States than in Sweden; but the push can only be understood in terms of the great difference between Sweden and the other two countries in the extent of the earnings disparity that now exists, a difference that is clearly and correctly seen by our elite respondents. Our Swedish respondents are citizens of a nation in which a great deal of income equality has been achieved—and they have mixed views about it. Some think that it has not gone far enough and would narrow the earnings gap even more; others feel that it has gone too far and would widen it. But this mixed view is within the context of very different general attitudes about a fair income distinction between top and bottom earners. Although many Japanese and American groups would reduce the income gap between the executive and the unskilled worker to a fraction of what they perceive it to be—in several cases to one-third of the perceived current level and, in the case of the leaders of the Buraku Liberation League, to about one-fourth—the resulting disparities would be on average well above those that Swedish leaders, including those of the more conservative groups, would consider legitimate.

The contrast among the three nations in what is considered a desirable income gap is seen graphically in Figures 6.2 and 6.3, which present data from Tables 6.3 and 6.4 in a way that highlights the differences among counterpart groups in the three nations. Figure 6.2 displays data on the top-bottom income gap and Figure 6.3 on the gap between the executive and the skilled auto worker. As Figure 6.2 shows, the views of the Swedish elites are of a different order of magnitude from those in the other two nations. Indeed, not only does each group in Japan and the United States favor ratios that are many times as large as those that their counterparts in Sweden consider to be fair, but there also is no overlap between the preferred ratios among the Swedish groups and those of the groups in the other two nations. Note, for instance, the contrast between party leaders in Sweden and in the other countries. The left party leaders in Japan and the United States favor an earnings ratio about three times as large as that favored by the conservative leaders in Sweden. The U.S. and the Japanese

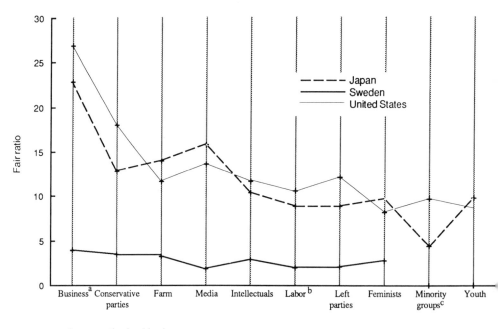

a.   Average, national and local.
b.   Data, for Sweden, from blue-collar union. White-collar and professional union scores,
       2.4 and 3.2 respectively.
c.   Buraku Liberation League in Japan, blacks in the U. S.

Figure 6.2. Attitudes toward a fair ratio between executive earnings and
          unskilled worker earnings

data track each other fairly closely—at least in contrast to the Swedish case. There is, however, a visible tendency for a more egalitarian set of views in Japan.

The latter point is seen more clearly in Figure 6.3. Sweden still stands out, but the Japanese data are quite distinct from those in the United States. The views of Japanese leaders lie between those of leaders in the two other nations and are, if anything, somewhat closer to those in Sweden than in the United States. This is especially clear in relation to the main established groups—business, labor, and the conservative and left parties. Leaders of these groups in Japan favor earnings gaps about one-half as great as do their counterparts in the United States. Indeed, the leaders of the conservative Liberal Democratic party in Japan favor an income ratio that is substantially smaller than that which the Democratic party leaders in the United States consider fair, not to mention that which their Republican counterparts would favor. These data clearly demonstrate

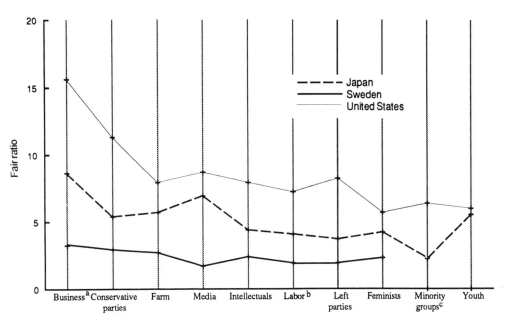

a. Average, national and local.
b. Data, for Sweden, from blue-collar union. White-collar and professional union scores, 2.1 and 2.7 respectively.
c. Buraku Liberation League in Japan, blacks in the U. S.

Figure 6.3. Attitudes toward a fair ratio between executive earnings and auto worker earnings

the greater egalitarianism in Japan compared with that in the United States, an egalitarianism obscured somewhat by the data on unskilled workers because of the age criterion used in that case.

In sum, the range of opinion as to legitimate income disparities hardly overlaps between Sweden and the other two nations. Japanese and U.S. leaders may be more consistently in favor of a narrowing of income disparities than are their Swedish counterparts, but they rarely if ever approach what the Swedish elites think of as a just income hierarchy. There is also a meaningful contrast between the United States and Japan. The differences between the parallel groups in the two nations are quite consistent, especially with regard to the executive/auto worker ratio. In almost all cases the Japanese leaders are more egalitarian regarding income disparities than their counterparts in the United States; this contrast is especially evident in the responses of the leaders of the main established groups—business, labor, and the political parties. Japanese views of the correct income disparity are in general not nearly as egalitarian as those in Sweden, but they are substantially more egalitarian than those in the United States.

One's Own Income

We have thus far presented data on the views of our respondents regarding income levels of various occupations. We also placed the respondents themselves on the income hierarchy and asked them what "someone at your level in your occupation" earns and ought to earn. These figures should correspond closely to what the respondents themselves earn and believe they ought to earn—except for those who consider themselves grossly overpaid or underpaid compared with others in a similar position. But such cases are likely to be rare and would represent personal deviations that would not affect what we are interested in—where the respondent's occupation falls in the hierarchy.

Our respondents vary, of course, in the jobs they have. In some cases the criterion for selection into the leadership sample was that a person hold a particular full-time job. This is the case for business leaders and people in the media, for instance. In other cases a particular occupation is not necessarily entailed in the selection criterion. Leaders such as labor leaders, farm organization leaders, leaders of challenging groups, and political party leaders were selected because of their institutional positions. In most of these instances the individual occupies the position as a full-time job, but in some cases the position may not represent the main employ of the individual. And for some of the leadership segments—the intellectuals, in particular—the category may contain a wide range of occupations. This range of occupations within a leadership group, however, does not affect the basic purpose of our question, which is to allow our respondents to place themselves on an income hierarchy compared to others. Where they place themselves will tell us how the income hierarchy in the three nations looks from the perspective of their occupations.

Given the range of respondent occupations, we find as we would expect a wide variation in the positions they perceive themselves to hold vis-à-vis the top and bottom of the earnings hierarchy. We will focus on what they regard as a fair disparity between themselves and those above and below them. Figure 6.4 presents data on the desired ratio between the income of someone in the respondent's job and that of an executive at the top of the income hierarchy. The nations are arrayed as in the previous data. In the United States, all the respondent groups accept as legitimate

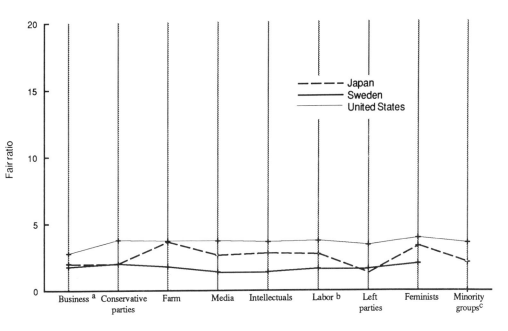

a. Average, national and local,
b. Data, for Sweden, from blue-collar union. White-collar and professional union scores,
     1.6 and 1.7 respectively.
c. Buraku Liberation League in Japan, blacks in the U. S.

Figure 6.4. Attitudes toward a fair ratio between executive earnings and
            respondent earnings

an earnings advantage between 3.5:1 and 4:1. (The exception is business, but the comparison with executives is redundant in this case.) Indeed, the uniformity across the various groups is quite striking—especially given the fact that they differ substantially in their own income and in the amount of the advantage that they perceive executives to have. Note that the more radical of the groups, such as blacks and feminists, join the others in accepting ratios of that magnitude: they agree with such conservative groups as Republicans and farm leaders and with such affluent respondents as leaders in the media regarding a fair income advantage of executives over themselves. Of course this does not imply that they agree with others as to how much executives ought to make—to earn three-and-a-half or four times as much as a black or feminist leader is not the same as earning three-and-a-half to four times as much as a leading figure in the media. These data round out the picture of attitudes toward top income earners in the United States. The leadership groups are almost unanimous in their desire to reduce the earnings of those at the top of the hierarchy, although they vary in how much of a reduction they desire. They agree, however, that such top earners ought legitimately to earn more than they themselves do—and the degree of that advantage is quite uniform across a quite heterogeneous set of elite groups. Wherever one stands on the income hierarchy, one accepts the same relative advantage for those at the top.

The Swedish data offer a definite contrast to those in the United States in terms of how much more an executive ought to earn. Swedish leaders believe an executive ought to earn at most twice as much as they themselves earn—and most leadership groups believe that the ratio should be even smaller. Note, however, that no group wants complete equality in earnings with the top executive (if they did the ratio would be 1.0); the Swedish respondents are relative egalitarians, not complete egalitarians. The Japanese data fall between these two patterns in terms of the advantage for an executive that the respondents would consider fair. The Japanese leadership groups show more heterogeneity than the leadership groups in the other two nations. Some Japanese leaders consider it appropriate that executives earn somewhat more than three times as much as they do. These ratios are similar to those found in the United States; farm leaders and feminist leaders fall in this category, as do bureaucrats. Other leaders believe the proper difference should be closer to 2:1, with the left parties considering a ratio of 1.6:1 appropriate—figures much more in the range of the Swedish data.

In sum, none of our sets of leaders are complete levelers. All consider it legitimate that top business executives earn more than they themselves do, but beyond that there is an important difference among the nations as well as an important similarity. The difference is in the level of advantage thought to be fair for an executive; the similarity is that each nation seems to have a distinctive level that holds across most groups. The across-group agreement is not as complete in Japan as in Sweden and the United States, but attitudes are fairly uniform there as well. It is as if there is a uniform accepted income ceiling in each nation, but the uniformity is in terms that are relative to the individual. In each nation there is substantial variation across groups in how much an executive ought to earn, just as there is variation in how much each respondent group thinks it ought to earn; but each group would place executive income in a similar relationship to its own.

The data comparing someone in one's own occupation with an unskilled worker at the bottom of the earnings hierarchy provide a similar contrast between Sweden and the other two nations (Figure 6.5). In Sweden, all groups consider a fairly low ratio to be fair; even business leaders opt for a ratio just slightly more than two to one. Some of the Swedish groups are quite strikingly egalitarian on this measure: leaders of the LO and of the Social Democratic party believe that they should earn only a marginal amount (a ratio of 1.2) more than the low-paid unskilled worker.

In the United States and Japan, the elite groups take less of an egalitarian stance. Labor leaders in both countries believe that they should earn about three times as much as an unskilled worker, and even the more radical challenging groups consider ratios of two to one or better to be appropriate. The data suggest that Japanese leaders are in favor of a somewhat wider gap than is the case in the United States, but it is likely that we are seeing the reflection of the ages of our leaders compared with a young unskilled worker.

In almost all cases it is interesting that the ratio thought to be fair is very close to the ratio perceived. For instance, labor leaders in Japan and the United States believe that the ratios between their income and that of an unskilled worker ought to be 3.3 and 2.9 respectively; they perceive that the actual ratios are 3.6 and 3.3. In other words, they believe that an income advantage over unskilled workers roughly equivalent to that which currently exists is fair. Again in Japan there is more variation than is found in the other two nations regarding the definition of a fair ratio.

In one sense the Swedish responses are more heterogeneous than those in the other countries. In Japan and the United States, most groups think that the ratio of their own income to that of a low-skilled worker is about

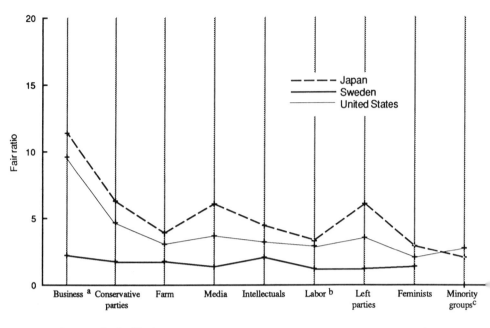

a. Average, national and local.
b. Data, for Sweden, from blue-collar union. White-collar and professional union scores,
    1.6 and 1.9 respectively.
c. Buraku Liberation League in Japan, blacks in the U. S.

Figure 6.5. Attitudes toward a fair ratio between respondent earnings and
unskilled worker earnings

right. In Sweden, some think that the ratio is about right, but others think
it too high or too low. The sharp difference between Sweden and the other
two countries, however, is in the narrowness of the Swedish perceived and
desired ratios: Swedish respondents do not see themselves as making
much more than an unskilled worker, nor do they believe that they should
do so. The least egalitarian group in Sweden, business leaders, consider
as fair a ratio of their income to that of the unskilled worker that is very
close in magnitude to that of the most egalitarian groups in Japan and the
United States. Looked at another way, business leaders in Japan and the
United States consider as fair an income gap four or five times the magnitude of that favored by their counterparts in Sweden. The contrast between Japan and the United States also remains, with Japanese leaders
willing to accept a smaller advantage over the unskilled worker—a distinction that is probably understated by the criterion of youth assigned to
the Japanese worker.

These data on the desired income gap between one's own occupation and a very high-paying occupation on the one hand and an unskilled occupation on the other highlight the Swedish income attitudes compared with those of the other two nations. The Japanese and American respondents live in societies in which they perceive a fairly wide income gap between themselves and executives above them as well as between themselves and unskilled workers below them. Most of the leadership groups find this situation less than fully acceptable and would prefer to see it changed; they would accomplish this by reducing the income of the top earner, and most of the groups would also raise the income of the bottom earner. At the same time, however, they would raise their own income so that the ratio between themselves and the bottom does not change, and they are willing to leave substantial earnings gaps between themselves and those above as well as those below.

To some extent these are egalitarian attitudes toward income. Leaders would reduce the absolute income of the top earners, and that is egalitarian. They would reduce the ratio between themselves and the top earners, and that too is egalitarian. Lastly, they would raise the absolute income of those at the bottom of the income scale, and that is also egalitarian. But this egalitarianism falters in two ways. As respondents raise the income of those at the bottom of the hierarchy, they raise their own proportionately and maintain the same ratio to the unskilled worker—no great egalitarianism there. Most of all, in their ideal world of equality they maintain a substantial gap in earnings between themselves and top-earning executives as well as between themselves and unskilled workers. They would make an unequal world less unequal but still retain a good deal of inequality.

Our Swedish respondents show a greater commitment to equality. For each leadership group the desired income gaps between those at the top and themselves and between themselves and those at the bottom are substantially narrower than is the case for their counterparts in the other two nations. The Swedish respondents want a world that is much more egalitarian than that desired by Japanese and American leaders. The current thrust of Swedish opinion, however, is by no means unambiguously egalitarian. Many believe that equality has gone too far and would reverse the leveling trend.

The analysis of attitudes toward income differentiation is as relevant to the question raised at the beginning of this chapter as to the explanation of income differences. Several types of explanation were mentioned: explanations in terms of market forces (higher earnings are commanded by occupations for which workers are in short supply); the nature of the work (occupations requiring more training, greater skill, or greater responsibility receive higher rewards); ideas about distributive justice (the normatively acceptable top and bottom levels of earnings as well as norms about fair income disparities influence income distributions); and government policies (government policies for taxes and transfers play a major role in determining income differentiation).

Our data cannot provide a definitive answer as to which explanation is most potent—there is probably some validity to each—but the data do tell us something about the issue. It is clear that the nature of the occupation does not by itself determine income differences. We study a similar range of occupations in each nation. The cross-national diversity in the income differences among them makes clear that other forces—be they government policy, cultural norms, or fundamentally different market conditions—affect the distribution of income. Furthermore, what is considered to be a just income distribution does not appear to depend on the nature of the occupation. If it did, one would expect consensus across nations on a fair income differentiation even if market forces or government policy led to different income distributions in reality. We find wide differences across nations, however, in what is considered just. Furthermore, the differences appear to parallel the income distribution that government policy fosters. This is clearly seen in the difference between Sweden and the other two nations—and especially between Sweden and the United States—in terms of what is thought to be a fair gap in earnings between those at the top and those at the bottom of the income hierarchy.

The data suggest that what is considered fair is at least partly contextual. The vast differences in how much inequality is considered fair are surely not unconnected to the vast differences in the actual earnings hierarchies across the nations. It is ambiguous whether the norms of just distribution follow upon and adjust to reality as created by public policy and private decisions or whether government policy and private income decisions follow upon and are affected by general cultural norms. Probably a little of each. One might suspect, however, that the current consensus in Sweden regarding a proper income gap represents an acceptance by all groups of the fait accompli of four decades of Social Democratic government.[21]

The contextual nature of attitudes toward income equality can be seen by considering a question we asked about the causes of poverty, a question we believed might help to explain differences among individuals and groups about a fair income distribution. How much inequality one accepts as fair should be closely related to the explanation one accepts as to the cause of inequality, in particular the extent to which one believes that differences in income depend on variation among individuals in skill and effort rather than on characteristics of the social and economic system beyond the control of any individual. If low income can be explained by individual incapacity or lack of motivation, the resulting difference in income among individuals is more easily justified. If one believes that income inequality results primarily from such characteristics outside the control of the individual as handicaps at birth, economic fluctuations, and discrimination, it is more difficult to justify differences in income.

Traditional descriptions of American views on equality would lead one to expect more "individual blame" in the United States, given the individualistic ethic held, with more or less intensity, by groups in America. In Sweden, however, there are so many more guarantees against poverty than in the American welfare system that one might expect more "individual blame" and less "system blame." In fact we found neither when we asked out elite respondents whether poverty was the fault of individuals or the fault of the social and economic system. They could place themselves on a seven-point scale somewhere between those two positions, and given the wide differences across the nations in the nature of the welfare system as well as the differences in the commitment to an individualistic ethic, the answers across the nations are remarkably similar. In each nation the average answer given by our elites falls just to the left side of the midpoint (4.0) of the scale—at 3.6 in Japan, 3.7 in Sweden, and 3.4 in the United States.

Figure 6.6 shows the answers to this question by leadership groups. The data for separate groups are quite similar across the nations: there is a fairly substantial gap between left groups and more conservative groups in the assignment of responsibility for poverty. More striking is the similarity among counterpart groups across the nations. The similarity is intriguing and somewhat surprising. We can speculate that, in assigning responsibility for whatever poverty exists in each nation, the groups make adjustments for the nature of the welfare system and perhaps even for their general cultural beliefs as to individual responsibility. Although there are clear differences among the nations in the degree to which the welfare system takes responsibility for the alleviation of poverty and equally clear (although less precisely measurable) differences in the degree to which individuals are committed to an ethic of individual versus social responsibility, these differences appear to be discounted. Groups assign blame

Is poverty the fault of the individual or the system?

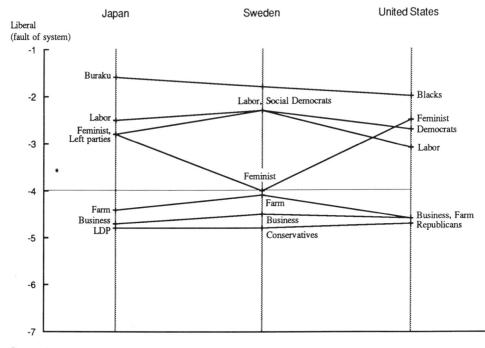

Figure 6.6. Attitudes toward the causes of poverty

for poverty within the context of each country. This still allows full rein for variation of views among leadership groups within each nation. Leaders of left and right parties and leaders of business and labor differ substantially within each nation in the assignment of blame for poverty, but their positions are relative to the national context. Similarly placed leaders come to surprisingly similar conclusions about the causes of poverty—but do so from premises that are relative to the situations in their own nations.

The cross-national data make clear that attitudes toward fair differences are not a function of universal characteristics of occupations. The variations across nations in what is thought to be fair for similar occupations as well as the similarities in belief about the causes of poverty suggest that these views are enclosed in quite varied structures of government policy. Yet the fact that these attitudes vary so much—and in a similar manner—among groups within each nation makes clear that they do not merely reflect the faits accomplis of government policy. They have autonomy.

7

Has Equality Gone
Too Far?
A Note on Sweden

The analysis of attitudes toward equality in each of the three nations has yielded some interesting differences and similarities. The differences are found most frequently in terms of how much equality is desired, as is seen in the differential commitment to the welfare state and the differential tolerance of income inequality. The similarities are largely in the divisions among groups within each nation: business, labor, and challenging groups line up as we would expect them to; leaders of the political parties are similarly arrayed as their locations on the left-right political continuum would lead us to expect them to be. The internal divisions within each of the nations are similar in pattern. They nevertheless vary with the context of political culture within which the divisions occur. Thus in Sweden, there is consensus in favor of the welfare state but more disagreement on radical redistribution. In the United States, there is consensus against radical redistribution but more division on the welfare state. Where there is division in each of the nations, the contending parties line up in a similar manner. The location of the division in the spectrum of public policies varies.

The same pattern of similarity of relative position within different political contexts is found in relation to the issue of how much income inequality is acceptable. In each nation there is a range of attitudes toward inequality of income, but the location of the range of views differs. In Sweden, the range is located in a quite egalitarian section of the full range of possible income disparities compared with the other nations. However, one of the striking characteristics of Swedish opinion is the combination of support for equality coupled with a notion that perhaps the welfare state and equality have gone too far. Glimmers of such opinions appeared in our overview of attitudes toward equality and in attitudes toward income equality. This attitude is, of course, not unique to Sweden. The issue of the limits of social intervention to foster equality is a general issue found in most welfare states. Indeed, it confirms the contextual nature of attitudes toward equality and the welfare state that such a debate is no less vehement in the United States, where the commitment of the government to welfare measures and to income redistribution is substantially less than in Sweden.

It is in Sweden, though, that the debate is most interesting. Sweden is the vanguard welfare state, the government whose public policy has the strongest redistributive effects. It is useful, therefore, to look more closely at the issue of the limits of equality and the welfare state in such a setting. It must be kept in mind, however, that any backing away from the welfare state and equality in Sweden is within the context of an already well-developed egalitarian commitment. If some Swedish leaders would move back from that direction, the level of commitment to welfare and redistribution would still be greater than that to which the most radical of leadership groups in Japan and the United States aspire.[1]

Three survey questions related to whether welfare-state measures and equality had gone too far in Sweden. Respondents were asked to express agreement or disagreement, using a four-point scale, with the following: (1) "In many respects things have gone too far with equality in this country"; (2) "Social reforms have gone so far in this country that the government should be decreasing rather than increasing social welfare benefits for citizens"; and (3) "It's too easy to get on welfare."[2] A historical data base using these questions in earlier elite and mass public surveys in Sweden allows us to trace changes over time in the proportion who believe that equality has gone too far.[3]

The overall pattern of responses to these three questions (Figure 7.1) shows the left groups—the Social Democrats and the leaders of the LO—well to the left side of the scale, as they were on all the basic welfare-state questions. They obviously disagree with the contention that equality and the welfare state have gone too far and oppose cutting back or slowing down social reforms. There is a slightly weaker welfare-state commitment on the issue of whether it is "too easy to get on welfare," more marked, interestingly, among union leaders than among Social Democratic leaders. Both groups register disagreement with the statement, but the difference in the mean response to that question compared with that of the others may indicate the beginning of concern about "welfare cheats."

With the Social Democrats and the blue-collar union leaders holding firm on continuing social reforms and the movement toward equality, the varying degrees of disagreement with that point of view among other leaders is interesting. If one simply looks at the farthest right groups in the

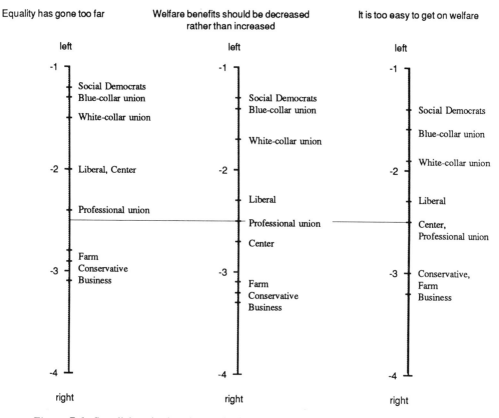

Figure 7.1. Swedish attitudes about whether the welfare state and equality
        have gone too far

survey, the Conservative and business leaders, one would conclude that
the pattern of cleavage on this issue is the same as for the issues of capitalism and radical redistribution discussed in Chapter 4. The left leaders
strongly disagree that equality has gone too far, the right leaders rather
strongly take the opposite position, although their mean response is not as
far to the conservative end of the scale. None of the conservative groups
is as far to the right as the Social Democrats and blue-collar unionists are
to the left on Figure 7.1. This contrasts with the questions about radical
redistribution where the conservatives are closer to their end of the scale
than are the left groups to theirs.

One does not, however, get a full picture by looking only at the groups
at the ends of the spectrum. Responses on the fairness of capitalism and
on radical redistribution among political groups other than the Social

Democrat/blue-collar union leaders and Conservative/business/farm leaders show that the left groups are almost alone in their belief in the unfairness of capitalism and in their support for radical redistribution. Liberal and Center party leaders as well as leaders of professional unions line up on these issues with the right groups. (White-collar union leaders are in the middle.)

This is not the case for the questions about whether equality has gone too far: here, these other groups, although split, tend to side with the Social Democrats and blue-collar unionists. On all three questions the white-collar union leaders, although somewhat to the right of the Social Democrats and blue-collar unionists, have a mean response that keeps them in the egalitarian camp. The professional union leaders are somewhat farther to the right, but, unlike on the issue of radical redistribution where they side with the conservative leaders, on these questions the professional union leaders are near the midpoint of the scale. The Liberal leaders show moderate opposition to the view that equality has gone too far. The Center leaders are generally slightly to the right of the Liberal leaders, although the two groups are very close.

Thus, a crucial feature of responses to the equality-gone-too-far questions is that, as of the time of the survey in 1978, there was no political majority for stopping social reforms or movement toward greater equality, provided the movement did not extend to such radical redistributionist measures as relatively equal pay for all people. The Conservatives and business leaders want an end to further social reforms, but leaders of two of the three nonsocialist parties, as well as nonparty groups in the middle such as white-collar and professional unionists, are ambivalent. What is similar about responses to the radical redistribution and the equality-gone-too-far questions is the polarization of Social Democrats/blue-collar unionists and Conservatives/business leaders. What is different is that on the latter questions the middle groups are split rather than siding with the conservative groups.

The issue of whether egalitarian policies and social reforms have gone too far was a new source of cleavage in Sweden in the late 1970s as compared with the previous decade. It is sometimes suggested, especially by Swedish Social Democrats, that the nonsocialists have tended to accept welfare-state measures only in retrospect, opposing them when they first are proposed and opposing new social reforms at any given time. This suggests one explanation for the opinion pattern seen here: the nonsocialists always support existing welfare-state measures but oppose further advances.

This is, however, an oversimplified view of the history of the Swedish welfare state. Two of these three questions were asked of Swedish members of Parliament in 1969. In addition, a basic welfare-state question about all but the old and handicapped getting along without social welfare benefits was asked in 1969 and replicated in our survey. Table 7.1 compares the 1969 results with our results for parliamentarians nearly a decade later.[4] The important point is the large shift in opinion on the equality-gone-too-far question between the two eras compared with the much smaller shift for the basic welfare-state question. Note how dramatic is the change for the Conservative members of Parliament on the former. In the 1969 survey all of the party leaders, including the Conservatives, disagreed on average with the statement that social benefits should be decreased, although the Conservatives just barely disagreed. Furthermore, in 1969 all three nonsocialist parties disagreed that equality had gone too far. The mean responses for the Liberal and Center members of Parliament on that question were as lopsided in support of social welfare as on the basic welfare-state all-but-the-old-and-handicapped question. By the late 1970s the conservative groups still supported the existing welfare state, as indicated by the latter question, but their positions on the welfare state's reaching its limits had changed. By 1978 they believed those limits had indeed been reached.

Two events in the 1970s, one specific to Sweden and one common to Western industrialized countries, may help explain these changes. In

Table 7.1.   Mean responses of Swedish parliamentarians on questions about egalitarian policies, 1969 and 1978. (The higher numbers are the more conservative answers.)

Question and group	1969	1978
Equality gone too far in Sweden		
Social Democrats	1.0	1.2
Liberals	1.4	2.3
Center	1.2	2.4
Conservatives	1.7	3.7
Decrease rather than increase benefits		
Social Democrats	1.2	1.3
Liberals	1.7	2.7
Center	2.1	3.3
Conservatives	2.8	4.0

Source: See note 4 to Chapter 7.

1976, as noted earlier, Sweden got its first nonsocialist government in almost forty-five years. With a Social Democratic government no longer in power, the deference to the proequality views of the Social Democrats that had built up over time in Sweden may have dissipated. People may have become less shy about expressing antiegalitarian views. In our Swedish survey we asked respondents whether they agreed with the statement that "in general, it has become easier to express unpopular opinions in Sweden since the change in government." Of our business sample, 51 percent agreed, as did 47 percent of the farm leaders, 36 percent of the professors, and—hardly surprisingly—67 percent of the leaders of the nonsocialist parties.[5]

In addition, Sweden fell into an economic crisis in 1976. The country had managed temporarily to avoid the effects of the OPEC oil price increases of 1973–74 by expansionary fiscal policies. This, however, entailed large wage increases that gradually undermined the competitiveness of Swedish export industries. Further, a number of important Swedish industries, such as steel, shipbuilding, and iron mining, were decimated by long-term shifts in comparative advantage in favor of newly industrializing countries. Beginning in late 1976 and extending into the time of our survey in 1978, bankruptcies of major firms and demands for emergency aid, particularly in shipbuilding and steel, became common.

As has been the case throughout the Western world, the Swedish economic difficulties of the 1970s, unlike those of the 1930s, strengthened the hand of conservative rather than radical forces. The Depression of the 1930s was interpreted as the result of a failure of the free market. Conservatives argued that the economic setbacks of the 1970s, by contrast, did not result from a failure of the market but from a failure of government policies, most particularly equality-oriented policies that reduced incentives to work and invest. This explanation did not convince everyone, certainly not in Sweden, but it was plausible enough to put the advocates of continued government efforts to reduce inequality on the defensive. The changes in responses we see in the data from 1969 to 1978 presaged a blossoming debate in Swedish society, and in Western societies in general, that still continues.[6]

Has Income Equality Gone Too Far?

We can obtain a more fine-grained look at the issue of whether equality has gone too far by examining the data on attitudes toward income equality. As we saw in the previous chapter, Swedish respondents favor an income distribution that is much more egalitarian than that considered fair by leaders in the other two nations. The ranges of opinion about what is fair do not even overlap—the most conservative Swedish group is more egalitarian than the most radical group elsewhere. But some Swedish leaders are uneasy about the extent of equality in Sweden. The egalitarian trend, they appear to believe, has gone too far.

We can get a better picture of what our Swedish respondents think about income distribution and the government's role in relation to it if we take into account their views on income before government intervention through taxes and transfers. In Sweden, as we have noted, respondents were asked about perceived income both before and after taxes and social transfers and about a fair disposable income after taxes and transfers. The three measures allow us to see how respondents perceive the impact of the government on earnings. Table 7.2 presents data for the three occupations we have tracked most closely: top executives, dishwashers, and automobile workers. Column 1 under each occupation shows the ratios of respondents' views of what the income from the occupation ought to be and what the income is *before* government intervention. All respondents believe that before taxes and social transfers executives earn more than they ought to earn. The ratios range from about 0.3—for blue-collar union leaders and Social Democrats (indicating that they believe that executives should earn about 30 percent of what they get before taxes)—to about 0.5—for leaders of the Conservative party. No group takes the position that the income received by an executive would be fair only if the government did not intervene.

Compare columns 1 and 2. The latter shows the ratios of respondents' views of what an executive ought to earn and the perceived income *after* government intervention. Note that some groups believe that the tax and transfer system overcorrects executive income. Business leaders think that executives are overpaid before taxes and transfers, but after taxes and transfers the ratio between what is fair and what executives are perceived to earn is larger than 1.0, indicating that they believe that business executives ought to end up with more than they in fact do. Similar ratios above 1.0 are found for such leadership groups as farm leaders and leaders of the Conservative party. Leaders of the blue-collar unions and Social Democrats, however, believe that business executives earn more than they should before taxes and transfers and that, although the tax and transfer system reduces that overearning, it does not reduce it far enough; they have ratios below 1.0 for the after-tax measure, indicating a belief that executives still earn more after taxes than they ought to. Other groups, all

Table 7.2. Attitudes toward income in Sweden before and after government intervention (ratios)

	Executive			Dishwasher			Auto Worker		
	Ought/ is before	Ought/ is after	Is after/ is before	Ought/ is before	Ought/ is after	Is after/ is before	Ought/ is before	Ought/ is after	Is after/ is before
National business	0.4	1.5	0.3	0.9	1.1	0.7	0.7	1.0	0.7
Local business	0.4	1.5	0.3	0.8	1.1	0.7	0.7	1.1	0.7
Farm	0.4	1.3	0.3	0.9	1.2	0.7	0.7	1.1	0.7
Blue-collar union	0.3	0.7	0.4	1.0	1.4	0.7	0.8	1.2	0.6
White-collar union	0.3	0.9	0.3	0.9	1.3	0.7	0.7	1.1	0.6
Professional union	0.4	1.3	0.3	0.9	1.1	0.8	0.7	1.1	0.7
Media	0.3	0.8	0.4	1.0	1.4	0.7	0.8	1.2	0.6
Professors	0.4	1.1	0.3	0.9	1.2	0.8	0.7	1.1	0.7
Women	0.4	1.1	0.3	0.9	1.2	0.8	0.7	1.1	0.6
Social Democrats	0.3	0.7	0.4	1.1	1.5	0.7	0.8	1.2	0.7
Center	0.3	1.0	0.3	0.9	1.2	0.7	0.7	1.1	0.6
Liberals	0.3	1.1	0.3	0.9	1.2	0.7	0.7	1.1	0.6
Conservatives	0.5	1.5	0.3	0.8	1.1	0.7	0.7	1.1	0.6

of whom believe that executives earn more than they should before taxes, have ought/is ratios after taxes that are closer to 1.0, indicating that the tax and transfer system brings executive incomes down to approximately where they belong. The data in those two columns reflect the pattern that we have seen thus far: some groups believe that the system has gone too far in correcting income inequality, some that it has not gone far enough, and some that an appropriate position has been reached.

The third column, which relates perceived income before and after taxes, illustrates the perceptions that our various leadership groups have of the extent of the tax bite. The range of estimates across groups is not great; most groups estimate that taxes and transfers reduce executive income to about a third of its pre–government-intervention level. But there is some difference between the left groups, such as blue-collar union leaders and Social Democrats, and the more conservative groups in their estimate of the size of that bite. Blue-collar union leaders, for instance, have a ratio of 0.4, whereas business leaders have a ratio of 0.3; the latter perceive taxes to take a more substantial chunk of executive income.

It is interesting to see how Swedish leaders perceive the impact of governmental intervention through taxes and social transfers on the income of the occupation at the bottom of the income hierarchy. Most groups believe that dishwashers receive a little more than they ought to before taxes and social transfers; blue-collar union leaders and the Social Democrats believe that they receive exactly what they ought to earn. After taxes and transfers most groups believe that dishwashers have smaller earnings than they ought to have. The ratios vary somewhat from the more conservative groups, who feel that their earnings are only slightly below what they should be, to the left groups, who feel that the earnings of dishwashers are substantially lower than they ought to be. What is interesting in these comparisons is the general belief that the tax and transfer system lowers the income of an unskilled worker rather than raising it. This general perception is seen in the third column under the dishwasher category. All groups perceive the tax and transfer system to have a somewhat negative effect on the earnings of the dishwasher: they are less well off after government intervention than before. It may be that our respondents focused more heavily on the impact of taxes than on the impact of social transfers. It is also possible that, given the range of collective consumption goods provided by the government, few believe that anyone's posttax income is, or should be, higher after taxes and transfers than before.

The data on the auto worker confirm what the other data have already told us. Before taxes and transfers auto workers are seen by all groups to earn somewhat more than they ought to. The range of variation is not very great, although the group differences are in the expected direction. After government intervention auto workers end up with somewhat less than they ought to have. And we can see in the last column the general perception across all groups that auto workers are somewhat worse off after government intervention than before.

These data help round out our understanding of attitudes toward equality in Sweden. They show a perception that the income of various occupations before taxes and transfers is higher than it ought to be. This position is shared by all groups with reference to top executives and skilled auto workers and held by many groups even with regard to very unskilled workers. They perceive government intervention as correcting this by lowering the earnings of all of these three occupations. But in most cases they see government intervention as overcorrecting. There is general agreement on this issue with regard to lower-paid occupations such as dishwashers and auto workers, and, more strikingly, many groups believe that the system also overcorrects the income of the top income group. In the latter case only a few of the leadership groups—leaders of blue-collar unions, the Social Democratic party, and to a small extent white-collar unions—believe that government-induced income redistribution is insufficient.

The situation is even clearer if we consider the views of leaders on the income gap between a top and bottom earner. Figure 7.2 contains a number of panels showing the perceptions of various sets of leaders of the income gap before and after government intervention as well as their views of what a fair gap would be. Business and farm leaders agree that government intervention reduces the income gap between executives and dishwashers; they perceive a high executive/dishwasher ratio before government intervention and a substantially smaller one after. Business leaders, however, believe that the reduction in income differentiation has gone too far; they think that the income gap ought to be bigger—not as big as it was before government intervention, but bigger nevertheless. Farm leaders would also like to see the gap widened, although their desired ratio differs only slightly from what they perceive the case to be after taxes and transfers. They believe that equalization has gone too far but only by a small amount.

The data on labor leaders neatly illustrate the differences among the three types of union leaders on redistribution. The views of blue-collar union leaders are in sharp contrast to those of business. Blue-collar union leaders agree with business that the system of taxes and transfers substan-

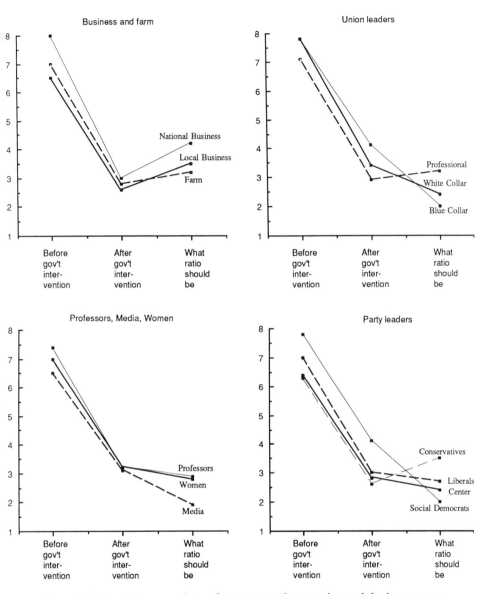

Figure 7.2. Swedish perceptions of government intervention and the income gap

tially reduces the gap between the two occupations, but the labor leaders believe that the reduction has not gone far enough. They see government intervention as narrowing the gap by half; they would narrow it again by somewhat more than half. White-collar union leaders take a similar position, although they want a more moderate additional reduction of the income gap. The leaders of the professional unions, however, agree with business and farm leaders that the income gap has been narrowed too much.

The two intermediate groups—professors and leaders of women's groups—take moderate positions. They see the gap as reduced by government intervention and believe that it ought to be reduced somewhat more but not very much. They see the effects of government intervention to be about right. Leaders of the media closely resemble leaders of the blue-collar unions, believing that government redistribution has not gone far enough.

In the panel containing the views of the leaders of the political parties we see encapsulated the three positions we have discovered: that government intervention produces too much, not enough, or just about the right amount of redistribution. Social Democratic leaders believe that things have not gone far enough; Conservative leaders that they have gone too far; and the two middle-of-the-road parties think that things are about as they should be. The data show the reactions to the Swedish experiment in income equalization across the spectrum of political views in that country. None of the party groups would return the income gap to its size before government intervention; and certainly none would think a gap as wide as that in the United States or Japan is acceptable. But there is an important difference in the degree of income redistribution that they consider appropriate.

8

Political Equality

Equality, in almost all its forms and along most of its dimensions, has become more and more a political issue. The modern state is responsible for the economic and social welfare of the individual in continually increasing ways. The distinction among our three nations in the extent of income equality can be understood only in the light of the differences among the nations in public policy. Nor is governmental involvement in equality limited to the economic sphere; in almost all its other aspects, equality is affected by public policy. To understand economic inequality as well as other forms of inequality, one also has to understand political inequality.

Political inequality refers to differences across individuals and groups in their influence over political decisions. Political inequality and inequality in other domains are closely intertwined. Economic resources can be converted into political influence despite attempts, which vary in their vigor and effectiveness from nation to nation, to limit such conversion. The one-person, one-vote policy aims at equality in political influence by creating a ceiling on the amount of political voice an individual can have. But many ways of exercising political influence circumvent that limitation; and most of those other means depend on the political use of economic resources. Conversely, political influence can be converted into economic resources: those with greater political influence can use it to foster policies that protect and enhance their economic position. The history of democratic elections and democratic political movements is in large part a history of attempts by disadvantaged groups to break out of the cycle whereby political and economic advantage reinforce each other.

Political equality is important not only because it affects and is affected by economic inequality; it is important in its own right—it is a goal in itself, not merely a means to an end. In this chapter we look more closely at the equality of political influence. The literature on economic equality is vast and constantly growing; it is rich with data and concerned with complex issues of measurement. There is a large comparable literature on political equality, which deals with citizen and group participation in democratic government and with issues such as what groups and citizens have access to political rights; who uses the rights; how effectively; and what classes, groups, or strata are excluded. All these traditional questions about the working of democracy relate to political equality. But the literature on political equality is not rich with data and is almost bereft of discussion of measurement. The reason, of course, is the problem that has always plagued the systematic study of politics: the absence of a clear metric of political influence.

The absence of such a metric creates both methodological and substantive problems. Methodologically it forces us to use surrogate measures that are indirect. Substantively, the absence of clear measurement means that the empirical question—who has more influence than who?—is unanswerable. The result is that political debates often turn on what *is* the case as much as on what *ought to be* the case, on the question of *who* governs? not who *should* govern? To complicate matters further, one's perception of what *is* the case is often colored by what one thinks the case ought to be. We shall return to this theme in the next chapter.

In our discussion of income we focused on a comparison of perceptions and values: what is the current income hierarchy and what would be a fair hierarchy. In the case of income we were also able to compare respondent estimates of income distribution with objective data. With political influence we focus on a comparison of perceptions and values as well; we lack, however, a body of objective data. Our analysis, then, is not of the "reality" of political influence in the three nations but of the perceptions of that influence structure by the various groups of leaders and their beliefs about what it ought to be.

The perceptions of our respondents are important in themselves, however. These leaders are among the main political actors in each society. Their beliefs about the real and ideal in relation to political stratification have real consequences. The disparity between a group's perceptions of the existence of political inequality and its values about how political influence ought to be distributed fuels desires for change in the influence hierarchy. As we shall see, the conflict that grows out of these differences is as much about perceptions (who is influential?) as it is about values (who ought to be influential?).

The perceptions and values of our leaders are also likely to be closely connected to the reality of influence. These leaders are sophisticated observers of the political process in their countries. Asking an informed participant is still, in political analysis, a highly credible technique of observation, and the views of these leaders on the power structure should give a good deal of insight into the actual nature of that power distribution. Because they are actors in the political process engaged in a contest over political position, however, their perceptions may be distorted by their partisan positions—especially in light of the ambiguity inherent in perceptions of influence. We shall therefore single out the perceptions of those leadership groups that are less partisan participants in the political struggle: intellectuals and leaders from the media. They are by no means fully objective but they may provide a somewhat more detached look.

Measuring Influence Beliefs

One of the classic methods for studying political influence is the reputational approach: one asks knowledgeable observers to rate individuals or groups in terms of their influence over political life in general or over some decisional area. The argument against the method is that it measures just what it says it measures: reputation for influence, but not necessarily influence itself. We begin our consideration of attitudes on equality of influence by considering reputations—that is, elite perceptions of the influence hierarchy. This approach suits our needs because we are interested in reputation: whom the various leaders perceive to be influential. A comparison of their perceptions and their values should provide insights into the nature of equality in the political sphere.

Our measurements are analogous to those dealing with income. As with income inequality, we are interested in the "is" and "ought" of influence. We asked our respondents about the relative influence of various actors in the political process. As with the measurement of perceived and desired income, we had to decide what was an appropriate measure of influence and whose influence we were to compare. And as with our income measures, our approach oversimplifies one of the most complex of concepts in social analysis. Yet it provides, we believe, quite revealing comparative data.

Our respondents were asked to compare a series of groups in terms of their relative influence over political life in their countries by placing each group on a scale ranging from "very influential" at the top to "very little influence" at the bottom. The groups to be compared were presented to the respondents at the same time. The comparative nature of the ratings provides a basis for measuring influence not against some absolute standard but as a relative matter. The relative nature of these evaluations needs underscoring. Given the nature of our scale, we cannot locate groups in some absolute influence position. We do not know in any precise way how much more influence one group is perceived to have than another, but we do know how they are ranked. It is clear that our respondents were able to make distinctions among the object groups; the task was not difficult and few respondents refused to make such ratings.

When we compared the "is" and "ought" of income, individuals with particular occupations seemed appropriate units. For comparisons of influence it seemed more appropriate to use collectivities as units. Income levels relate to individuals, political influence adheres to collectivities. In what follows and in the next chapter it is important to keep in mind the collective nature of the units involved because it affects our results. As we shall see, many respondent groups consider labor unions to be as influential as or more influential than big business. These respondents would certainly have ranked the average top executive as more influential than the average factory worker (although it is not clear that they would have put the executive above an average union leader). We shall return to this issue in the next chapter. We raise it here simply so that the reader will be forewarned of the difference in the units used for economic and political influence.

We asked our respondents to rate the actual and desired influence of most of the groups we had sampled as well as some additional target groups. The set of target groups about which we asked differs somewhat from nation to nation, but there is a good deal of similarity. We asked questions about the main economic actors in our respondent sample: business, labor, and farmers. We also asked about the main intermediary groups: parties and the media. Lastly, we asked about challenging groups in each nation; these include the various groups in our respondent sample—feminist groups, black groups, the Buraku Liberation League—as well as consumer groups in Japan and the United States and environmentalists in Sweden. In Japan bureaucrats formed one of the target groups as they did one of the respondent groups. Because the collectivities about which we asked include many of the groups that formed our elite sample, we can see how sets of leaders rated the influence of their own group in comparison with that of others.

The measurements, to repeat, are not of the actual influence of these groups but of their perceived influence. The metric we use cannot tell us where the respondents put the target groups in absolute terms because there is no absolute interpretation of a ranking on the scales we use. But because the ratings are comparative, we do know if a respondent perceives a target group to have more or less influence than another and how the respondent would rank them in his or her ideal world of political influence. These ordinal ratings are crucial to and sufficient for our argument.

Perceptions of Influence

Figure 8.1 shows the rankings the various respondent groups gave to the target groups about which they were asked. It reports a large amount of data because numerous respondent groups were asked to rate numerous target groups in each country. Out of this variety, however, some quite striking cross-national similarities appear. One such uniformity is the high influence rating given the media in each country. Each respondent group in each of the three countries rates the media in the top three of the influence groups. In Japan, the media are ranked at the top by every group except the media elites themselves, and in the United States, the media are always at the top or very close to it. Some Swedish groups place the media a bit lower but always in the top three.

That the media are viewed in the same way in three nations so diverse is an arresting finding. The debate about who governs has generated an enormous political science literature, but almost all of this literature, whether of the pluralist or "power elite" school, centers on the political influence of economic classes or of interest groups organized along (mostly) economic lines. Virtually none of this vast literature highlights the influence of the media—a group that makes no campaign contributions, controls no factors of production, and has few votes—much less suggests that the media might be the most influential elite group in society. The closest anything in the literature comes to the suggestion of media power is the suggestion of a "new class" of professionals not tied to traditional interest groups.[1] Yet our respondents agree in believing that the media are very influential. That influence must come from the important assets the media have available: the control of information, the ability to appeal to people based on general ideas of what is right and wrong, and the related ability to put public officials in a positive or shameful light.

Along with the media, business is usually at or close to the top of the influence hierarchy. In Japan, bureaucrats and political parties are sometimes ranked higher, but in such cases business follows just behind. Labor ranks high in Sweden and the United States but is closer to the middle of the rankings in Japan. The high ranking of business along with the media is hardly surprising; the data confirm what we would have expected. But they are a useful confirmation of the uniformities that exist across quite

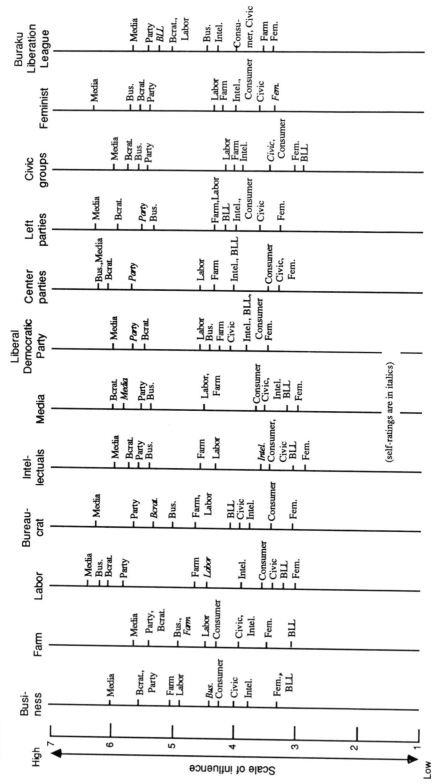

Figure 8.1A. Perceptions of influence: mean ratings of target groups by respondent groups in Japan

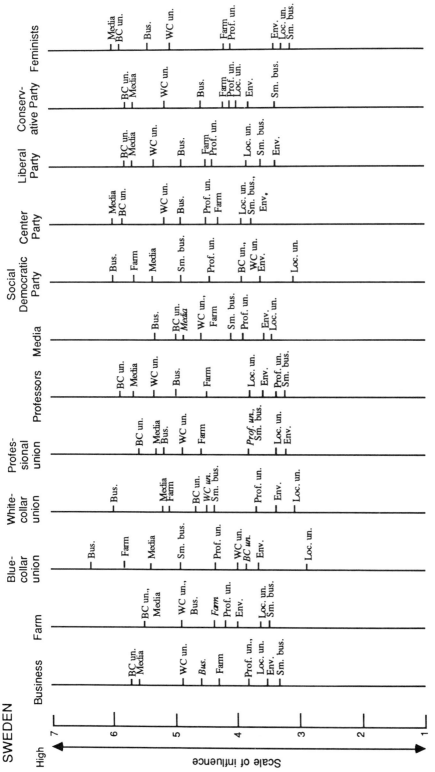

Figure 8.1B. Perceptions of influence: mean ratings of target groups by respondent groups in Sweden

UNITED STATES

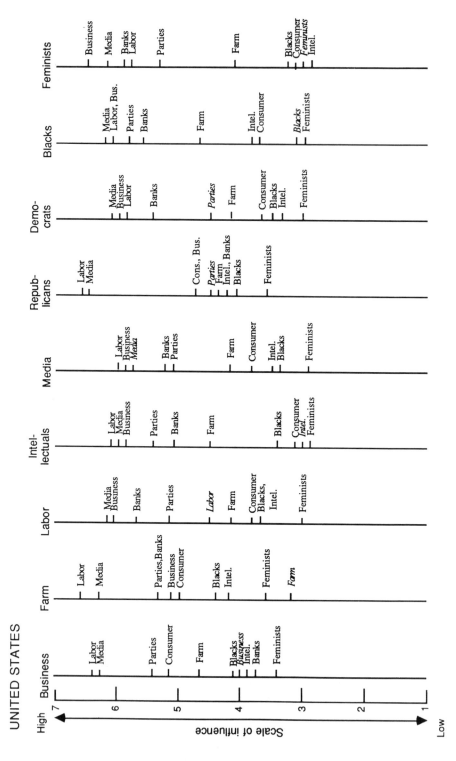

Figure 8.1C. Perceptions of influence: mean ratings of target groups in the United States

different nations. In addition, the existence of such similarities helps anchor our analysis when we begin to find differences across the nations.

The nations are similar in another way. In each case the challenging groups are generally rated low in influence. The set of "new" groups varies but they generally fall at or near the bottom of the influence hierarchy. In the United States feminist groups are almost universally considered to be the least influential of those about which we asked, and black and consumer groups are fairly low in influence as well. A similar situation exists in Japan: feminist groups, the Buraku Liberation League, consumer groups, and civic groups all cluster near the bottom of the hierarchy. And in Sweden environmentalists occupy a similarly low position. In all three nations, thus, the political struggle is perceived in broadly similar terms: between business and labor groups with a good deal of influence and challenging groups with considerably less.

Within this broad outline there are, however, many variations. The individual patterns in each nation are complex, as one would expect given the number of groups making a large number of ratings. Some interesting differences and special patterns can be noted. One is that, though the media rank high all over, the rank is higher in Japan and the United States compared with Sweden. Each respondent group in Japan, except the media people themselves, rate the media at the top of the list, and in the United States the media are always at or near the top. Swedish groups rate the media lower. Another interesting difference is the contrasting position of organized labor in Japan in relation to the other two countries. In both Sweden and the United States, big labor (the LO in Sweden and labor unions more generally in the United States) are close to or at the top of the influence hierarchy, close to business and well above the farm sector. This is especially striking in Sweden because our survey took place shortly after the overthrow of the long-dominant Socialist government. (As we shall see below, before the change in government the position of the LO was even more unquestioned.) In Japan, labor is quite low on the influence hierarchy, well below business and slightly above or below the farm sector depending on the respondent group.

A full appreciation of the perceptions of influence in each nation requires a closer, more contextually based analysis than is possible in this comparative work.[2] A few comments may be useful here, however, on each of the national patterns revealed in Figure 8.1. They cannot answer the question of who rules Japan (or Sweden or the United States), but they can tell us something of what leading actors in the political process perceive to be the case.

In Japan, the media reign supreme. Every group places them at the top, often with a substantial gap in rating between them and the next most influential group. The only exception is the group of media representatives themselves, but even they rank the media very close to the top. The media are placed at or near the top in influence by leaders in all three nations, but the Japanese place them in a more unambiguously top position than elsewhere. What is particularly interesting in Japan is that the media are generally seen as antiestablishment and opposed to the government in power. Their high ranking must, therefore, be seen in juxtaposition to the establishment, which ranks just below them.

The media may be perceived to be the most influential single institution, but the weight of their influence probably does not match the combined weight of the three groups that are ranked closely behind them. All groups—across the entire political spectrum—place the bureaucracy, political parties (the reference appears to be to the LDP), and business as the next set of influential institutions.[3] This is consistent with the dominant model of the power structure in Japan, which has been one of a ruling triumvirate with the alliance of the LDP, the bureaucracy, and big business having the overwhelming influence over the policy-making process. According to this view, the three institutions support each other: the LDP needs bureaucratic expertise in formulating and implementing policies; it also needs the contribution of business to finance expensive election campaigns and party management. Business and the bureaucracy, in turn, strongly support the LDP regime because the former wishes to maintain the free enterprise system and the latter wants the LDP in power so that the policies it initiates will be ratified in the Diet.[4]

It is interesting, further, to note the lack of consensus on the relative positions of these three groups, despite the consensus that they are all near the top of the hierarchy. There is definite agreement about who makes up the dominant coalition, less clarity as to their relative position within it. Most groups put the bureaucrats above parties and business, but several place parties above bureaucrats, especially noteworthy among these being the bureaucrats themselves and the LDP leaders. The former may be manifesting a form of influence denial (a subject to which we shall return), but the latter clearly are not. Similarly some disagreement exists about the relative position of business, although there is relative consensus that business is not, in contrast to some interpretations of Japanese politics, the dominant force.[5] Most put business below bureaucrats and parties, but labor, some of the challenging groups, and the leaders of the center parties put it above the parties. This ranking may reflect relatively recent changes in the hierarchy of political dominance in Japan, where the previous controlling position held by the bureaucracy has been challenged by the increased power of politicians who more frequently have their way in conflict with the bureaucracy. In turn, politicians are more influenced by interest groups, of which business is the prime example, than was previously the case. This shift would make the relative positions of the three groups somewhat uncertain.[6]

There is an interesting difference between the established and opposition groups in their relative ranking of the bureaucracy and parties. The established groups—the LDP, bureaucrats themselves, business and farm leaders—rate the bureaucrats on a par with or a little below the parties. Opposition groups tend to put the bureaucrats above political parties in influence. This suggests that outsiders see a more tightly controlled bureaucratic state whereas insiders see the bureaucracy as subordinate to the party system. Whether the latter take this view because of their clearer perception of reality or because it is more appropriate for the bureaucracy to take the lesser position we cannot tell.

As noted above, one striking difference between Japan and the other two nations is the relatively low rating of labor. In Sweden and the United States, labor is almost universally placed in the top three groups and often at the very top. The only exceptions are the ratings by labor of its own influence and the ratings of its closest allies. In Japan, by contrast, labor is found toward the middle of the influence scale in many cases. In the other two nations labor is consistently rated above the farm sector in influence, but in Japan it is seen as similar to or sometimes below. This ranking seems to be consistent with the relatively weak position of organized labor in Japan. The proportion of the work force unionized is relatively low compared with a nation such as Sweden. The level of unionization is commensurate with the low level in the United States, but the Japanese labor unions have not been able to develop the close relations with a successful political party that labor in both Sweden and the United States have succeeded in doing. Labor represents a larger sector of the economy than does the farm sector, which represents only 10 percent of the work force, but the closer ties of the farm sector to the ruling party compensate for that. Labor stands in opposition to the ruling LDP party and the triumvirate of business, the LDP, and the bureaucracy, but the farm sector trades votes with the ruling party for patronage and policies. And business, although it might otherwise oppose government subsidization of agriculture, accepts such policies because it realizes the importance of maintaining a winning electoral coalition. The long-term domination by the LDP, allied with business and the farm sector but not with labor, has left unions generally outside of the decisional structures that make economic policy in Japan. Furthermore, Japanese unions have been predominantly enterprise unions, a factor that has severely limited the influence of organized labor on the larger national economic and political scene.[7] The data also underscore the central role of the LDP-bureaucracy-business grouping that is seen to be the dominant governing coalition. Farm groups are generally perceived to be more influential than labor—despite the greater size and activity of the latter—perhaps because of their greater closeness to this dominant coalition.

Challenging groups are at a low level in the hierarchy in the Japanese influence ratings. The data suggest that leaders in Japan see the media as the leading opposition force. Their control over channels of information and opinion balances the power of the main established influential sectors more than does the influence of antiestablishment challenging groups. The challenging groups share the view as to their lower influence except for the Buraku Liberation League leaders who rate their influence quite high, higher than other groups rate them. This may be a misperception on their part or alternatively it may, in fact, be due to local successes; the BLL may be more effective than others fully realize. They have had a relatively high level of influence with the bureaucracy and a good deal of success with the Socialist party. Furthermore, the "harmonization" (*dōwa*) campaign led by local governments has resulted in many concessions. This success on the local level may be more salient to the BLL leaders than to many others. This is consistent with the fact that the bureaucrats and opposition party leaders rate their influence highly. (See Table 8.2 below for some data supporting this interpretation.)

In Sweden, there is less consensus on the relative influence of groups than there is in Japan. Although the media are generally rated as quite influential, their influence is sometimes rated below that of the blue-collar union, business, and farm organizations. Furthermore, there is less agreement on the relative positions of labor and business, unlike the consensus in Japan that the latter is more influential than the former. One source of this uncertainty may be the change in the Swedish government that took place about two years before our survey, a change in which the Social Democratic rule of more than four decades was overturned in favor of a conservative coalition. This change may have reduced the clarity of the influence hierarchy in Sweden. As we shall see below, the impact of the change in government was differently interpreted by different groups in Sweden.[8]

The fact that the media in Sweden are accorded a high position but not quite as high as they are given in Japan and in the United States probably reflects the somewhat different role that the media play in Sweden. Daily newspapers are usually closely attached to one or another political party, which reduces somewhat their independent influence. Political reporting on television is generally considered to be oriented to the left (a perception consistent with what we found in the attitudes of the TV and radio personnel in our study), and this reduces its influence.

An interesting feature of these data should be noted. First, there is a pattern to the lack of consensus on the relative power of labor and business. Labor and its political allies rate their own position as relatively weak and that of business (and farm groups) as strong. Business and its political allies do the opposite: they believe themselves weak and labor strong. This pattern continues with regard to other groups less closely aligned with the labor-business cleavage—conservative groups generally see the media as more powerful than left groups do—and even with the nonestablished organizations: left groups see environmentalists and local unions as relatively weaker and small business groups as relatively stronger than do conservative groups. Groups tend to downplay their own power and that of their allies.

In the United States, labor, business, and the media all vie for top place in influence. In general, challenging groups are seen as much less influential, although we see some striking differences between established and challenging groups in their views of their relative influence. Note the relative positions of business and consumer groups: most groups see business as much more influential than consumer groups, but business perceives the opposite to be the case, and Republican and farm leaders see business and consumers as about equal in influence. The latter groups see consumers as marginally more influential than business. Business, in contrast, sees consumers as having quite a substantial advantage over it. We shall return to this as a general phenomenon shortly; it is mentioned here as an illustration of the sense of beleaguerment that business apparently has in the face of new challenging groups. To take an even more striking example, business leaders consider black organizations to be more powerful than business. No other group shares that view.

The material in Figure 8.1 represents the perceptions of the various elite groups of the influence situation in their countries. When we considered income differentials, we turned from data about perceptions to data about actual income from census records and the like, which allowed us to compare the perceptions of elite groups with reality. We cannot do this in connection with influence, there being no such objective data. The elite perceptions may contain the misperceptions and distortions introduced by the varying vantage points of the elite groups. How can we distinguish a correct perception from a misperception without an anchor in objective influence measures? In the absence of external, objective data, we cannot; but by comparing the perceptions of particular groups one may be able to locate the bases for systematic distortion of the influence situation—distortions that are, as we shall see in the next chapter, an important part of the conflict over influence.

The data we need are all in Figure 8.1 because we have there the varying views that the elite groups have of the same sets of actors—the way in which business, labor, and other groups view the influence of business, the comparison among groups in the way they perceive their own influence, the perceptions that others have of them, and so forth. We begin with a simple influence-denial hypothesis: in the absence of objective measures of influence, groups will tend to underrate their own influence and that of their friends while inflating the influence of those opposed to them. Such a distortion, we believe, is psychologically sound in that individuals are less likely to notice instances in which their own views are accepted than instances where their views are thwarted. Such distortions may be reinforced by the fact that they can also be politically useful: they become the basis of claims for equalization of political influence which, given one's perception of one's own weakness, would be beneficial to oneself.

Let us begin with the two main contenders for political influence—business and labor. They are generally seen as quite influential. Figure 8.2 shows their mutual perceptions. In each country we find the same pattern: business leaders believe that labor is more influential than business; labor leaders believe that business is more influential than labor. Each believes that it enters the political contest at a disadvantage to the other. We cannot tell whose lens is more distorted, but it is clear that reality is seen in a systematically distorted way by one or probably both actors.

The systematic distortion of the degree of influence of one's political adversary extends beyond the perceptions of these antagonists. It is also found in the perceptions that other actors have of business and labor. We compared the views of the leaders of several political parties in each country on this subject. We might expect the political parties to share the perspective of their allies—to see opponents as more powerful, allies as weaker. There is, however, one additional element here. We assume that groups are more aware of the influence of others than of their own. The

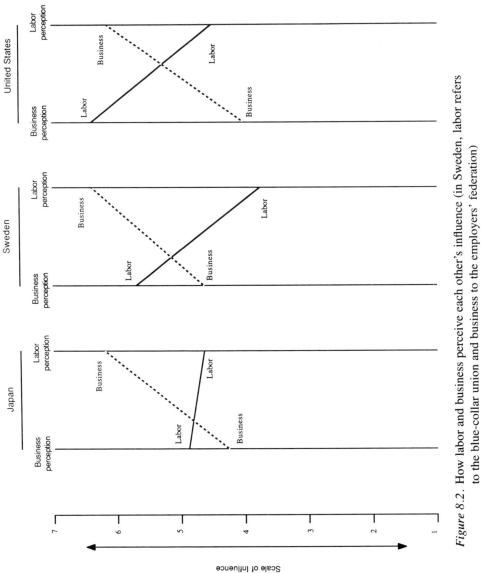

Figure 8.2. How labor and business perceive each other's influence (in Sweden, labor refers to the blue-collar union and business to the employers' federation)

implication of this for the perceptions that groups have of the influence of their allies is unclear. Parties of the left closely allied with labor are likely to have a heightened sensitivity to the power of business, just as labor has. But these parties may also be sensitive to the power of labor in a way that labor itself is not, and for the same reason that labor and left parties are aware of business power. Labor power is a friendly force for left parties vis-à-vis business. Within the coalition of the left, however, labor power may be a challenge to the left parties and this will heighten their awareness of it. The same may be said for business and conservative parties.

Figure 8.3 provides evidence for such a pattern of perception. Party leaders see those on the other end of the political spectrum as more influential than those allied with them. The left parties see business as more influential than do the more conservative parties; the conservative parties see labor as more influential than do the left parties. However, party leaders do not underrate the influence of their powerful labor and business allies to the extent that those allies underrate themselves. A comparison of Figures 8.2 and 8.3 shows that in each case party leaders perceive their allies as more influential than the allies see themselves. For example, the Swedish blue-collar union places itself at 2.9 on the influence scale, whereas Swedish Social Democrats place it at 4.0. Similarly, Republicans in the United States rate business about one unit higher on the influence scale than business places itself.

In addition, political parties recognize the influence of their most well-established allies. For example, the Democrats see labor as almost as powerful as business, and the LDP sees business as close to labor in power. In Sweden we find a similar pattern, although one has to look for it more carefully. It should be remembered that our survey was taken shortly after the Swedish Social Democrats lost, for the first time in more than a generation, their position as governing party. The leaders of that party did not see the main labor federation as particularly powerful after the Socialists' electoral defeat. When we asked retrospectively about the influence of the Swedish groups before the change in government, however, we found the same pattern as in the other two nations—the Social Democratic party leaders rated their labor allies very high before the change in government—indeed, well above business in influence.

The differential perceptions that labor and business (as well as their allies) have of their respective influence led us to consider whether a pattern of influence denial is found among all the contending groups. Does each group think that it is less influential than it is—or, at least, than others think? To answer this question, it would be useful to have an objec-

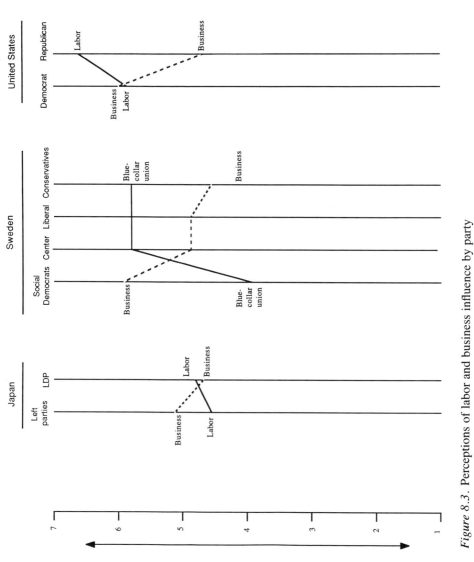

Figure 8.3. Perceptions of labor and business influence by party

tive measure of influence, but such, as we have pointed out, eludes us as it has eluded all political scientists; we have only perceptions. Because we must rely on perceptions, it would be desirable to focus on those of objective observers who are not involved in the conflict among contending groups and who do not see the influence situation from a partisan perspective. In our leadership samples we have some groups that might fill that role: intellectuals and media people. They were not chosen for their commitment to one side or the other in the conflict between labor and management or between challenging and established groups. They are also, we hope and believe, informed observers of the political scene. As individuals, however, they have their own positions to the left or right, and as a group they may tend in one direction or the other—thereby biasing their perceptions. Thus, for objective observers we turn to those members of our intellectual and media samples who describe themselves as politically moderate. If, as we assume, their perceptions are not systematically distorted in one direction or another, they can provide a good bench mark for determining whether all our contending groups underrate their own influence.

The data on this question as shown in Figure 8.4 indicate a tendency in the direction of influence denial but hardly a firm and uniform pattern. In the United States all groups but the feminist leaders see themselves as less powerful than the observers see them. The underrating of influence is only marginal for black leaders but quite pronounced for farm, labor, and business leaders. A similar underrating of influence takes place in Sweden. The blue-collar union and the business federation underrate their influence the most compared with the ratings assigned them by the media and intellectuals, but the other unions and the farm organization tend to underrate theirs as well. Only the professional union (SACO) overestimates its influence in comparison with the estimate of intellectuals. This, however, may be a somewhat redundant evaluation, because the intellectuals in Sweden were selected from the professoriate, who would themselves be members of SACO. Thus the low estimate of the organization's influence by the intellectuals may just be a low estimate by rank-and-file members of SACO—that is, a form of influence denial.

The Japanese data are somewhat at variance. Business leaders, as elsewhere, underrate their influence. Labor and farm leaders rate their influence roughly in accord with the ratings given by the observers. The two challenging groups—feminist leaders and leaders of the Buraku Liberation League—believe that they have more influence than the observers

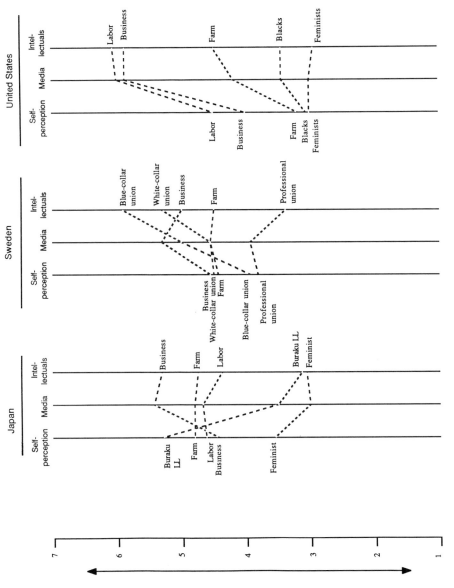

Figure 8.4. Self-perceptions of influence of contending groups compared with views of mediating groups

attribute to them; in the case of the Buraku Liberation League the gap is quite substantial.

The data are not completely unambiguous but a pattern does emerge. It is not the case that all groups underrate their own influence compared with the ratings of objective observers. Challenging groups—feminists in Japan and the United States and the leaders of the Buraku Liberation League—see themselves as more powerful than the observers do, and the other challenging group for which we have data—blacks in the United States—rates its influence in roughly similar terms as do the observers. In the cases where challengers rate their influence high, it is unclear whose perception is off the mark. Is it that feminists overrate themselves or that journalists and intellectuals underrate them? It may be a combination of the two. The Buraku Liberation League, it would seem, does go beyond what one might consider a reasonable estimate; the misperception probably comes in good part from that side. Organizations representing disadvantaged groups may have a good deal of influence on the local level, however, influence of which they are aware but that might not receive wider attention. We will return to this point in a moment.

The intriguing finding is the difference between challenging and established groups. It is among the best-established groups that we find the clearest evidence of influence denial. The most notable case is business: in each nation business leaders underrate their own influence by a substantial amount in relation to the observers' ratings. Labor does so as well, especially labor in the United States and the LO in Sweden. In Japan, where unions do not have as established a political position, labor's perception of itself is not out of line with the perceptions others have of it.

Our general assumption that groups underrate their own influence may need revision. The groups that see themselves as less influential than others see them seem to be those that have well-established channels of access to the government through party and/or bureaucratic channels. Business is well established in all three nations, labor in the United States and Sweden. Labor's position in Japan is more problematic, with the major labor federation linked to the opposition in a situation of long-term dominance by the Liberal Democrats and with many unions subordinate to particular firms. The data suggest that established political groups have a special advantage: they can exercise substantial political influence without even realizing that this is the case. Easy and routinized access to decision makers is not perceived to be influence but rather normal contacts among colleagues. Indeed, one can argue that not only may business exercise influence over the state without realizing it, but it may also exercise influence without doing anything. The data presented here are compatible with a structuralist view according to which business interests dominate in running the economy, not because business leaders directly impose their will on the government, but because the government itself takes the initative to provide for the needs of business in order to maintain the economy in general and to maintain the conditions for its own revenue.[9]

The special unrecognized and sometimes indirect influence of established groups suggests also that such groups will be especially sensitive to challenge. Their own position is secure, but that very security makes them less aware of their own influence and more uneasy about new groups that might challenge it. That this is the case can be seen if we compare the rating given by business of the influence of challenging groups with the rating the challenging groups give of business. On the assumption that the views of the moderates in the media and among intellectuals represent a realistic estimate of influence, we can ascertain how much business and the challenging groups overestimate or underestimate each other's influence. Table 8.1 reports those instances where we have obtained mutual perceptions of business and challenging groups, and the data support our expectations. Business overrates the influence of feminists and of minority groups more than the feminists and minority groups overrate business. In fact, in Japan the challenging groups do not overrate business at all. Contending groups may be sensitive to each other's influence, but those in positions of established influence appear more likely to overestimate the challenges to them than are challengers to overestimate the entrenchment of those established. No wonder the defense of privilege is usually more vigorous than the challenge to it.[10]

The data on mutual perceptions of influence might appear to suggest

Table 8.1. Overrating of the influence of opposition by established and challenging groups. Rating by opposition is compared to rating by observer. The first figure under Japan, for instance, indicates that Japanese business rates feminists 0.4 higher than do the "neutral" observers.

	Japan	U.S.
Business rating feminists	+0.4	+2.3
Feminists rating business	0.0	+0.8
Business rating minority group	+0.5	+1.1
Minority group rating business	−0.5	+0.4

that the members of our leadership sample live in fantasy worlds. Business is either deceiving itself or us when it reports a level of influence not much better and sometimes worse than that of some of the newest and least well-established challenging movements. But there is some evidence that this is related to how various leadership groups actually experience the government. In Chapter 3 we presented data on the amount of contact that various leadership groups had with government officials. We also asked the leaders how successful were such contacts and found that some of what we assumed to be the most well-connected groups report less success in their contacts with government officials than do some of the groups with less well-established connections. In Table 8.2 we show the percentage of business leaders and labor leaders, on the one hand, and leaders of challenging groups, on the other, who report that the contacts they have with government officials—their legislative representative or a local official—are generally successful. Established group leaders, despite what we might expect, are less likely than are leaders of challenging groups to report such success. We do not know the full circumstance of these con-

Table 8.2.   Percentage of those who have contacted government officials who report such contact as generally successful

Country and contacting group	Individuals contacted	
	Legislators	Local officials[a]
Japan		
Business	26	29
Labor	28	25
Feminists	41	32
Buraku	37	37
Sweden		
Business	27	42
Blue-collar union	27	36
White-collar union	37	41
Feminists	47	50
United States		
Business	27	38
Labor	23	21
Blacks	43	55
Feminists	35	34

a. In Sweden, these are bureaucrats.

tacts, in particular the specific goal that the contactors are seeking; but it is likely that feminist leaders, black leaders, and leaders of the Buraku Liberation League seek different types of response and, more important, have different expectations as to response. Their requests may be narrower, and success, we would expect, is more salient than failure to them in comparison with business leaders. Business and labor, on the other hand, may be less appreciative of success but very sensitive to failure. The data in Table 8.2 also help us understand the high evaluation by the Buraku Liberation League of their own influence position. In Chapter 3 we showed that the BLL leaders were more likely than any other group to report contact with a bureaucratic official and among the most likely groups to report contact with a local official. Table 8.2 shows that they are also substantially more likely than business or labor to report success when they make such contacts. Their evaluation of their position does not appear to be based on fantasy but on evidence of how their expectations are fulfilled from contact with the government.

Who Should Have Influence?

Thus far we have considered the perceptions by groups of the influence structure of their societies. Of equal importance is the issue of the influence structure that they would *like* to see. On this the situation is unequivocal: almost all groups would prefer to see themselves as the most influential social sector. This is seen on Figure 8.5, which parallels Figure 8.1 in format except that respondents are reporting whom they would like to see in an influential position rather than whom they actually see. The exceptions to the rule that groups prefer to see themselves at the top of the influence hierarchy are few, and these groups place themselves quite close to the top. Intellectuals in the United States and Japan would like to be near but not at the top of the influence hierarchy (we do not have parallel data on these groups in Sweden). Similar (quite moderate) self-denial is found among the media in Sweden and among the feminists and bureaucrats in Japan. (Japanese bureaucrats express the belief that they ought to be below the political parties in influence but above any other actors.) Our respondents certainly are not reticent about seeking influence: if we compare the perceptions about influence in Figure 8.1 with the desired influence hierarchy in Figure 8.5, we find, not surprisingly, that each group desires an increase in its own influence—in many cases by a fairly substantial amount.

There is one interesting exception: representatives of the media in each

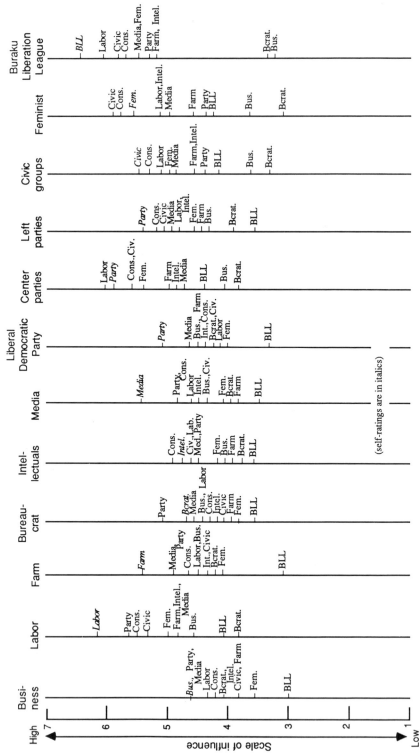

Figure 8.5A. Attitudes about influence: mean ratings of amount of influence groups *ought* to have in Japan

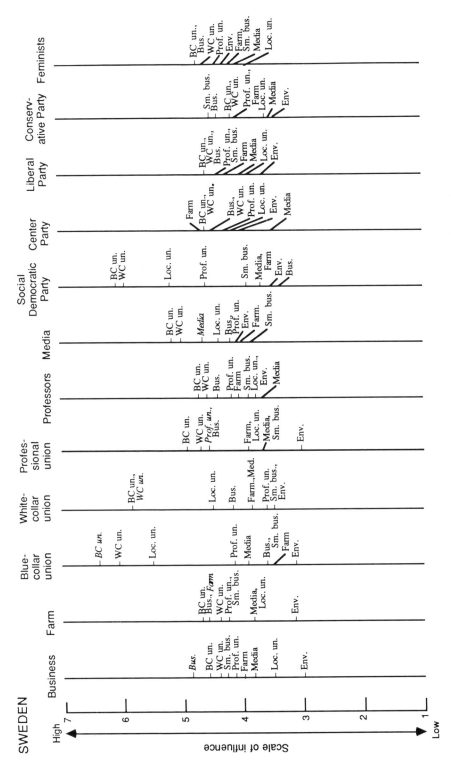

Figure 8.5B. Attitudes about influence: mean ratings of amount of influence groups *ought* to have in Sweden

UNITED STATES

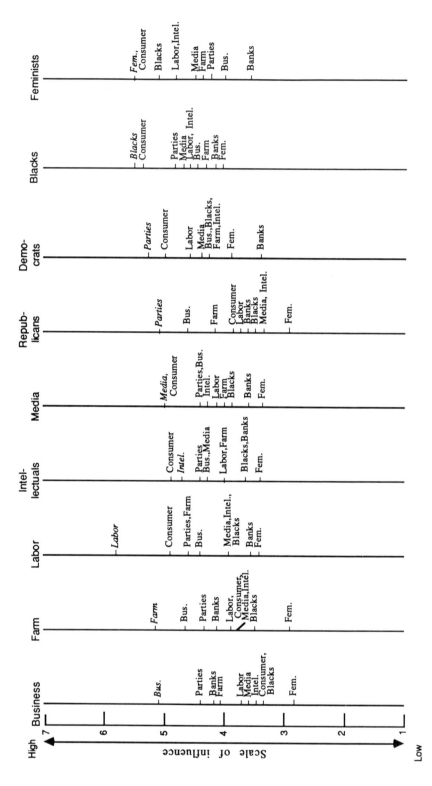

Figure 8.5C. Attitudes about influence: mean ratings of amount of influence groups *ought* to have in the United States

country would prefer to have *less* influence. The perception of media influence that they share with most other groups apparently does not rest easily with them. They perhaps feel more comfortable with a reportorial and interpretive role than with an influential one. Only two other self-denying groups can be found: both governing groups in Japan, the LDP leaders and the bureaucrats, believe that parties and the bureaucracy, respectively, are too influential. The reason for these positions is not certain. For the LDP leaders, it may be that they responded to the question on the influence of parties with the other parties in mind (the question asked about parties in general, not about particular parties). As for the bureaucrats, it is true that they would reduce their own influence, but they would also reduce the influence of the others they see as being influential. Indeed, as they perceive influence in Japan, they are less influential than the media and the parties (they must refer to the LDP), and they would prefer a situation in which they were more powerful than the media and less powerful only than the parties. The latter deference to the parties probably represents a nod to political control over the bureaucracy.

The data on influence provide a rich picture of the political world as the various groups in our sample perceive it to be and as they would wish it to be. We can examine these data from a variety of perspectives. We can consider how each of the groups in each nation views political influence: from the perspective of Japanese business leaders, for instance, who has influence in Japan and how would they like that to change? Or we can determine how the groups in our leadership sample view the particular groups about whom we asked: what do the leadership groups in the United States, for instance, think about the amount of influence that American business has and ought to have? We will take the latter perspective because it captures more effectively the influence structure in each of the nations. By looking at, say, the responses regarding the role played by business in the influence structure in each nation—the leaders' perceptions of its actual role and the role that groups believe it ought to play—we learn more about perceptions and values in relation to the political process than we would if we organized the data in terms of the views of each of the groups of respondents that we sampled.

In each of the three nations one of the main political polarities is that between business and labor. Although they have many interests in common—for instance, a strong international economic position for their nations—they are also often antagonists in the economic and political spheres. As we have seen, labor and business are arrayed at the opposite ends of the scales of attitudes toward economic equality, and they tend to be allied with different political parties. Figures 8.9 and 8.10 contain the views of the various leadership groups as to the influence that business and labor have and ought to have in the respective nations. (For ease of comparison, Figures 8.9–8.13 are gathered together in an appendix at the end of this chapter.) We use an arrow format. For each of the respondent groups in each nation we present an arrow that begins at the influence level the respondent group *perceives* the target group to have. The point of the arrow is at the influence level that the respondent group believes the target group *ought* to have. The attitudes that the various groups have toward business are quite clear and not too dissimilar across the nations. Almost all groups believe that business has too much influence. Indeed, it is only business itself that believes it has less influence than it ought to have. In Japan and Sweden, the leaders of business feel that it ought to have somewhat more influence than it does, but they do not want a dramatic increase. The business community in the United States stands out in the extent to which it believes itself to be weak and believes that it ought to be much stronger. In each of the three nations the survey of leaders was conducted under a government generally considered sympathetic to business—a Republican administration in the United States, the Liberal Democratic party in Japan, and a nonsocialist government in Sweden. The particular position of the American business leaders must be seen in this light. Despite the fact that Republican administrations are generally more sympathetic to business and despite the close proximity of business to Republican leaders on all of the scales of political attitudes, American business considers itself to be a somewhat deprived and oppressed segment of society. This view is shared by no other group. Of all the groups studied, Republican leaders are most supportive of American business, but even they believe that business has more influence than it should have.

Our data do not allow us to determine whether business leaders have as much influence as others perceive them to have and even less so to determine whether they have more influence than they ought to have. But the data do testify to the quite uniform belief held by most sophisticated leaders in these countries that the business community has more of a voice than it ought to have.

Labor is not viewed much more favorably, although the picture is more mixed. The influence of labor is considered to be too high by all the respondent groups in the United States, with the exception of labor itself. All groups prefer a substantially weaker labor movement; the desired reduction of labor influence is of a similar magnitude to the desired reduction of business influence. It is interesting to note that the Democratic leaders also believe that labor's influence is much too great, despite the fact that labor is in many ways the closest ally to the Democratic party. Although Republican leaders also want to reduce the influence of their closest ally, business, the magnitude of that desired reduction is much less than that which Democrats wish for labor. Clearly, organized labor is both ally and rival to the Democratic leadership.[11]

The relationship of the Democrats to labor in the United States contrasts with the relationship of Social Democratic leaders to labor in Sweden. In Sweden, as in the United States, most leadership groups would reduce the influence of labor, but Social Democratic leaders, in contrast, would increase its influence by a substantial amount. The difference between Sweden and the United States in the attitudes toward labor of its closest party ally reflects, we are sure, the different structural relationships in the two countries between party and unions. In Sweden the alliance is close and long-term; in the United States the Democratic party's ties to labor are historically strong but the two institutions are quite separate and often at odds. In addition to labor itself and the Social Democratic leaders, respondents from our sample of Swedish TV journalists also support an increase in labor influence, reflecting the general pattern of support for labor and the Social Democrats among that group. The negative view of the other groups toward labor is particularly striking in light of the fact that the Social Democratic party had lost office for the first time in four decades. As we shall see in the next section, the views of labor influence would have been much more negative had the Social Democrats remained in office.

The attitudes toward labor in Japan are more complicated. As we have seen, labor is generally considered to be fairly low on the influence scale, lower than the position of its counterpart in Sweden and the United States. The likely reason is the long-term dominance of the government by the LDP, the ally of business, the farm sector, and the bureaucracy. Unions in addition have had a relatively low profile in Japan, often being attached to particular companies and usually decidedly nonmilitant. Some groups, however, believe that labor is too influential, the groups being those one might expect. Business considers labor too influential and labor considers itself not influential enough. The leaders of the various social movement groups, feminists, civic movements, and the BLL, as well as the opposition parties, share labor's view and would raise its influence. On the other side we find business, bureaucrats, and the leaders of the LDP. Farm leaders, intellectuals, and media leaders would leave labor's influence roughly as it is.

In each of the nations we asked about the influence of a broad public interest type of group—consumer groups in Japan and the United States and environmentalists in Sweden. There is a distinctive pattern in each nation, as shown in Figure 8.11. In Japan, all groups except business and farm leaders believe that consumers ought to have more influence. The expected differences appear between more conservative groups and less conservative ones. In the United States, there is much more definitive polarization with some groups wanting a substantial increase in consumer influence and others a substantial decrease—a difference that is paralleled by differences in perception of how much influence such groups have. Business, farm organization leaders, and Republican leaders see the consumer groups as quite influential and would have them less so; consumer groups are seen as a threat to their position. Labor and Democratic leaders are joined by the challenging groups, media people, and intellectuals in regarding consumers as weak and wanting them to be more powerful. These data probably reflect the fact that consumer groups are more salient and powerful in the United States than in Japan. There is, moreover, a greater dispute in the United States over the extent of that power.

In Sweden, the distinctive characteristic is the relative consensus on the degree of environmentalist influence and the extent to which it ought to be changed. There are those who would raise the influence and those who would cut it, but the magnitude of these changes is much less than in the other two nations.[12]

We also have data on the attitudes toward the influence of feminist groups in Japan and the United States (Figure 8.12). Feminists, as we have seen, are perceived to be relatively low in influence. In Japan, there is quite widespread support for an increase in that influence. The feminists themselves are a good bench mark to evaluate the degree to which other groups support an increase in their influence: they would raise their own influence by a substantial amount on the influence scale. It is interesting that a number of other groups are as supportive of them or almost so; these include labor, the center parties, and the other challenging groups. All other groups would also increase the influence of feminists, although for some of the more conservative groups—business, farm leaders, and the leaders of the LDP—the difference between "is" and "ought" is statistically insignificant and they might better be thought to prefer the status quo. The farm leaders represent one of the more culturally conservative groups in Japan, yet even they believe that feminist groups have too little influence. It is interesting that, of the three ruling coalition groups—business, the bureaucracy, and the LDP—it is the bureaucratic leadership that is most supportive of an increased voice for feminist groups. This is consistent with a view of the "top-down" reform role of the bureaucracy in connection with various issues of gender equality (see Chapter 10). In sum, feminist groups in Japan may challenge the traditional order but that challenge is either so moderate (their demands are not considered extreme) or so weak (they have little chance of accomplishing much) that their level of influence is not considered a threat, even by the most established groups. No group thinks that they have too much influence.

In the United States, the position of feminist groups is more controversial. Feminists themselves would raise their own influence substantially, but no other group shares that view. The Democratic leaders and black leaders believe that feminists should have more influence than they do, but they would not put the feminists in the high position the feminists would like for themselves. Members of the more conservative triad—business, farm leaders, and the Republican leaders—believe that the feminists have already attained more influence than they ought to have. The difference from Japan may lie in the fact that American feminists have greater salience and more influence; they not only challenge the existing distribution of benefits but also are perceived to be successful enough to be threatening—hence they ought to have their influence cut.

In both Japan and the United States, the challenge from disadvantaged minorities leads to quite varied and potentially conflictual evaluations of their influence (Figure 8.13). In each case the minority group itself believes that it should have a good deal more influence than it has and a good deal more influence than any other group would give it. Leaders of black groups in the United States see themselves as relatively low on the influence scale, a perception shared by other groups, and would raise themselves substantially. Leaders of the Buraku Liberation League in Japan see themselves as much more influential than others see them and would like to be more so. In each country the leaders of most left groups also believe that the minority group should have more influence but to a much more modest degree than does the group in question. The views of two left groups that would not raise the influence of the minority group stand out. In Japan, leaders of the left parties believe that the BLL has too much influence. In fact, the negative view of the BLL comes from the left party leaders affiliated with the Japanese Communist party, a party that has had a strong rivalry with the BLL for the leadership of the buraku people, not from their allies in the Socialist party.[13] In the United States, labor leaders would raise the influence of black leaders by an amount so small as to be statistically insignificant. Militant minority leadership clearly can be a threat to groups on the left as well as to those on the right. The groups on the right, as we would expect, believe that the minority groups are too influential. Note in Japan that the bureaucrats, who believe that feminist groups should have more influence, take the opposite view of the BLL. In all likelihood this reflects a response to the more militant and direct tactics of the BLL.

Electoral Change and Group Influence:
The Swedish Example

The analysis of the relative influence of groups that we have presented is static; it deals with what the leadership groups perceived at a particular time and what they preferred at that time. Influence, of course, can wax and wane. We have characterized certain groups as established, others as challenging, the assumption being that the former are long-term influentials in the political process, the latter more recent entrants. The challenging groups we have selected, representing feminist and minority interests, are relative newcomers. They argue for the recognition of types of inequality that were not earlier on the political agenda, although they may be long-standing ones. These groups clearly have positions of influence, low though some of our leaders find them to be, that are substantially higher than would have been found to be the case ten or so years before our study.

The same variation over time can be found for the more established groups. Although they have had a more continuous role in the political process, their relative influence is surely subject to fluctuation. One possible source of such fluctuation is the varying fortunes of the political parties with which they are allied. Two quite different expectations are possible in relation to the varying party role.

1. The distribution of group influence in a society might be independent of the particular governing party or coalition. If this were the case, a change in government would make little difference in the relative positions of the leading societal actors. This situation would occur where policy making is outside of the realm of party competition—dominated by permanent bureaucracies or conducted through intersector bargaining on social and economic councils. Party alternation would also be unimportant if the politics of party competition and elections were merely a facade behind which a politics of group influence were conducted. Lastly, party alternation would make less difference if resources for political influence were independent of electoral outcome: the less important was control

over votes or access to legislators of sympathetic parties, the less significant would a change in government be to the influence of a group.

2. The alternative expectation is that influence positions are highly contingent on who controls the government. Some parties favor certain groups. As party government changes, the relative influence of groups is seriously affected. The latter assumption is more compatible with democratic elections than is an influence hierarchy impermeable to the effects of party alternation.

Our study of Swedish leaders offers a unique opportunity to see whether the influence hierarchy in Sweden—at least, as it is perceived by the leaders in our sample—was affected by the change in the Swedish governing regime in 1976, when the Socialists, who had dominated Swedish parliamentary life for four and a half decades (alone or in coalition), were replaced by a conservative coalition. In our elite survey, conducted about two years later, we asked our respondents for their perceptions of the influence of various groups before the change in government and at the time of the survey. The answers to the two questions as well as to the question as to how much influence groups ought to have allow us to see how elite groups think influence changed.

Five major actors in the Swedish political process—the major business federation (SAF), the farm organization (LRF), the blue-collar workers' union (LO), the white-collar union (TCO), and the professionals' union (SACO)—are groups whom one would expect to be seriously affected by the change from a Socialist government to a more conservative one. In particular, one would expect a major change in the influence position of the SAF and the LO. Figure 8.6 shows to what extent the leaders of these groups perceive their own influence to have changed after the change in government. The figure shows, for each of five leadership groups, how much influence they believe their own group had before the change in government, how much it has after the change, and how much it should have. By tracing the progression on the figure from "before" to "after" to "should," one can see how each group thinks things were, how they are, and how they would like them to be.

The business and farm leaders perceive the change in government to have had a similar effect on their influence positions: they believe that their influence was quite low before the government change and that the overthrow of the Social Democrats raised their influence substantially. However, they still consider themselves to be only moderately high on the influence scale. Neither group thinks its new influence level is quite high enough; each would like to see itself somewhat higher.

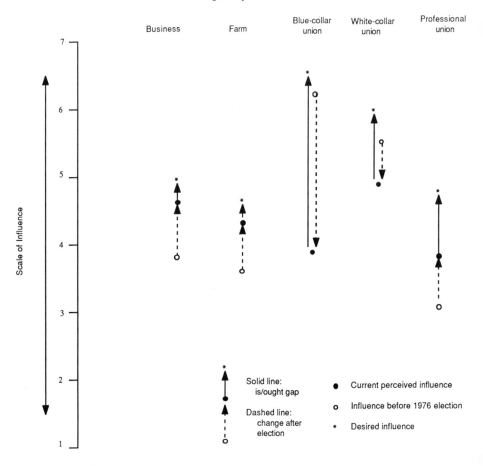

Figure 8.6. How Swedish groups see the impact of the 1976 election on their own influence

The contrast between business and farm leaders and leaders of the LO is striking. The latter group perceive a major decline since the election; their influence—as they perceive it—has plummeted from near the top of the scale to close to the bottom. Labor obviously believes that things were substantially better before the change in government—but even then not quite good enough. Their preferred influence position is a little higher than what it was under the Socialist government. Thus business and labor each indicates a small amount of dissatisfaction with its influence position under its "own" regime. The LO felt more influential under the Socialists than after their defeat, but they appear to believe that they should have been somewhat more influential before the change in government. Under the conservative regime, business feels more influential than previously—but not quite influential enough.

Leaders of the TCO, the white-collar union, look upon the change in the government in much the same terms as do the leaders of the LO. They were better off before the change, although they would have liked even more influence under the Socialist government. The change they perceive, however, is not as great as that which the LO perceives. The TCO leaders do not believe themselves to have been as influential as the LO was under the earlier regime, nor do they believe that they lost as much after the change. The leaders of the professional union, SACO, are relatively dissatisfied with their influence position under both regimes. They consider themselves to have been relatively uninfluential before the change in government, somewhat better off after the change, but still well below where they would like to be. A comparison of the leaders of the three union federations reflects the closeness of each to the Socialist government: the leaders of the LO believe their influence to be most closely related to the existence of a Socialist government; the leaders of the TCO have a more moderate dependence; and SACO believes itself to be more influential after the removal of the Socialist government.

The data in Figure 8.6 make clear that the various leadership groups see their own influence as substantially affected by the change in government. But in addition to the self-perceptions of the leadership groups we wish to examine the relative positions of the various groups vis-à-vis their adversaries in the political process. Perhaps the most important issue is whether a change in government actually rearranges the *hierarchy* of influence: did the change in government from a labor-oriented Socialist regime to a more business-oriented conservative coalition reverse the positions of union and management? We cannot give an objective answer, but we do have the perceptions of the various groups. If our generalization about influence denial is true, we would expect business and labor to differ on how much the former was helped and the latter injured by the change in government: labor should see the change as more devastating for its relative position than business sees it as increasing its influence.

Figure 8.7 shows the perceptions that business and labor have of the impact of the change in government on their relative influence positions. For contrast, it also shows the views of media people and professors of the impact of the government change on labor and business. We expect the latter to have a more balanced view.

Compare the perceptions of business and labor in the left two sections of Figure 8.7. Each of the arrows shows the change in the influence posi-

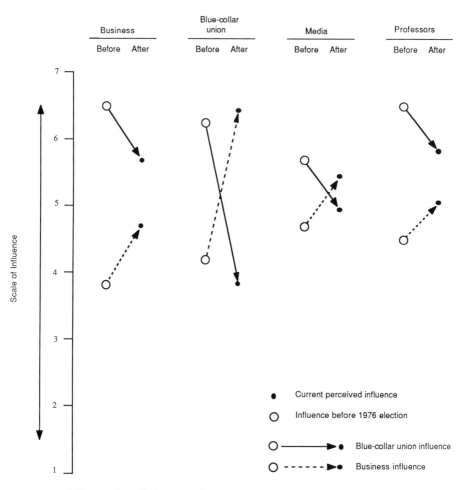

Figure 8.7. Perceived influence of labor and business leaders before and after
the Swedish election of 1976 (as seen by business, blue-collar union
leaders, the media, and professors)

tion of labor or business as they perceive it. Business perceives the change
in government to have narrowed substantially the wide influence gap between itself and labor, but it does not believe that the change in government turned the influence hierarchy upside down; it still sees the LO as
significantly more influential than the SAF. Labor's view is in sharp contrast. Its perception of the situation before the change in government is
similar to that of business: labor does not believe its advantage over business under the Socialist government was as wide as business believes it to

have been, but the business and labor perceptions of the influence gap before the change in government are not very different. Where labor differs from business is in its perception of what happened after the change in government. Labor sees the change as turning the influence hierarchy on its head: it was previously more influential than business; it is now much less.

Lastly we can look at the perceptions of the samples from the media and the professoriate. The two groups differ somewhat. The professors see the change much as does business—as narrowing the gap between the influence of business and labor but not reversing their positions. Media people see the gap as having been essentially eliminated, but they do not see business as having gone as far ahead as does labor.

The data certainly do indicate that a major change in government such as that which overturned the long-term Socialist rule has an impact on the influence positions of groups—or, at least, it is certainly perceived to have such an impact. Furthermore, the data show different perceptions on the part of labor and business, each seeing the change as less favorable to itself than its antagonist sees it. Both agree that the change enhanced the position of business at the expense of labor, but labor sees the advantage turning much more sharply against itself.

Because this asymmetric perception is particularly crucial to our overall argument about conflicts over influence—an argument to which we shall turn in the next chapter—it might be useful to add more data on the perceived consequences of the government change on the degree to which business and labor believe that they can deal successfully with the government. We asked our respondents about the extent to which they found their contacts with the government to be successful. (These contacts were discussed in Chapter 3.) The percentage of business and labor contactors who report such success is shown in Figure 8.8, with the added distinction between contacts before and after the change in government. Business reports somewhat more frequent success after the government change in contacts with members of Parliament and with members of the cabinet but almost no change in relation to bureaucrats. In contrast, labor leaders report a substantial collapse of their ability to achieve success with MPs and cabinet members after the change in government and a decided decline in the responsiveness of bureaucrats as well. Thus, not only is there an asymmetric view of the degree of damage done to labor and the gains made by business in the defeat of the Socialist government, but there is also a disjunction in the perceived scope of the weakening of labor's position. Business sees the elected government as more responsive but sees no

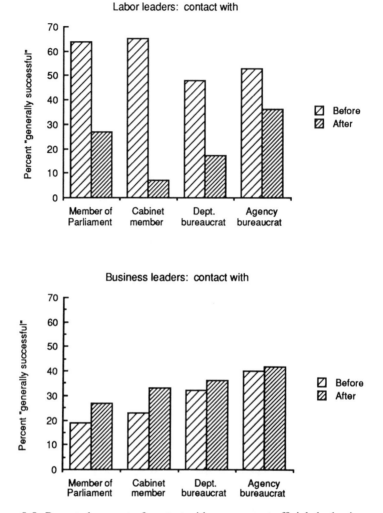

Figure 8.8. Reported success of contact with government officials by business and labor leaders before and after the Swedish election of 1976

change in the bureaucracy. Labor sees the government change as having a devastating effect on its position with the elected government and as damaging its position with the bureaucracy as well. We cannot tell who is correct about the bureaucracy in terms of how sensitive they are to governmental change in how they respond to the claims of various groups, but the data clearly support our contention about differential sensitivity of groups to a gain or loss of political influence.

In sum, the data support our contention that groups are likely to see themselves as weaker than their antagonists see them. Furthermore, the data support our contention that established groups are likely to be much more sensitive to loss or threatened loss of influence than are less advantaged groups to be sensitive to their influence position. This greater sensitivity on the part of the established group manifests itself in an overestimation of the threat that challenging groups pose to it. Labor was well established under the Socialist regime; labor, business, and the more neutral observers, media and professors, all agree on this. If we take the perceptions of the observer groups as a bench mark, we find labor overreacting to the change; they see their own decline in influence as more severe than other groups appear to think is warranted.

The struggle over political influence, this suggests, is likely to be greatly affected by the perception of where groups are on the influence scale—especially the self-perception that groups have. This importance of perception gives the contest over influence a special character. That issue is examined in the next chapter.

Appendix

Figures 8.9–8.13, on the following pages, show the views of the various leadership groups in Japan, Sweden, and the United States toward the influence that select interest groups have and ought to have in the respective nations.

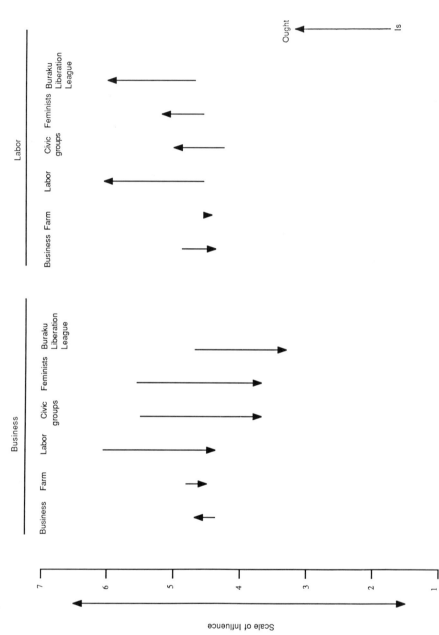

Figure 8.9A. Attitudes of the main contending groups toward business and labor influence in Japan

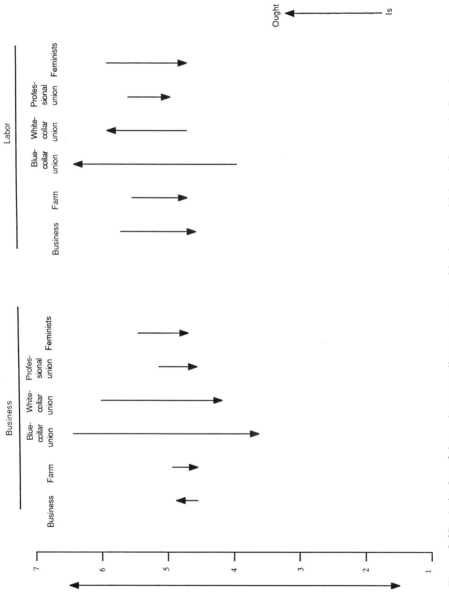

Figure 8.9B. Attitudes of the main contending groups toward business and labor influence in Sweden

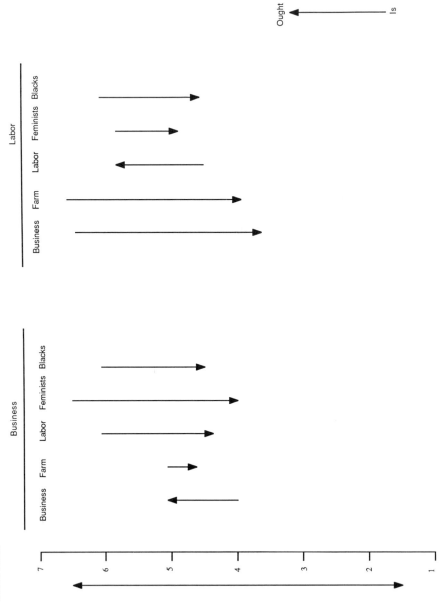

Figure 8.9C. Attitudes of the main contending groups toward business and labor influence in the United States

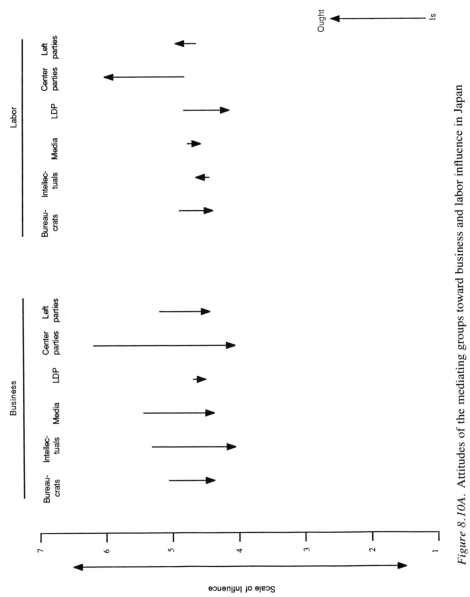

Figure 8.10A. Attitudes of the mediating groups toward business and labor influence in Japan

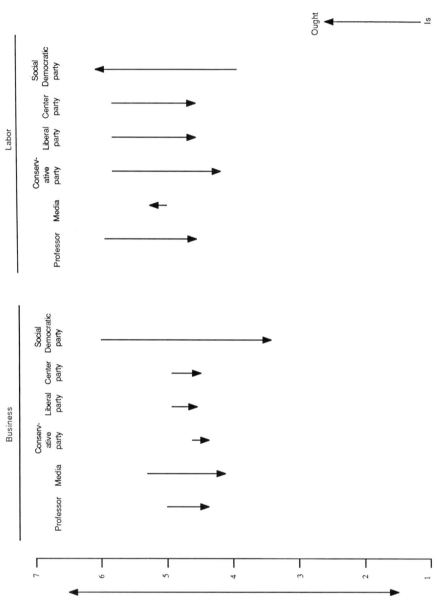

Figure 8.10B. Attitudes of the mediating groups toward business and labor influence in Sweden

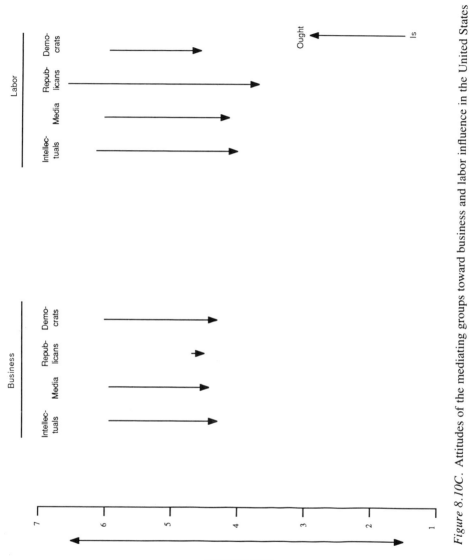

Figure 8.10C. Attitudes of the mediating groups toward business and labor influence in the United States

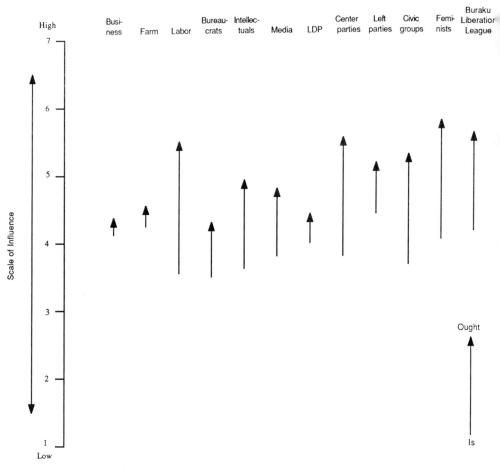

Figure 8.11A. Attitudes toward consumer group influence in Japan

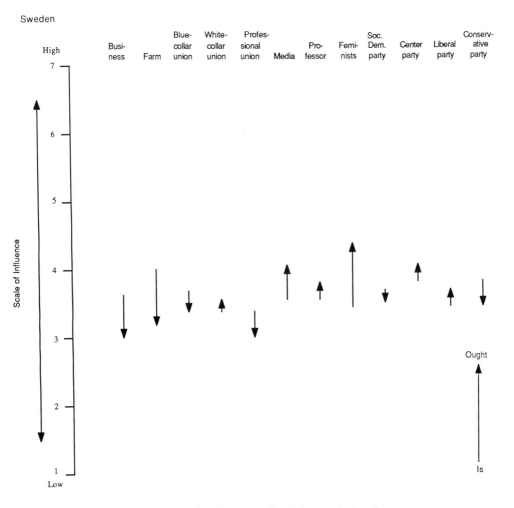

Figure 8.11B. Attitudes toward environmentalist influence in Sweden

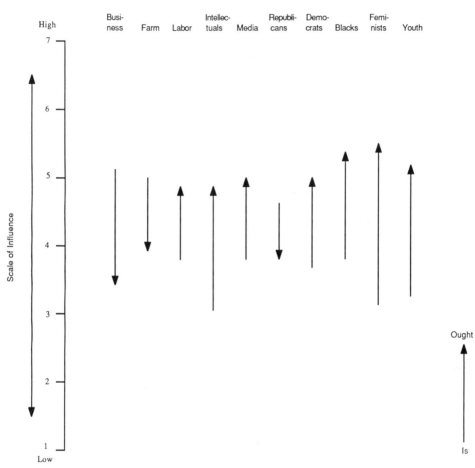

Figure 8.11C. Attitudes toward consumer group influence in the United States

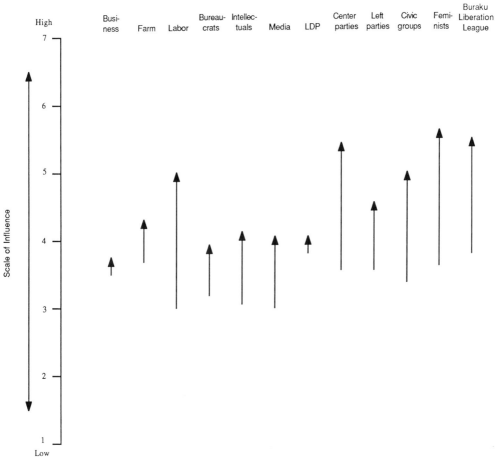

Figure 8.12A. Attitudes toward the influence of feminists in Japan

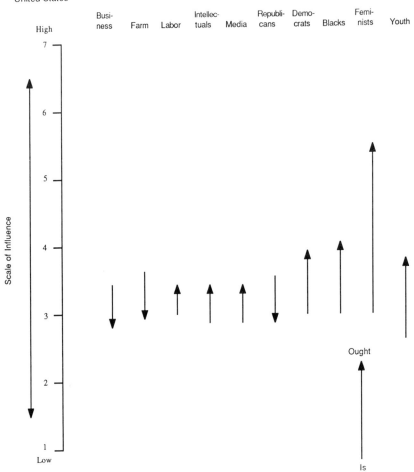

Figure 8.12B. Attitudes toward the influence of feminists in the United States

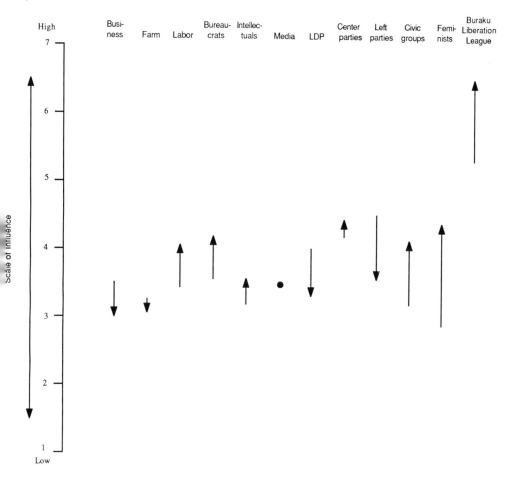

Figure 8.13A. Attitudes toward the influence of minorities in Japan

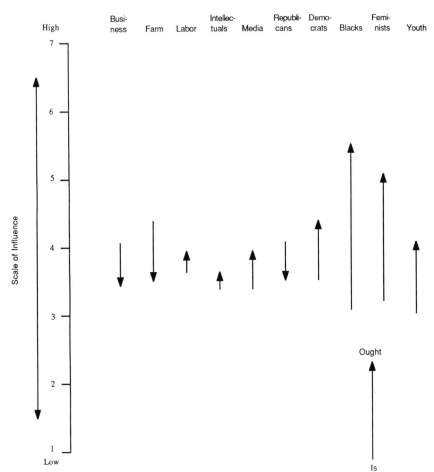

Figure 8.13B. Attitudes toward the influence of minorities in the United States

Political and
Economic Equality

Political conflict is often, perhaps usually, about inequality. One party resents advantages held by another, and the other party struggles to preserve them. Or each party perceives the other to be advantaged, in which case the redress that each seeks makes the other feel even more disadvantaged. Such political conflict can be about many kinds of advantage. Inequities in the distribution of income or the distribution of land, inequality in the right to pursue particular occupations or live in particular places, differential respect or recognition, disparities in life chances and opportunities—all these can become the substance of political conflict among classes, ethnic groups, races, regions, or religions, or between men and women. Often the political conflict is about politics itself, about inequities in the distribution of political rights or inequalities in political influence. Disparities in political influence or in the possession of those political rights that allow one to seek such influence generate particularly sharp conflict, as we shall shortly see.

Conflicts about inequality are, of course, not easily divisible into ones that are about this or the other specific goal. They are usually about multiple forms of inequality. Indeed, the struggle over one form of inequality almost inevitably involves others. We have stressed the close connection between political and economic inequality, how political advantage can be used to protect or increase economic advantage and, conversely, how economic advantage can be converted into political influence. However, although economic and political inequality are usually intertwined, they are different and generate different kinds of disputes. In this chapter we compare political and economic inequality to show how the two—because of some differences between economics and politics—lead to different kinds of conflict. One might expect conflict over economic inequality to be more intense and virulent than conflict over political position. The former deals with income and, therefore, with the ability to acquire the basics of life and a decent standard of living. As we shall see, the opposite is the case: political inequality creates the more irreconcilable difference.

Several features distinguish economic from political inequality and affect the nature of the struggle over each.[1]

Measurement. As we have pointed out, there is no clear metric for the measurement of political power and influence. Political scientists have long lamented the absence of a metric equivalent to money in economics. The absence of such a metric, it is argued, has impeded the development of political science into the more fully quantified and abstract science that is modern economics. Some have drawn the analogy between political influence and money. Political influence is to politics what money is to economics: each is a general medium that can be used to achieve a multiplicity of goals—money in the market and influence in the political arena.[2] The comparison is quite apt conceptually but less so methodologically. The fact that amounts of money can be easily observed and measured whereas amounts of political influence cannot creates a profound difference between the two.

The distinction in terms of measurability is not, however, absolute. Despite the existence of money, the measurement of income is by no means unambiguous: income can be defined in various ways. How much income an individual has may depend on the conceptual categories used. Various forms of income can be hidden by deception. The distinction is, nevertheless, real. It is relatively easy to compare the incomes of two individuals or two groups of individuals. When it comes to political influence, such comparisons are much more difficult. Indeed, much political debate both among political scientists and political practitioners is on the question of who governs rather than on the question of who should govern. This was quite clear in our data in the previous chapter. One of the most striking characteristics of the data on influence was the systematic perceptual disparities that were found whereby groups overrated the influence of their opponents and underrated their own. The absence of a precise political metric has not only a profound methodological effect on political science but also a profound substantive effect on actual politics.

A constant-sum game. Income and influence differ in another important way: politics is more likely to be a constant-sum (or zero-sum) contest than is economics. This too has consequences for the conflict over each form of inequality. In an expanding economy one person's gain is not necessarily another's loss. Indeed, because economic growth depends on incentives and income differentiation, another's economic gain may often redound to your benefit. This is not to argue that economic conflict may not partake of a constant-sum game at times; in the absence of economic growth, conflict over income can approach a zero-sum game.[3] But such is not the normal state of economic conflict. If envy ruled all and if people evaluated their own economic positions in relative rather than absolute terms, one could only lose from someone else's gain. Although there is evidence that people do make such relative judgments of their economic position,[4] most people—and certainly the elite with whom we deal— would accept the fact that income differentiation may benefit even those at the bottom of the income hierarchy.

The conflict over political influence, however, is more likely to be a constant-sum game: an increase in your political influence diminishes mine proportionately. Political influence is inherently relative in a way in which income is not. If General Motors increases its profits by 10 percent and thereby increases the income of its stockholders, that does not necessarily imply a diminution in the income of members of the United Auto Workers or even a diminution in the income of stockholders of the Ford Motor Company. The increase in General Motors' income per se does not take away from the income of its employees or its business competitors. But if one political party increases its number of votes by 10 percent over its previous electoral performance, that fact per se diminishes the political strength of the opposition party. The same is true for the contest among interest groups for influence over a legislature and among rival legislative factions for influence over legislation. In the world of politics, your strength is my weakness.[5]

One can imagine a situation in which political influence is not a zero-sum game. If one had a growing polity—where the power of the state and the range of its activities were expanding—the political influence of all or most groups could increase at the same time.[6] Or if there were a pluralist utopia in which government policy were dispersed into many policy arenas, it might be possible for all groups to become more influential in the domains of policy with which they were concerned without thereby detracting from the influence of others busy in different policy arenas. However, expanding polities usually involve intense conflict over the direction of that expansion, and a pluralist utopia where everyone gains and no one loses is unlikely given finite governmental budgets and a crowded policy agenda. Thus, although the conflict in economics may sometimes approach a constant-sum game and the conflict in politics may sometimes involve positive sums of influence where all can gain at once, on balance political conflict is likely to be closer to a constant-sum contest than is economic conflict.

The absence of a clear political metric and the constant-sum nature of the conflict in the political domain have a profound effect on the nature of the conflict over political influence and make that conflict quite different from that over economic well-being. That, at least, is our expectation. The absence of a clear metric in the political realm creates greater uncertainty among those involved in the contest over political influence. Such contestants, as we have already seen in the previous chapter, perceive the world of influence very differently from each other. They tend to underrate their own influence and overrate that of their opponents. Their opponents, of course, take the opposite position. In the absence of some more objective measure, the issue cannot be settled. The conflict over influence becomes one over both values and perceptions: Who should have influence and who should not? Who has it and who does not? In contrast, the conflict over economic equality is, we expect, likely to be over what ought to be the case rather than what is the case. Groups will differ over the interpretation of income data, but there *are* data and that should limit the range of empirical claims that can be made about income distribution.

Political conflict also differs from economic conflict because there is a constant sum of political influence but a variable sum of economic reward. It makes one's relative political position crucial in a way that one's economic position is not. The mere fact that another group has influence means that one will want to reduce it. Furthermore, how much influence reduction is necessary to achieve a satisfactory position for a particular group will be judged in relative rather than absolute terms. A satisfactory solution to a felt inequity in income distribution might be to lower the income of the rich and raise the income of the poor in order to reduce the gap between them. But those lower on the income scale might accept an income gap that still left them less well off than those at the top. They might indeed think such a gap redounded to their benefit. On the influence side, a reduction in the gap between more and less influential groups would not provide a satisfactory outcome for the less influential if they remained in a subordinate position. This suggests that those who feel themselves deprived in political influence are likely to want radical redistribution whereas those similarly deprived in economic position may take a more moderate position.

The difference between the domains of politics and economics in terms of measurability and the constant-sum nature of the contest mutually reinforce each other to give political conflict a particular bite. The constant-sum nature of political conflict means that those perceived to be more influential are perceived to be a threat. The lack of a clear metric means that political rivals have quite different perceptions of the influence hierarchy. They perceive their rivals to be more influential than they are. Thus, each sees itself as threatened by the other, and each sees its rival's attempt to gain more influence—an attempt that the rival considers merely a redress of its own disadvantaged position—as making an inequitable position even more inequitable.

This is what makes the contest over politics more virulent than that over economics. In economics, some may want to achieve greater equality and others may oppose it, but both sides will agree on who is better off and who is worse off, and those worse off may be willing to settle for something less than total reversal of the situation. In politics, there is much less agreement as to who is better off and who is worse off. Furthermore, those who perceive themselves to be worse off will want a complete redress; they will want to change their position relative to the better-off. Because the various parties who believe the influence structure to be unfair begin from quite different perceptions of what it actually is, each will see the other's position as fully illegitimate.

At least this is what we expect to be the case. We can use our data on perceptions and values about equality in the political and economic domains to test our expectations. Our overall approach is somewhat different from that of the previous chapters when we considered income and influence inequalities separately. There our concern was of necessity more contextual; we focused on differences among the nations and among groups within each nation in the amount of equality desired. The particular configuration of groups in each case was of interest to us. Our concern in this chapter is not with the specific configuration in each nation but with some general patterns of values and perceptions as they apply to income and influence. We are interested in similarities this time—similarities across the nations and among the leadership groups in each nation. In particular, we hypothesize certain similarities in the way attitudes on income differ from those on influence. If similarities can be found in the pattern of attitudes in three nations with such heterogeneous cultures and among such a wide range of groups within each nation, the validity of the above distinctions about political and economic conflict will be strengthened.

Our principal expectations are the following:

1. If the conflict over influence approximates a constant-sum game, leaders will want to see their own influence changed so that it exceeds that of the groups they perceive to be more influential. In so doing, they will reverse the influence hierarchy. On income, more of a variable-sum game, they will prefer a narrowing of the gap between those at the top of the

earnings hierarchy and themselves but not necessarily a reversal of the hierarchy.

2. The same distinction between income and influence applies to the relationship between those perceived to be at the top of the hierarchy and those perceived to be at the bottom. The leaders may want to narrow the income gap between the top and bottom, but they will not want to flatten or reverse the hierarchy. (The extent to which leaders want a narrowing should vary from group to group.) As for influence, it is more likely that groups will want to see the hierarchy radically flattened or perhaps reversed. This will, of course, be partially contingent on where each group perceives itself to be.

3. Disagreement across groups within each nation in their views on income inequality is likely to be greater on the issue of what the income distribution ought to be than on what the income distribution is. Because there is no comparable metric for influence, disagreement is likely to be at least as great on the "is" of influence distribution as on the "ought."

4. The constant-sum nature of influence conflict coupled with the disagreement over the facts of the influence distribution will make for greater polarization of group positions in relation to influence than in relation to income.

In the analysis that follows we compare political with economic inequality—or, rather, we compare the beliefs and attitudes of the various leadership groups on the two types of equality. To do so, we must deal with the issue of the absence of a common metric. There is no metric for political influence so that one could compare its distribution with the distribution of income or wealth. Even when one turns to beliefs and attitudes on inequality, there is no common metric. We have measures as to how much income inequality and how much influence inequality our respondents consider to be just, but the scales are not directly comparable. Nevertheless, we believe that comparisons across the two domains are legitimate. Although we cannot equate distances on the income scale with distances on the influence scale, we can validly compare ordinal positions from domain to domain. The ratings that our respondents made of the actual and desirable income and influence for the various target occupations and target influence groups were relative ratings. In each domain they were faced with the full array of targets before any were rated, and the ratings reflected how respondents felt one target should be located in relation to others. Thus we can ask reasonable comparative questions across the two domains: Do respondents want their income to be higher, the same, or lower than that of a business executive? Do they want the influence of their group to be higher, the same, or lower than that of big business? As we shall see, the two domains differ substantially in the hierarchical order that respondents perceive and the order they would consider to be fair.

Second, we compare across the two domains only indirectly. In each domain we have many measures relating to equality: the perceptions and values a number of respondent groups have about a number of target groups. Our comparisons across the domains are of the relations among these measures within each domain. In Figures 9.1 and 9.2 we first compare "is" with "ought" in relation to one's own income and then in relation to the income of the top earner—that is, the group perceived to be most advantaged. The two is/ought pairs are then compared with each other to see how a group's view of the fairness of its own income relates to its view of the income of the most advantaged. These comparisons are all within the domain of income and all use the same measurement scale. A similar set of comparisons is made within the domain of influence. Only then are the *patterns* of attitudes in each domain compared with each other. This use of embedded comparisons, which is repeated in various forms in the following analysis, allows us to compare from domain to domain despite the fact that there is no common metric. It allows us to ask, albeit indirectly, whether respondents see a greater need for equality in one domain than in the other.

The Top Earner versus One's Own Position

In the chapter on income equality we examined how respondents viewed their own income in relation to that of the top earner. And in the chapter on influence equality we considered their views on their own influence versus that of the group perceived to be most influential. We begin our analysis of the difference between income and influence inequality by comparing how respondents place themselves vis-à-vis the top person or group in each domain. Because conflict over influence has a constant-sum quality, relative position should be everything; income, however, is less intensely competitive. One would therefore expect leaders to be willing to tolerate a wide gap between their own income and that of the top earners but to be less tolerant of a similar disparity in influence between themselves and those they perceive to be most influential. That this is the case for each group in each nation is seen in Figures 9.1 and 9.2.

In Figure 9.1 we compare how each leadership group views its own income and the income of the occupation it perceives to earn the most—

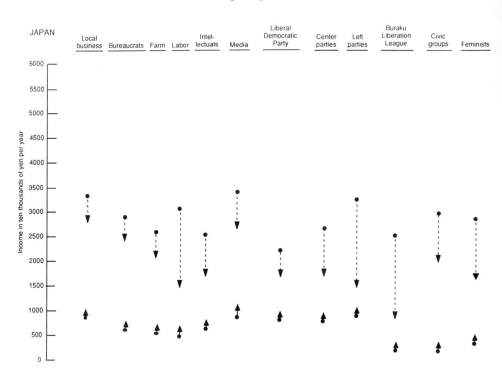

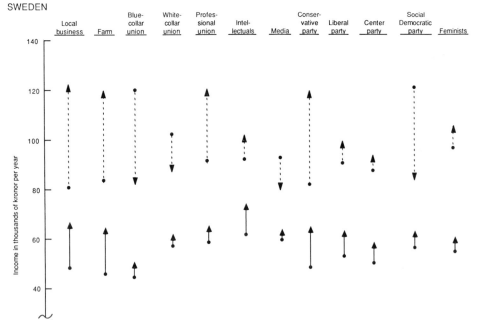

UNITED STATES

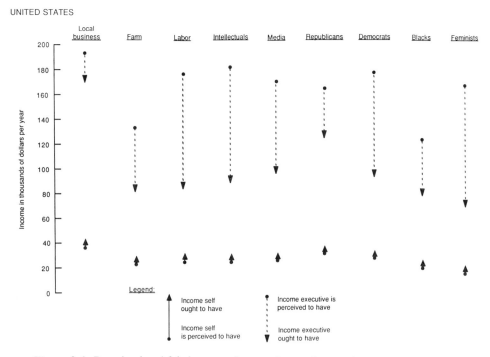

Figure 9.1. Perceived and fair income of respondent and executive (based on logged data). See note 16 to Chapter 6.

business executives in the majority of cases—in terms of what it thinks is the case and what it would consider fair. The data come from answers to the questions: what does "someone at your level in your own occupation" earn and what should he or she earn, and what does a top business executive (or other highly paid individual) earn and what should that person earn? We use an arrow format similar to that used in the previous chapter. Each arrow at the bottom of each graph refers to the respondent's own group, and goes from "is" to "ought." It begins at the income that the group, on average, reports for itself. The head of the arrow marks the income the group thinks would be fair. The dashed arrows at the top of the graph refer to the income of top earners, what it is perceived to be and what each group thinks it ought to be. The pattern is quite uniform across

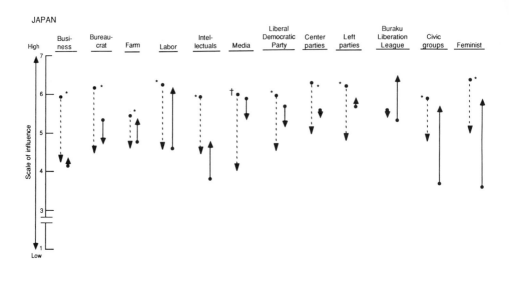

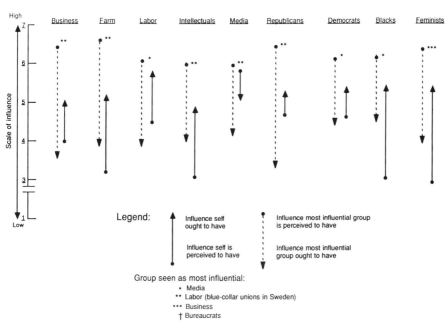

Figure 9.2. Perceived and fair influence of respondent and most influential
group

the three countries. Each leadership group thinks its own earnings ought
to be more, but not very much more. In contrast, most groups would
reduce top earner income more substantially. It is significant, however,
that in each case the increase in income that a group thinks it deserves,
combined with the much larger decrease it wants for top earners still does
not remove the gap between the two.[7] The amount of income change desired varies from group to group and across nations as we have already
seen. What is significant is the underlying uniformity revealed on Figure 9.1.

Figure 9.2 uses the same format to indicate where each group thinks it
currently stands within the influence hierarchy and where it would like to
be. We also place within the influence hierarchy each group's perception

of the group it considers most influential as well as the influence it thinks that group should have. The bottom set of arrows shows each group's view of its own influence. All groups—with the exception of the media in each country and bureaucrats in Japan—want to move themselves up. The positions of the arrows for the most influential groups indicate where the groups place the top influentials relative to themselves. We cannot directly compare the amount of movement that groups want on the income scale with the amount of change they want on the influence scale, but we can compare the impact these movements would have on the hierarchical order of groups on the two scales. From that perspective the movement is greater on the influence than on the income scale.

The uniformity among groups and across nations is striking. All groups want considerable rearrangement of the influence hierarchy. Each group wants to raise itself so that it has more influence than the group it considers most influential. Even the media leaders and the Japanese bureaucrats who would lower their own influence fit into this pattern of reversing the influence hierarchy: although they would lower their own influence, they would reduce the influence of the top group much more, thereby reversing their relative positions. In contrast, American, Swedish, and Japanese leaders would leave the income hierarchy intact. Each group desires an increase in income, but the amount of change does not challenge the fact that the top earner should continue to earn more than they. The difference between Figures 9.1 and 9.2 is consistent with the extent to which income and influence each approximate a constant-sum game. That each group moves itself to the top (or very close to the top) of the influence hierarchy is what one would expect in a constant-sum conflict. It is not enough to do better than one is currently doing; one has to do better than others are doing. The cross-national similarity in the income/influence difference— especially across so many varied groups within three nations—is compelling.

How to Treat Those Better Off

We can consider more generally the way in which the leaders would treat the income and influence hierarchies by examining how they would deal with those at the top and the bottom of the hierarchy. If our suppositions about the similarities and differences between political and economic equality are correct, we should find that leaders want to cut the income and the influence of those at the top of each hierarchy. The higher a group is on each hierarchy, the greater the cut that will be desired. But because political conflict tends to be more constant-sum, the equalizing effect should be greater in that domain than in the domain of income. In other words, for both income and influence we should see an equalizing tendency, but the result should be a more radical equalization in relation to influence.

For both income and influence, the higher a group's position is perceived to be, the more drastically the leaders want to reduce it. Figure 9.3 plots the relationship between the average income (on a log scale) that our leaders perceive an occupation to earn and the average change in income that they desire for that occupation. Each point on the graph represents an occupation. It is clear that the leaders would raise the income of those at the bottom of the hierarchy and cut the income of those at the top. The proportional changes are greater as one moves to the top or bottom of the scale. (In Sweden the relationship is curvilinear, with cuts for the top and a raise for the bottom, but little change for those in the middle range.) Figure 9.4 plots the parallel relationship between the average influence a target group is perceived to have and the average change in influence that the leaders desire for that group. Each point on this graph represents a target group. The same treatment accorded to income is accorded to those high or low on the influence scale: the lower the group is, the more it is raised; the higher it is, the more it is cut.

Figures 9.3 and 9.4 refer to averages across all of the leaders, which can be misleading if there is a wide variation in the views of different leadership groups. But a similar tendency is found when we look at each leadership group separately. Table 9.1 reports the correlation between the perceived level of income and the percentage change desired, as well as the parallel correlation for influence for individual leadership groups. In virtually every case the relationship is strongly negative: the more each group perceives an occupation to earn or the more influence it perceives a target group to have, the more it would like to lower its income or influence. The single exception is in Sweden, where the more conservative groups—business, the Conservative party, and farm leaders—think that income redistribution has gone far enough if not too far in their country and do not favor cutting the earnings of higher paid occupations. The correlations are negative for business and conservative party leaders in the other two countries, although, as we would expect, not as negative as those for the other groups.

The data in Figures 9.3 and 9.4 and Table 9.1 suggest little difference

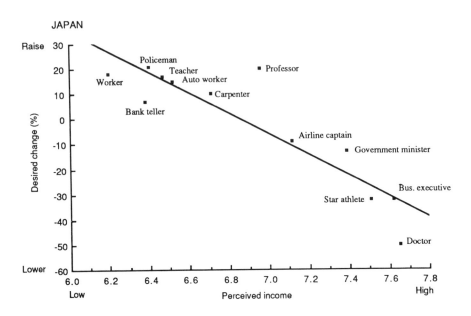

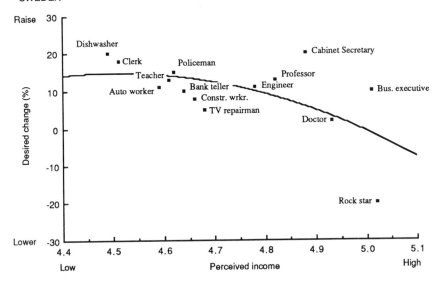

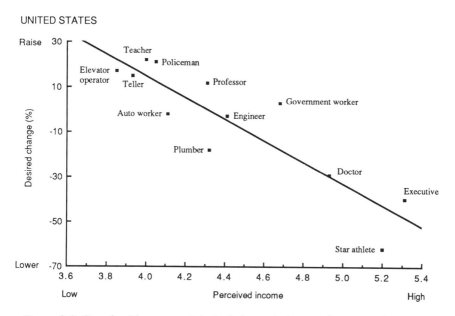

Figure 9.3. Perceived income and desired change in income for occupations
(based on logged data). See note 16 to Chapter 6.

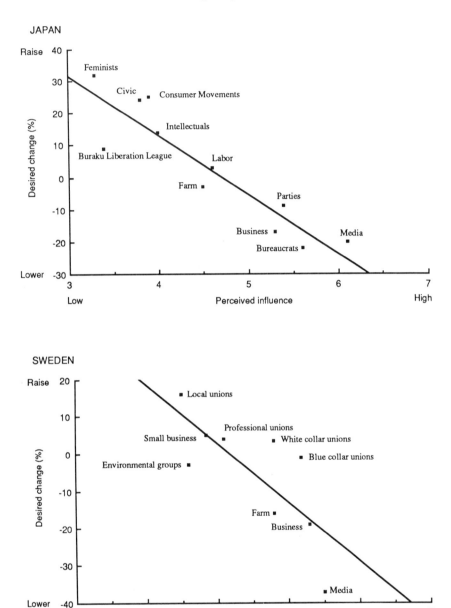

JAPAN

SWEDEN

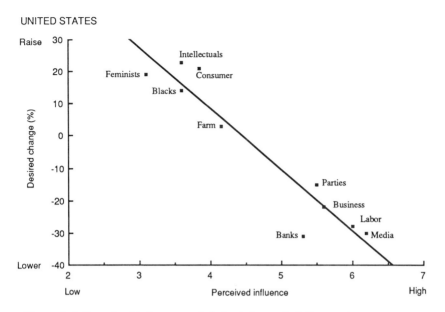

UNITED STATES

Figure 9.4. Perceived influence and desired change in influence for target
         groups

between income and influence. The more of either a group is seen to have, the larger the proportional cut that the leaders want to make. We do, however, expect a difference between influence and income. We do not expect the leaders to seek to rearrange the income hierarchy; we do expect them to propose a substantial reordering of the influence hierarchy. This suggests that, although respondents would take proportionally more away from those well endowed in either influence or income, the degree to which they would do this should be much greater for influence than for income.

The data confirm this. In Figures 9.3 and 9.4 we looked at the relationship between how much an occupation or target group is perceived to have and how much respondents think the present amount of income and influence should be *changed*. In Figures 9.5 and 9.6 we consider the relationship between how much a target group is perceived to have and how much the leaders think it ought to have after whatever changes in income or influence the respondents think are necessary to achieve a fair distribution. The relationship in Figure 9.5 between the income from an occupation

Table 9.1. Correlations of perceived position and desired change for the income from various occupations and for the influence of target groups

	Income	Influence
	Correlation of perceived income with desired change[a]	Correlation of perceived influence with desired change[b]
Country and group		
Japan		
Business	− .45	− .85
Bureaucrats	− .58	− .89
Farm	− .72	− .74
Labor	− .97	− .85
Intellectuals	− .85	− .93
Media	− .69	− .83
Liberal Democratic party	− .61	− .82
Center parties	− .90	− .74
Left parties	− .97	− .91
Buraku Liberation League	− .97	− .64
Civic groups	− .94	− .91
Feminists	− .94	− .89

Table 9.1 (*continued*)

Country and group	Income	Influence
	Correlation of perceived income with desired change[a]	Correlation of perceived influence with desired change[b]
Sweden		
Business	.58	− .87
Farm	.07	− .82
Blue-collar union	− .94	− .92
White-collar union	− .78	− .72
Professional union	− .14	− .76
Intellectuals	− .49	− .91
Media	− .91	− .67
Social Democratic party	− .96	− .90
Center party	− .64	− .89
Liberal party	− .63	− .90
Conservative party	.45	− .93
Feminists	− .79	− .92
United States		
Business	− .42	− .71
Farm	− .76	− .76
Labor	− .92	− .69
Intellectuals	− .80	− .90
Media	− .80	− .80
Republicans	− .70	− .67
Democrats	− .80	− .87
Blacks	− .86	− .93
Feminists	− .88	− .97

a. Correlation between the (mean) income that members of a group believe each occupation generates and the change in income desired for each occupation.

b. Correlation between the (mean) influence that members of a group believe each target group has and the change in influence desired for each target group.

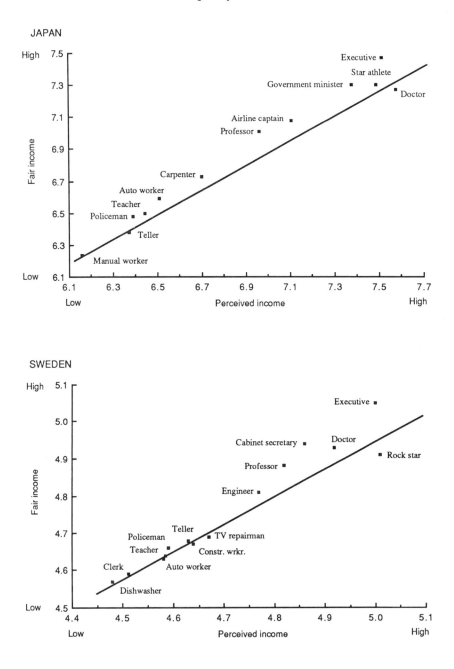

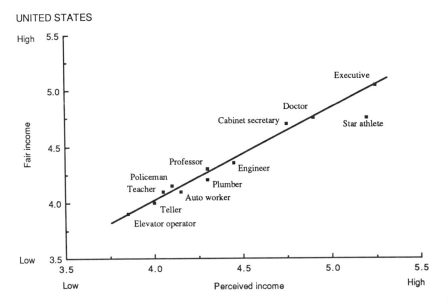

Figure 9.5. Perceived and fair income for occupations (based on logged data).
See note 16 to Chapter 6.

and what would be considered fair is clear and positive: the leaders feel that occupations currently generating higher incomes ought to do so. This figure contrasts sharply with Figure 9.3, which showed that the greater the income from an occupation, the more our respondents feel earnings ought to be cut. Nonetheless, the two figures do not contradict each other. Executives are thought to earn more than the other occupations. The leaders would decrease executive incomes,[8] but they want executives to remain at the top of the income hierarchy. The cut reduces the distance between top and bottom occupations but leaves the hierarchy intact.

Figure 9.6 contrasts sharply with Figure 9.5. When we plot the influence that target groups are perceived to have against the influence the leaders think they should have, we discover no relationship. The sharp cut in the influence of those at the top—reflected in the data in Figure 9.4—

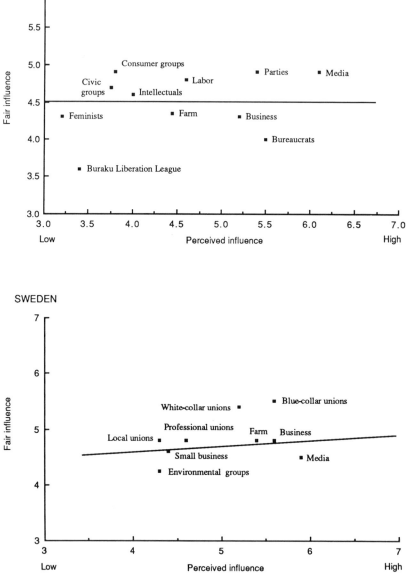

JAPAN

Fair influence

6.0
5.5
5.0   Consumer groups
                                        ■ Parties   ■ Media
     Civic   ■ Labor
     groups   ■ Intellectuals
4.5
   ■ Feminists   ■ Farm   ■ Business
4.0   ■ Bureaucrats

3.5   ■ Buraku Liberation League

3.0
   3.0   3.5   4.0   4.5   5.0   5.5   6.0   6.5   7.0
   Low   Perceived influence   High

SWEDEN

Fair influence

7
6
                                    ■ Blue-collar unions
         White-collar unions ■
5   Professional unions   Farm Business
   Local unions ■   ■   ■   ■
              Small business   ■ Media
            ■ Environmental groups
4
3
   3   4   5   6   7
   Low   Perceived influence   High

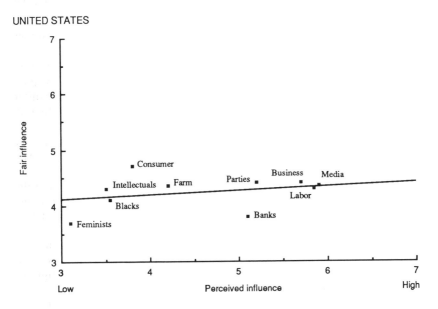

Figure 9.6. Perceived and fair influence for target groups

results in the flattening of the influence hierarchy as seen in Figure 9.6.

The contrast between the leaders' views on income and influence may be likened to the difference between a progressive and a confiscatory tax. The leaders apply a progressive tax to income: a higher proportion of income is taken from those near the top of the scale. The tax is, in fact, progressive in both a positive and a negative direction: those who are perceived to have low earnings are given an income boost—the lower the perceived income, the bigger the boost. But the progressive tax does not upset the income hierarchy. It leaves the top earners with substantially higher earnings than those below them. With regard to influence, however, the leaders apply a confiscatory tax to those they perceive to have higher influence and a countervailing negative tax to those seen as very low in influence. The difference between the two domains is striking: in the economic domain, they propose marginal changes in the status quo, but the income hierarchy remains; in the influence domain, something closer to full equality of result is desired, with each group ending up with similar influence.

Again, the contrast between Figures 9.5 and 9.6 could be misleading because the data are averaged across all leadership groups, which are quite heterogeneous in their views on income and influence equality. They differ on how much income equality they want; some are much more egalitarian than others. They are more agreed on the amount of influence equality they want; equality of influence is seen as a good thing. But they vary widely on whom they want to be high or low on the influence scale. The leadership groups must therefore be considered separately.

Table 9.2 presents the correlations within each leadership group of the perceived and desired income of the various occupations as well as the parallel correlations for perceived and desired influence of the target groups. The pattern of correlations indicates that the contrast between income and influence reflected in Figures 9.5 and 9.6 applies to each leadership group. For income the relationships are all strongly positive: each group believes that the target groups that currently earn more ought to earn more (even if they have received substantial cuts). The point deserves underlining. The groups range from leaders of business and conservative parties to groups that take more egalitarian positions, such as leaders of liberal parties, union leaders, and feminist organizations. Across all these groups, including the more egalitarian, the strong positive correlations indicate acceptance of the existing income hierarchy. No group wants to change it.[9]

For influence, the pattern is quite varied. For some groups the correlation is positive, although by no means as positive as the parallel correlations between income perceptions and income values. These groups are generally satisfied with the influence hierarchy as they perceive it. Those most satisfied with the influence hierarchy tend to be the more conservative groups: business, farm leaders, and leaders of the Liberal Democratic party in Japan; business and farm groups in Sweden as well as leaders of the professional workers' union; Republicans in the United States. For other groups the degree of satisfaction with the influence structure is less. For intellectuals in Japan and most of the major economic groups in the United States, the correlation hovers around zero; there is no relationship between what they perceive and what they would like. For some groups out of the governing circles such as feminists in the United States, leaders of the Buraku Liberation League in Japan, and leaders of the major Swed-

Table 9.2. Correlations of perceived and fair positions for the income from various occupations and for the influence of target groups

Country and group	Correlation of perceived income with fair income[a]	Correlation of perceived influence with fair influence[b]
Japan		
Business	.98	.67
Bureaucrats	.97	.57
Farm	.98	.67
Labor	.97	−.18
Intellectuals	.98	−.06
Media	.97	.45
Liberal Democratic party	.99	.61
Center parties	.92	−.04
Left parties	.76	−.49
Buraku Liberation League	.96	−.46
Civic groups	.97	−.08
Feminists	.99	−.42
Sweden		
Business	.97	.30
Farm	.95	.38
Blue-collar union	.96	−.37
White-collar union	.95	.25
Professional union	.94	.68
Intellectuals	.93	.33
Media	.92	.35
Social Democratic party	.95	−.55
Center party	.96	−.07
Liberal party	.96	.65
Conservative party	.95	.05
Feminists	.93	.37
United States		
Business	.92	.20
Farm	.93	.11
Labor	.97	.15
Intellectuals	.93	.40
Media	.93	.10
Republicans	.90	.37
Democrats	.95	.17
Blacks	.98	−.01
Feminists	.91	−.68

a. Correlation between the mean of the income that members of a leadership group believe each occupation generates and the mean of the income it ought to generate.

b. Correlation between the mean of the influence that members of a leadership group believe each target group has and the mean of the influence it ought to have.

ish blue-collar union and the Social Democratic party (the survey was conducted in Sweden shortly after the Socialists' loss of power after forty years in office), the correlation is strongly negative; these groups would reverse the influence hierarchy they perceive to exist. They appear to levy more than a confiscatory tax on high levels of influence; in addition, they levy a negative penalty tax to subsidize those low in influence.

To recapitulate, attitudes toward influence approximate what we would expect in a constant-sum contest more than attitudes toward income do. Relative position appears to be what counts in relation to influence. Whereas each group of leaders is satisfied with the current income ranking of occupations, their views on influence rankings are more contingent on how they perceive the hierarchy. Some groups would adjust the hierarchy somewhat, others want to flatten the hierarchy, and still others would reverse it. Almost all would put themselves on top.

Perception versus Values

The conflict over positions of influence, this suggests, is more likely to be intense than the conflict over income because groups and individuals want a more radical change in the former hierarchy than in the latter. The conflict is made more intense by another feature of influence, the fact that there is no clear metric regarding who is where on the influence hierarchy. A major distinction between influence and income has to do with the relative importance of disagreements in perception and in values. We have suggested that conflict among groups over income would be conflict over what ought to be, not over what is. The groups would agree more on the actual income of various occupations than on what would be fair earnings. With regard to influence, however, both norms and perceptions—both "ought" and "is"—are in dispute. Indeed, the "is" may be even more in dispute than the "ought," because there is significant agreement in democratic societies on the norm of equal political influence. Thus we may expect more consensus across groups on what should be the case in relation to influence than on what is the case.

This difference between income and influence can be tested with the "is" and "ought" questions in each domain. For income we take several pairs of occupations, each pair consisting of a higher-paying and a lower-paying occupation. We calculate an "is" and an "ought" ratio for each pair—that is, how wide each individual perceives the income gap to be and how wide he or she wants that gap to be. We also calculate such "is" and "ought" ratios for the influence of pairs of groups, where each pair contains a more and a less influential group. We then have two types of ratio between the positions of those high and low on each hierarchy: "is" and "ought" ratios for income; "is" and "ought" ratios for influence. Our hypothesis is that the variation across our leadership groups on the "ought" of income is greater than the variation on the "is" of income; and that the variation on the "is" of influence is as great as or greater than the variation on the "ought" of influence.

These ratios are calculated for each individual leader and then averaged for each leadership group. The measure of consensus is the coefficient of variation of these mean ratios across groups. The larger the coefficient of variation, the greater the disagreement among the groups on that particular ratio. The results of these comparisons are reported in Table 9.3. In the United States and Sweden, the data clearly support our hypothesis. For income, there is more consensus across groups on the "is" than on the "ought." The coefficients of variation are substantially larger in relation to desired income than to perceived income; groups agree more with each

Table 9.3. Variations among groups in ratios of perceived to desired income and perceived to desired influence

	Coefficient of variation of group mean ratios					
	Income				Influence	
Country and group	Is	Ought			Is	Ought
Japan						
Executive to auto			Business to labor		.11	.18
worker	.26	.33	Business to feminists		.16	.21
Executive to young			Business to Buraku			
manual laborer	.11	.40	Liberation League		.22	.26
Sweden						
Executive to auto			Business to blue-collar			
worker	.16	.35	unions		.51	.28
Executive to			Business to environmentalists	.21		.14
dishwasher	.17	.24	Small business to blue-collar			
			unions		.44	.28
United States						
Executive to auto			Business to labor		.29	.16
worker	.12	.33	Business to feminists		.23	.19
Executive to			Business to civil rights			
elevator operator	.12	.40	groups		.30	.18

other on the actual income situation than on the desired income situation. The pattern for influence is the reverse. The coefficients of variation are higher for the perceived ratios than for the desired ratios, which indicates more consensus on how things ought to be than on how things are. In Japan, the income comparisons are consistent with our hypothesis; they show somewhat more variation in ideal income than in the perception of current income. The difference between perceptions and values is in the opposite direction from our expectations in the domain of influence, but the difference is relatively small. This is especially true for the widest influence gap—between business and the Buraku Liberation League—where the degree of consensus is about the same for perceptions and values. When, furthermore, one compares this narrow disparity in the degree of consensus on perceptions and values with the wide disparity between perceptual and value consensus in relation to the widest earnings gap—that between an executive and a young manual worker—the expected distinction between influence and income clearly appears. On the whole, the data are consistent with our point that influence is less precisely measurable than income, the result being that the former is the more likely subject of political debate.

Differences in the perception of the political hierarchy are what one would expect given the difficulty of obtaining objective measures of political influence. The combination of these differences in perception with the constant-sum nature of political conflict results in a conflict over political position that is more intense than that over economic position. Disagreements about the reality of the influence distribution exacerbate political conflict and impede the attainment of greater political equality. There may be general agreement on a norm of political equality, but the constant-sum nature of political equality and the ambiguity of political reality prevent that norm from leading to more equality. Each group thinks that it is deprived in terms of influence and that its adversaries have an advantage.

The result is that the general normative consensus loses some of its equalizing potential. If one of the contending groups were in a position to do so, it might try to equalize the distribution of influence; but if it did so according to its own perception of reality, it would only make the situation more unequal from the perspective of other contending groups. Indeed, consensus on the norm of political equality heats conflict because the differing perceptions of reality lead each side to think that the other is violating that norm. Politics, of course, is not just the conflict of organized groups, and the equalizing norms have an effect on less-committed political actors. But the variations in perceptions of reality inhibit the ability of equalizing norms to influence the behavior of partisans.

Consider, for example, the views of labor and business. In all modern democracies business and labor represent two poles of political conflict. Figure 8.2 showed for each of the three nations the mutual perceptions that business and labor have of each other's influence. In the eyes of business, labor is the more powerful of the two. Labor believes the opposite. The reversal of positions illustrated in this figure is of substantive importance. It is not merely that there is disagreement about the facts of influence; the disagreement is systematic. Groups underestimate their own influence and overestimate that of their adversaries.

Once one begins with such divergent perceptions, the fear of falling behind in influence leads to sharply contradictory views as to what is fair and just. Figure 9.7 illustrates how business perceives the threat posed to it by labor. The left side of Figure 9.7 shows, for each country, labor's perception (business has more influence) and how labor would like to change things (labor should have more influence than business). This part of the figure aptly reveals how groups would overturn the influence hierarchy as they see it.

The position of labor as illustrated on the left panel of Figure 9.7 is rather threatening to business, but it becomes even more threatening given the way business perceives the world, as illustrated on the right side of Figure 9.7. Business perceives labor to be more influential than itself. If one were to change the world that business *perceives* in the direction that labor *wants,* one would find an already disadvantaged business community undergoing further deprivation. Business and labor would be separated by almost the entire range of the influence scale with labor at the top. Surely business would consider this illegitimate.

Figure 9.8 turns the tables and presents the situation as labor would see it. The result is similar. Labor faces a situation it would perceive as going from bad to worse. The outcome in Japan and Sweden is not as bad for labor as it is for business largely because business in those two nations does not want as large an increase in its influence as labor does (the surveys in each country were conducted with business-oriented conservative governments in power). In the United States the situation is symmetrical: business believes itself as disadvantaged in influence vis-à-vis labor as labor believes itself to be vis-à-vis business. The outcome for labor if business had its way would be as bad as the outcome for business if labor had its way.

JAPAN

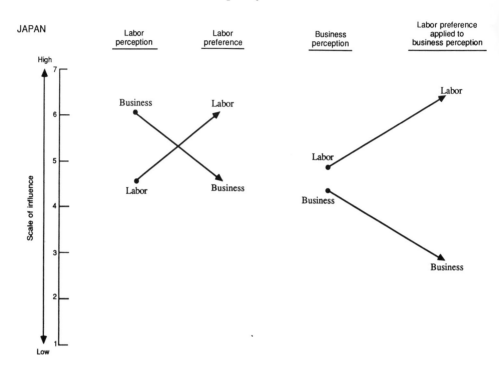

SWEDEN

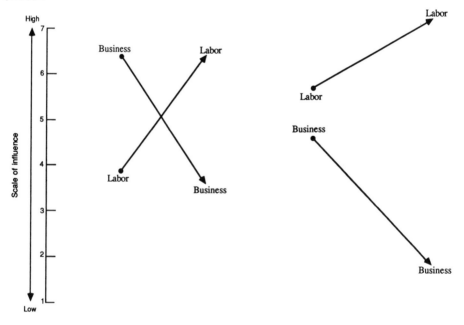

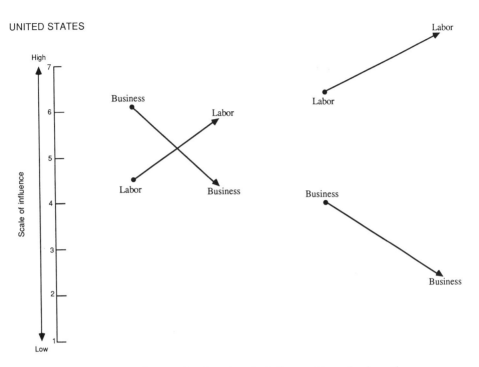

Figure 9.7. Labor's preference for changing the influence hierarchy from the perspective of business

Conclusion

The conflict over influence may be more intense than the conflict over income despite the seemingly greater normative consensus on influence. Leaders in three very different countries dispute the proper size of the income gap but they agree that the ranking of income groups should stay the same. A narrowing of the gap may be threatening to those at the top, but the threat is moderated by the consensus that those at the top should remain there. For influence, groups want a complete reversal of position. To turn a hierarchy upside down is more threatening than merely to constrict its range.[10]

The conflict associated with changing the influence hierarchy is even more severe because the antagonists have such different perceptions of where they and where their adversaries are. Each group, viewing the preferences of the other in terms of its own perceptions of influence, sees itself as starting from a deprived position and becoming even more deprived. It

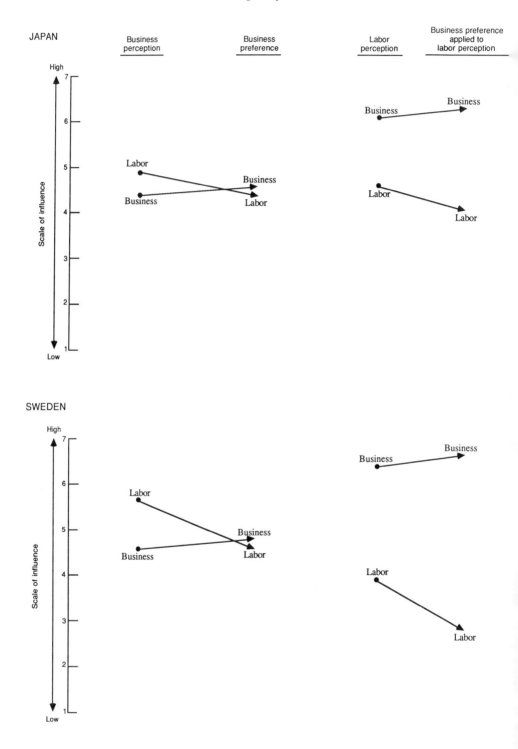

UNITED STATES

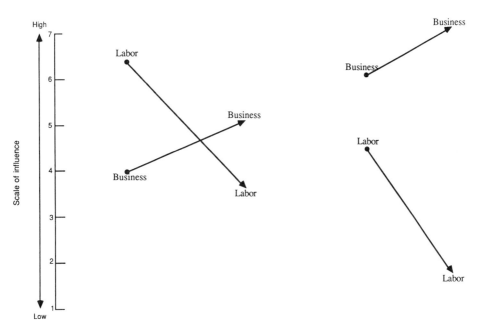

Figure 9.8. Business's preference for changing the influence hierarchy from the
perspective of labor

also sees its opponent, already at the top of the influence hierarchy, as
demanding more influence. Such a conflict calls into question the legitimacy of the demands of the other group. The groups generally agree about
a fair distribution of influence: it is a relatively equal distribution in which
no group dominates the others. But groups do not agree on what changes
would produce such a fair influence distribution. The evidence from the
United States, Japan, and Sweden lends support to our original contention:
although equality may be more of a normative ideal in politics than in
economics, incongruent perceptions and the constant-sum nature of politics make the attainment of equality as unlikely in political as in economic
affairs, and the same factors make political conflict generally more virulent and violent.[11]

10

Gender Equality

Demands for equality for women are an example of a challenge from the outside to the established political systems of the three countries. Feminist movements of varying strengths were active in the United States and Sweden during the period around the turn of the century and in Japan during the democratic interlude in the 1920s. In the former two countries these movements focused their efforts on women's suffrage. Broader demands for equality for women, however, never achieved much ongoing salience in the political systems of any of the countries. In the mid-1960s feminist movements revived and pressed new, often more radical equality demands, as did other groups previously excluded from power, such as disadvantaged minorities in the United States and Japan.

This chapter examines feminism as an example of new equality-related demands on the political system. We seek to understand how the political systems of the three countries have reacted to the demands and, in turn, the effect of their reaction on the form the demands took. As we shall see, the positions taken by the leaders we sampled reflected the way in which established institutions accommodated new views of the nature of equality, and in each nation the means for expressing the new demands took a particular shape. (Because our main theoretical interest here is in the initial reaction of the political system to new demands being made on it, our discussion focuses on the first years of the new feminism starting in the mid-1960s.)

We begin with Sweden, where a suffrage movement arose around the turn of the century as part of a general movement for extending the right to vote to groups that did not have it, including most industrial workers. The government granted suffrage to women in 1921. An important actor in the struggle for suffrage was the Fredrika Bremer Federation, founded in 1884 and still the only important feminist organization in Sweden. Also, the major political parties established women's federations, which played an important role in raising feminist demands during the 1920s.[1]

When the feminist movements revived in the 1960s, the earliest public stirrings of new feminist demands in Sweden came in books and articles that received widespread attention. A 1961 essay called "The Conditional Emancipation of Women," by a young writer named Eva Moberg, stirred the most interest.[2] Moberg argued that it was not enough to accept the view that women should work outside the home. As long as men did not take on more responsibilities within the home, women would face "double work" responsibilities, whereas men would have only responsibilities outside the home. The emancipation of women would then be only "conditional." Moberg's attempt to change the values of both women and men about the behavior regarded as typical for their sex was common to Swedish feminist writings of this period.

Perhaps the most significant feature of the emerging feminist movement in Sweden was the response to it by the party system. The Social Democrats incorporated feminist demands into the traditional cleavage lines of Swedish politics. No significant new feminist organizations formed to press the demands, and the feminists behaved quite moderately.

The Social Democrats made gender equality into their issue by subsuming it in the general issue of equality. To do so, they shifted the movement's emphasis from changing values and attitudes to changing the status of women in the workplace. Deemphasizing attitude and value change made feminism less threatening to socially more conservative working-class Social Democrats.

The ideological integration of feminism into the Social Democratic movement culminated with the adoption in 1972 of the program statement "The Family in the Future: A Socialist Family Policy" by the Social Democratic Women's Federation.[3] This program both incorporated feminist demands into general Social Democratic ideology and placed at the center those demands that fit best into that ideology.

The report began by noting that "in line with our basic values, the goal for social policies should be to bring about equality, security, and democracy. The same goal must apply to family policies. It is therefore clear that family policy measures must be made part of a total political strategy, a strategy that has as its goal a classless society."[4] The closing pages affirmed that "we have in our family policy program gone outside the traditional boundaries and widened the meaning of the term 'family policy.' Worklife has been placed in the center."[5] At the same time, although not rejecting outright sex-role issues, the program downgraded them: "We are favorably inclined towards information- and attitude-influence, but it is our view that they have only limited significance."[6]

Also in 1972 the Social Democratic government established the Delegation for Equality between Men and Women as part of the Office of the Prime Minister. Making the delegation part of this office was unusual and interesting. Had the delegation been part of a normal ministry or government agency, civil-service rules would have restricted the organization's ability to use political criteria in hiring. Had it been a freestanding organization established by Parliament, Swedish custom would have dictated that its governing board include representatives of all political parties. Because it was part of the prime minister's office, unusual for an organization with operational responsibilities, the government could keep it under closer political control.[7]

The delegation immediately concentrated on measures to improve the situation of women in the workplace. It added a hundred new positions to deal with women's labor market problems at the agency for training and job placement. It also obtained a subsidy for firms that hired women for traditionally male jobs (and vice versa). Its most widely publicized activity was a series of pilot projects where women were put onto construction sites or men into daycare centers.[8] The government also introduced provisions to protect the job status of women on maternity leave.

The development of the feminist movement in the United States shows both similarities and differences with Sweden. Like Sweden, the United States had a movement for women's suffrage in the second half of the nineteenth century. The movement culminated in the national extension of the right to vote for women by the Nineteenth Amendment in 1920. Unlike the Swedish movement, however, the American effort had no ties to a broader movement for universal suffrage, because all white men already had the vote, and there was no contemporary movement for restoration of the suffrage to southern blacks.[9] Also unlike those in Sweden, no American feminist organizations survived in any significant way after women won the vote.

In the United States, as in Sweden, the first stirrings of new feminist demands also came through writings, in particular two best sellers, Betty Friedan's *Feminine Mystique* (1963) and Kate Millett's *Sexual Politics* (1970).[10] Friedan attacked the view that women should regard femininity as a blessing. Believing there to be a general assumption that women should not work, she wrote a polemic against the view that excessive attention by women to a career was "unfeminine." Millett took a different tack: writing from a Marxian-influenced perspective, she presented sexual domination as a prototypical form of domination by some human beings over others.

In the United States, these early writings were not followed, as in Sweden, by efforts to seek out the political parties. Furthermore, neither the American political parties nor any of their major figures tried to incorporate these new ideas into their public positions. Instead, in 1967 feminists formed a new organization, the National Organization for Women (NOW), in which Betty Friedan took a leading role.

NOW's original purpose was to act as an interest group to lobby the Equal Employment Opportunity Commission (EEOC), a government agency, on sex discrimination.[11] The new organization petitioned the EEOC to hold hearings about a guideline permitting newspapers to publish want ads under "Help Wanted—Male" and "Help Wanted—Female" headings. NOW sought to abolish this practice in cases where members of both sexes could compete for the jobs. In December 1967 NOW led mass picketing of EEOC headquarters, the first organized march of the modern feminist movement.

NOW continued to act as an interest group outside the establishment. In its early years it organized many sit-ins and demonstrations: protests against policies on help-wanted ads, sit-ins at bars that did not admit women, rallies for the legalization of abortion. A New York City demonstration in 1970 attracted thirty to fifty thousand people and received extensive media coverage, marking the beginning of widespread recognition of a new women's movement.[12]

Feminist organizations made little effort to moderate their stands to appeal to larger political constituencies. Among themselves, they disagreed about attitudes toward radical cultural phenomena within their movement, such as separatism and lesbianism. NOW passed a resolution in 1971, over the opposition of Betty Friedan, stating that "the oppression of lesbians [is] a legitimate concern of feminism."[13] NOW itself had to contend with significant opposition on its left from radical feminist organizations.

This is not to say that American feminists failed to interact with political or governmental institutions. They did so prodigiously, but they generally acted by putting pressure on institutions—particularly government agencies and the courts—from the outside. Efforts to pressure the EEOC on various issues were a central early activity. Virtually all government affirmative action policies emanated from decisions of government agencies rather than legislative decisions involving party leaders.[14] In the courts feminists won decisions striking down protective state laws regarding women, and they took their campaign for abortion rights to the courts.

During this period the feminists were not allied with either political party, and neither party offered them particular support. For example, the passage by Congress of the ERA in 1971 was not really a Democratic issue.[15] In fact, much of the momentum came from within the Nixon administration. The Democratic chairman of the House Judiciary Committee, Emanuel Celler, had for years refused to hold hearings on the ERA; and the Democratic chairman of the Senate Judiciary Committee, Sam Ervin, prevented the bill from coming to the Senate floor after it had passed the House in 1970. Yet by the time the amendment passed both houses in 1971, it had broad bipartisan support.[16] When a national lobbying organization for the ERA was formed in 1975, it had two chairpersons, one Democratic and one Republican.[17] And a study of state legislatures that ratified or rejected the ERA found that, outside the South, an equal number of ratifying states had Republican-controlled legislatures as Democratic ones. (In the South, where rejection was common, legislatures were Democratic-controlled.)[18] The pattern was similar for abortion. In New York, where political lobbying for abortion was most extensive, the political initiative was taken not by Democrats but by Republican Governor Rockefeller. American feminists sought support wherever they could.[19]

By contrast, in Japan the women's movement, both traditionally and in the period around the time our survey was conducted, was weaker than in either Sweden or the United States. During the westernization that followed the Meiji Restoration of 1868, some feminist stirrings contributed to a general movement for westernizing political reform. The Public Meeting and Political Societies Law of 1890 and the Peace Police Law of 1900, directed against reformist forces, prohibited women from joining any political organizations and even "from attending meetings where political matters were publicly discussed." In 1919 *Shin Fujin Kyōkai* (the New Women's Society) was formed by Raicho Hiratsuka and Fusae Ichikawa to lobby for the removal of the ban on women's attendance at political meetings. In 1922 both houses of the Diet approved a revision of the Peace Police Law that removed the restriction.

After the New Women's Society dissolved in 1924, Ichikawa and others formed a a broader organization, *Fusen-Kakutoku Dōmei* (Federation to Secure Women's Suffrage). The federation succeeded in having the House of Representatives pass in 1930 and 1931 a revision of electoral law giving women limited suffrage in local elections. This bill failed, however, in the conservative House of Peers and thus never became law before World War II. The federation itself was forced to dissolve under wartime regimentation in 1940.[20]

The main breakthroughs for women's rights came after Japan's defeat in World War II. The American occupation introduced suffrage for women in 1945, and the Japanese constitution promulgated in 1947 declared the principle of gender equality. These changes were brought in under American auspices, though it would be an exaggeration to regard them, as Pharr does, "as the accidental by-product of Japan's defeat in World War II."[21] Some Japanese groups actively supported these changes, and immediately after the defeat of World War II, even before the start of occupation, Japanese feminists had established a committee to promote women's rights. The group tried to persuade the Japanese government to introduce women's suffrage, and the Japanese Cabinet had, in fact, decided to promote it one day before the issuance of directives for five basic reforms, including women's suffrage, by the American occupation forces.[22] In November 1945 *Shin Nihon Fujin Dōmei* (New Japan Women's League) was established with Ichikawa as president. Renamed *Nihon Fujin Yūkensha Dōmei* (League of Women Voters of Japan) in 1951, it has actively promoted women's rights in Japan, even after Ichikawa's death in 1981.

With the consolidation of postwar Japanese democracy, many women's organizations have emerged, often associated with the "progressive" political parties or trade unions, as well as associations of women involved in various professions such as nursing and law. The women's associations with ties to labor unions and left parties (Socialists and Communists) have pressed for equality between men and women in the workplace, but they have failed to persuade either unions or left parties to consider gender equality a major issue. As a result, progressive parties and unions in Japan have not incorporated the issue of gender equality into their programs to the same degree as have their counterparts in Sweden.

Since the mid-1960s in Japan a number of civic movements on environmental protection, food safety, and other causes have emerged; many women have participated in such movements.[23] But although radical feminist movements appeared on the fringes of Japanese politics in the early 1970s, they have been weaker and less vocal than such movements in the United States.

Nonetheless, during the decade between 1975 and 1985, the United Nations Decade for Women (in the middle of which our survey was conducted), there was much debate and concern about gender equality in Japan. According to Hanako Nuita, three factors contributed to this.[24] The first was governmental (bureaucratic) initiative. The Women and Minors Bureau of the Labor Ministry, which was set up during the American occupation and survived the postoccupation backlash with the support of women's organizations,[25] promoted the Equal Employment for Men and

Women Law during the decade. Despite opposition by business and only lukewarm support from the governing LDP party, the law won passage in 1985. Its content, however, was diluted. In addition to passing this law, the government established during this period a Headquarters for Promoting Plans for Solving Women's Problems, headed by the prime minister. In 1975 it prepared a National Plan of Action to improve the status of women. The second factor in the debate about gender equality was the alliance of women's associations, which maintained independence from the government and exercised pressure through autonomous conventions and movements.[26] The third factor was mass media support for more equality for women.

The left parties in Japan raised the feminism issues earlier than did the LDP, although the left's commitment was always moderate. Before the 1970s LDP leaders were more likely to avow antifeminism. Since then, with international pressure to respond to the UN's call for gender equality, they have become more supportive of women's rights. Despite the LDP's commitment to traditionalist values, it has grudgingly endorsed legislation to comply with guidelines on gender equality adopted by the UN during the decade of women. The Socialist opposition has often criticized government proposals on these matters as insufficient, but the Socialists vote for them because they are better than nothing.

The three nations differ not only in the character of their feminist movements but also in the progress women have made in moving out of positions of traditional inequality. Our survey illustrates the relative advances in terms of the percentage of women respondents in the various elite groups in our survey. Except for party leaders in Sweden and the United States, where the samples included a substantial number of women as a reflection of deliberately designed party structures, our elite respondents were chosen not because of their gender but because of their positions. As material presented earlier indicates, the percentage of women among our leaders is rather low in all three countries but generally highest in Sweden, somewhat lower in the United States, and by far the lowest in Japan.[27] For example, 3 percent of the national business leaders in Sweden were women, 2 percent of the American ones, and none of the Japanese ones. (Interestingly, the proportion of women among leaders of farm and intellectual groups is higher in the United States than in Sweden.)

Data on the mass public regarding women's attitudes toward a change from traditional roles reflect the results of our survey. In a 1975 survey commissioned for the Japanese government, 83 percent of Japanese women agreed that it was a good rule that "the husband works outside and the wife takes care of the home." In a similar survey in 1982, 71 percent of women agreed. This latter figure compared with agreement among only 34 percent of American women and 13 percent of Swedish women surveyed as part of the same government-commissioned research.[28] In the 1975 survey 49 percent of Japanese married women said they wanted their male children to receive a university education, whereas only 19 percent wanted their female children to do so.[29]

Feminism and the Political System

New equality demands, such as those of the feminists, challenge the established distribution of benefits in a modern democracy. One might, therefore, hypothesize that established organizations, unhappy about sharing power or benefits, might resist new views. At the same time, however, in each of these countries there exist established organizations of the left that support equality-related changes, and these groups might welcome new feminist demands. To explore these alternative hypotheses, we will examine two questions: First, how great is the distance between feminist leaders and leaders of established organizations on issues of gender equality as well as on other equality issues? Second, how great is the difference on feminist issues among leaders of different established organizations themselves?

The answer to the first question will show how far outside the existing range of political and social attitudes leaders of groups raising new equality demands stand. The attitudes of feminist leaders—on issues of gender or economic equality or both—might be quite distinct from those of all established groups, including the established groups of the left. In that case feminists would truly be standing outside the system. Alternatively, the attitudes of feminist leaders on these issues might fall within the boundaries of political debate among established organizations—perhaps on the left side of established debate but nonetheless not outside those parameters. This in turn might be the result of past changes in views—either because feminists themselves were "tamed" and became more moderate or because leaders of established organizations modified their views to take account of feminist demands.

Before turning to the attitudes of feminist leaders and other leaders on issues of gender equality, we should note some differences in the national samples of feminists that have an impact on these observed differences. The American sample consists mostly of leaders of newly established feminist organizations. The Swedish sample, by contrast, includes leaders of the older Fredrika Bremer Federation, which has a reputation for non–Social Democratic leanings; indeed, results we presented earlier show that a majority of our Swedish feminist sample vote for nonsocialist parties and are more likely to know nonsocialist than Social Democratic politicians personally. One might contend, therefore, that the relative moderation of the Swedish feminists we report is an artifact of our sampling a predominantly nonsocialist group. We would, however, argue against that interpretation. We chose the Fredrika Bremer Federation as a source of feminists not because it was nonsocialist but because it is the major feminist organization in Sweden. The fact that the major Swedish feminist organization is moderate is itself a crucial part of the story we are telling.[30]

We should also explain that the sample of Japanese feminists included both leaders of feminist organizations and female leaders of Japanese citizens' movements. We can, however, distinguish between these two types of leaders on the basis of a question in the Japanese survey where respondents were asked what kind of organization was "most important" to them. This allowed us to distinguish between those leaders who listed feminist organizations as most important to them and those who listed other kinds of organizations. As we shall see, these two subparts of the feminist sample differ significantly in their views. It is also significant, however, that only about one-third of the sample of feminists said that they identified predominantly with feminist groups—an indication of the weakness of feminism in Japan.

The feminist leaders in one country are a different breed from those in another. They are located in different organizational structures with different histories. In each nation, therefore, the answers to the first question on positions of feminist leaders relative to those of established leaders will reveal how much mainstream political debate has encompassed the feminist movement. Figure 10.1 presents the relevant data on the positions of feminist leaders and of male leaders of political parties and business and labor organizations on the two feminism-related seven-point-scale questions that were asked in all three countries: whether women should stay at home to raise families or work outside the home and whether a failure by women to advance reflected failure to try hard or discrimination.[31]

On these two feminism questions the mean scores show that in Japan and the United States feminist leaders are considerably to the left of the leaders of the established left political party and to the left of trade union leaders. This appears to be even more strongly the case in the United States than in Japan. These results change, however, when we refine the Japanese data by differentiating between those feminist leaders who are in

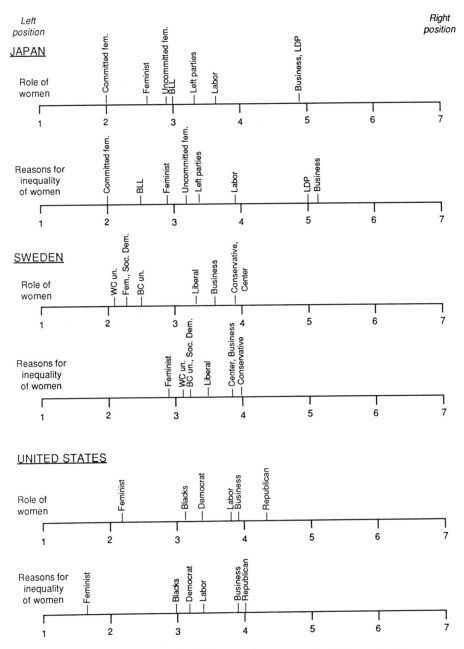

Figure 10.1. Mean scores on feminism questions among feminists and male leaders

our sample because of their identification with decidedly feminist organizations and those who are leaders of civic organizations. This comparison is found in Figure 10.1 where we distinguish between these two types of feminist leaders in Japan. The feminists who define themselves as committed are much farther to the left of the left party; they fall in a position quite similar to that of the American feminists. In Sweden, by contrast, we do not find feminist leaders in such a distinct position. The views of feminists are quite similar to those of Social Democratic and trade union leaders, both blue-collar and white-collar.

This difference between the United States and Japan on the one side and Sweden on the other arises not from differences among the views of feminists but from differences in the views of the leaders of the left party and the trade unions. Although one must be careful in directly comparing responses to a given question in different countries, the mean scores on the question about the proper role for women are very similar for the feminist leaders in all three countries. The differences among the countries in the distance of these leaders from the leaders of the established left arises from differences in the position of leaders of established left organizations. In Sweden, leaders of the established left organizations strongly endorsed feminist positions. In the United States and Japan, these leaders were on average more cautious in supporting feminist demands than were feminist leaders themselves. On the question of reasons for the inequality of women, the pattern differs in that American feminist leaders take a very radical view.

We followed this same procedure for the two radical redistribution questions we highlighted earlier in Chapter 4, to see whether feminist leaders were outside the mainstream of established parties and organizations on equality-related issues other than feminism. The results in Figure 10.2 show that American feminist leaders are outside the mainstream of established debate not only on issues of gender equality but on other equality-related issues as well. In Japan, by contrast, feminist views on issues of radical redistribution resemble those of the established organizations of the left. They are, in other words, within the left mainstream. In Sweden, feminist leaders take center to slightly right of center positions on issues of radical redistribution.

In addition to looking at whether feminist leaders fall outside the mainstream, we considered whether demands for gender equality fall within the already existing cleavage structures within each nation. We were concerned with the extent to which these demands are encompassed by the existing party system and the issues that differentiate the parties. One

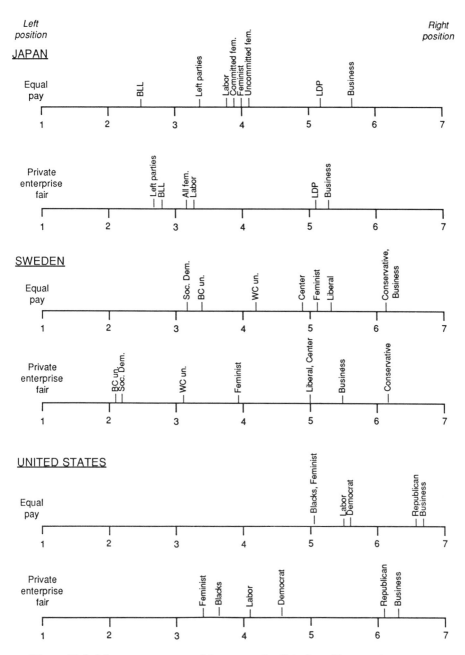

Figure 10.2. Mean scores on equal-income and political-conflict questions among feminists and male leaders

measure of this would be how much the leaders of the major parties differ on these new issues: feminist demands might crosscut existing sources of cleavage, thus dividing existing parties and organizations internally. Views about feminism would then not display the same patterns of partisan support and opposition that characterize more traditional equality-related issues. Alternatively, feminist demands might fall into existing patterns of partisan cleavage either because these demands naturally fit into the existing cleavage pattern (like the issue of abortion in a country whose party system is divided between Catholics and anticlericals) or because the parties had succeeded in redefining the issue in terms of existing cleavage patterns. The distinction is important: in the former case, the issue just happens to coincide with the traditional cleavage pattern between parties, although that coincidence may be not without consequence; in the latter case, the parties actively appropriate a new issue. This distinction, as we shall see, differentiates the party responses in Japan and Sweden.

Data on this subject appear in Table 10.1, which is based on the data displayed in Figure 10.1 that reports the mean attitudes on the questions dealing with the role of women and gender equality. Table 10.1 shows that left and right party leaders are generally relatively far apart on feminism issues in Sweden and Japan, relatively close in the United States. A similar difference across the nations is found between the two established cleavage groups in each nation, business and labor.[32]

These results are confirmed by data displayed in Table 10.2. There we compare across the nations the ability of partisan affiliation to predict the positions on the feminism factor of the members of the established organizations. We present similar data on the ability of partisanship to predict attitudes on our welfare-state scale—chosen because it represents the traditional dimension on which political parties differ.[33] Thus we can see

Table 10.1.   Distance between left and right groups on feminism issues

	Role of women		Reason for inequality	
	Distance between left and right parties	Distance between labor[a] and business	Distance between left and right parties	Distance between labor[a] and business
Japan	1.5	1.1	1.5	1.6
Sweden	1.6	1.2	0.8	0.6
United States	0.4	0.1	0.8	0.5

a. In Sweden these are blue-collar union leaders.

Table 10.2. Relative importance of party affiliation on different political dimensions
(United States and Sweden, entire sample of males
in established organizations, beta weights)[a]

Issue	Japan	Sweden	United States
Traditional welfare state	.54	.78	.59
Feminism	.54	.58	.27

a. The regression equation also included the following as independent variables: age, sex, income, education, father's education, mother's education (United States and Sweden only). Beta weights for these variables are not reported here.

Table 10.3. Correlation between scores on traditional
welfare-state and feminism factors
(entire sample, established groups only)

Japan	.45
Sweden	.55
United States	.31

whether partisans divide on the newer issue of gender equality in the same way that they divide on the more traditional issues of economic welfare. The data in Table 10.2 are beta weights for party affiliation in the three countries in regression equations for leaders of established organizations. The dependent variables are factor scores on welfare-state issues and feminism issues respectively; and the independent variables, in addition to party affiliation, are sex, age, income, and education.

In Japan, party affiliation does as well in explaining feminism factor scores as it does in explaining welfare-state factor scores. In Sweden, party does not explain feminism scores quite as well as it explains welfare-state scores. The drop-off in Sweden, however, is less significant than in the United States, where party affiliation does a much poorer job of explaining attitudes on feminism issues than it does on the welfare-state issues around which partisan cleavages traditionally were formed. Moreover, as Table 10.3 shows, the correlation between factor scores on the welfare-state factor and those on the feminism factor is considerably higher in Sweden and Japan than in the United States.

The data indicate that party differences are more closely aligned with positions on feminism in Japan and Sweden than in the United States. In the United States, the parties, divided on traditional welfare-state issues, did not, initially, differentiate in a similar manner on gender issues. In Japan and Sweden, we find greater partisan differentiation between the parties: party leaders differ on matters of gender equality, and the partisan affiliation of other leaders is closely correlated with their views on gender equality.

Sweden and Japan are, nevertheless, far from identical in this respect. In Sweden, the alignment of partisanship with gender position is part of a distinct set of policy positions taken by the parties—in particular, the effort of the Social Democratic party to embrace gender equality and to make it a concomitant of a more general and traditional position on social and economic equality. In Japan, the partisan difference appears to derive less from deliberate position taking by the parties than from partisan cleavage on the question of "traditional Japanese culture" versus "progressive Western culture." Westernization represented more of a culture shock to Japan than to Western countries, and many westernizing reforms (including an improved status for women) were introduced under foreign occupation. It is, therefore, hardly surprising that attitudes toward westernization divided Japanese parties earlier than Western party systems. (As a result, despite the Socialists' economic policies, better-educated people and white-collar workers in Japan are more likely than their counterparts in most other countries to vote for the left, because of sympathy with their views on westernizing values.)[34]

Gender equality falls naturally into that existing source of partisan cleavage. The parties did not have to do anything new to adapt to the issue. On questions of radical redistribution, as we have stated, Japanese feminists, unlike their counterparts in either the United States or Sweden, look like the mainstream Japanese left. This further suggests that feminism as an ideology, and feminists as people, fit well with established left ideology in Japan. Yet Japanese feminists (especially those from feminist organizations) take positions on feminist issues to the left of the left party. Thus the established left in Japan appears unwilling to move farther in the direction of the feminists than they might anyway be inclined to go.

Feminism and the Political System in the Three Countries

Our data provide some confirmation for the view that support for feminism is less widespread among Japanese leaders than among American and Swedish leaders, although the statement needs qualifications. The views of feminist leaders themselves, on both the questions of whether it is better for women to work outside the home and of whether women are held back by discrimination, are surprisingly similar in the three countries (Figure 10.3). Furthermore (again bearing in mind the caution with which intercountry comparisons on a given question must be interpreted), the views of Japanese Socialists and union leaders differ little on these two questions from those of their American counterparts, although the Japanese are considerably less profeminist than Swedish Social Democrats and unionists. The big difference is in the attitudes of conservative groups in Japan compared with those in the other two countries: liberal Democratic and business leaders in Japan are more conservative on feminism issues, by a fairly wide margin, than their American and Swedish counterparts. These Japanese leaders clearly stand on the conservative end of the scale on both questions, whereas their counterparts in the United States and Sweden hover around the center. In addition, Japanese Socialist leaders have about the same views on feminism issues as American Democratic leaders. This similarity suggests the relative conservatism of the Japanese left on feminism issues, because the Japanese Socialists are usually much more liberal than American Democrats.

In looking at the reaction of the political system to new feminist demands—taken here as an example of how the political systems of the three countries react to new demands posed to them—we see Sweden and the United States as polar cases. In Sweden, there were strong feminist currents in the society, and the party system succeeded in channeling the currents. By interpreting feminist demands as another example of demands for greater economic and social equality, the Swedish Social Democrats succeeded in overcoming potential resistance from culturally conservative working-class supporters. Cleavages on feminism in the Swedish political system closely resemble cleavages on more traditional equality issues. Furthermore, feminists themselves did not stay outside the political system; they had a champion in the Social Democrats, and their own views were relatively moderate.

The American data paint a different picture. In the United States, as in Sweden, feminist currents were strong. But unlike Sweden, the United States has a relatively weak party system. The parties were unwilling and unable to channel the issue, at least as of the time of our survey. The data show that party affiliation explains some of the cleavages on feminism in the United States, with Democrats somewhat more to the left and Republicans somewhat more to the right, but party explains feminism cleavages much more poorly in the United States than in Sweden (or than in the United States itself on traditional welfare-state issues). In the United States demographic factors such as age, education, and sex explain more

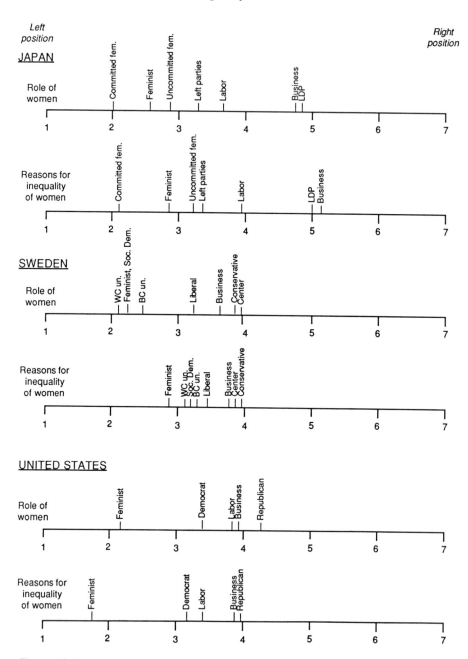

Figure 10.3. Mean scores on feminism questions among party samples (males
only) and feminists

of the variance in attitudes. Without a strong champion in the existing system and with the party system playing a relatively small role redefining the issue along traditional cleavage lines, feminist leaders in the United States remained somewhat outside of and more radical than the established system, not only on feminist issues but on other issues as well.

The Japanese case is somewhat intermediate. It shows feminists standing outside and to the left of the established system as in the United States (especially if we identify the small group of feminist leaders from decidedly feminist organizations). But we also find party doing as good a job of organizing attitudes on feminism as in Sweden. We have interpreted these results as an indication that feminism simply has had less impact on the established Japanese political system. Attitudes on feminism track traditional partisan cleavages in Japan not because some part of the established political system has worked actively to make that happen by interpreting feminist demands in a way that makes them consistent with traditional partisan cleavages, as in Sweden, but because in the Japanese political system feminism is not a source of crosscutting cleavages in the first place. One traditional source of partisan cleavage in Japan has been around issues involving traditionalist values, and feminism easily fits into that established cleavage pattern without the need for the parties to do much. Nonetheless, Japanese feminists still stand more outside the political system. Although the issue reproduces the normal pattern of partisan cleavage in Japan, the center of gravity of the debate is somewhat to the right. Socialist leaders have not moved nearly as close to feminist leaders as have Social Democratic leaders in Sweden. Japanese feminists are more isolated.

That the United States has a relatively weak party system and Sweden a relatively strong one is not new information. What is, however, interesting to observe is the impact of those differences in the strength of party systems on the ability to organize and take control of new equality issues such as feminism. Such an ability in turn has implications for the ability of the political system to respond to such new demands. By giving feminists a strong champion in the existing system, the Swedish party system encouraged resolution of feminist demands. It also encouraged feminists to direct their attention to working within the political system rather than casting stones on the system from the outsider's position that was the fate of their sisters, initially at least, in the United States.

11

Conclusion

We began this book by describing some intriguing differences among three nations in their degree of economic inequality. We also considered differences in other forms of inequality: inequality in influence over politics, inequality between women and men, and inequality between dominant majority groups and disadvantaged racial, ethnic, and other minority groups. How does one explain such differences? Not, we believe, by any single factor or in any simple way. There are multiple inequalities, they are closely related one to another, they have many sources. As political scientists, we are particularly interested in how various kinds of inequality affect politics and how government policies affect inequality. These concerns led us to consider elite values. There are many other factors to weigh if one wants a full view of the struggle over inequality, but values play a central role.

We have presented a great deal of data about such values. Before considering the implications of these data for the puzzle posed at the beginning of this book, we shall summarize what we have found. The empirical findings are, we believe, of great interest.

Summary of Major Empirical Findings

Our data provide a good deal of information about inequality in the three nations under study. As in any comparative study across nations, we find likenesses as well as differences among the nations. And as in most comparative studies, the more interesting likenesses are those in which particular patterns within nations recur across the nations—where, for instance, groups differ in similar ways from nation to nation, or various types of equality display similar differences one from the other in each country.

Who are the leaders? In all three nations leaders tend to be male, well educated, and middle-aged or older. They have high-status occupations and come from families with relatively high status. The exceptions are leaders of organizations with a particular occupational clientele such as labor unions and farm organizations.

Women are greatly underrepresented in leadership positions in all nations, especially in established organizations. They have had the least success in business. Women attain a significant share of leadership positions only in women's organizations and in organizations, such as some political parties, that have a special section or particular positions allocated to women. Our data show, however, that women have moved into leadership positions in other sectors with more success in Sweden and the United States than in Japan.

Leaders' political influence and activity. The various leadership groups are well positioned politically. They are acquainted with a wide range of political figures and are politically active in ways that the mass public is not. In all three nations we find a uniform pattern as to the modes of access and activity of the leadership groups. Leaders of challenging groups know people in the government but they are less likely than established business leaders to know people in the bureaucracy or high in the executive ranks. Instead, these challenging leaders have more ties among legislative representatives and people from the media. As a result, they lean toward outsider rather than insider activity. They use legislative rather than executive channels, and they more often try to influence the public than to influence governmental insiders.

Attitudes toward the welfare state and redistribution. We found patterns of consensus on some matters, disagreement on others, and the issues on which there is consensus or disagreement vary from nation to nation. The United States stands out somewhat from the other two nations: leaders disagree about the basic social policies of the welfare state but agree on issues of redistribution; all groups, including the most radical, oppose redistributive policies. In the other two countries, all groups accept the basic programs of the welfare state, but they disagree on redistribution. Thus in Sweden and Japan, redistribution is in question; in the United States, it is out of the question.

In each nation the various groups take predictable stands on these issues: labor and left parties generally favor the welfare state and redistribution, business and right parties usually oppose such policies. But two interesting exceptions to these stands form a mirror image of each other. In the United States, we find evidence for the well-known exception to the pattern of political attitudes in Europe: leaders of the party of the left, the Democrats, and leaders of labor unions reject the idea of income redistribution. In Sweden, there is also an exception to general patterns found elsewhere: the business community and the Conservative party support the welfare state.

Structure of equality attitudes. In all three nations we find a similar structure of attitudes toward equality. Attitudes toward the social support functions of the welfare state form a separate dimension from attitudes toward radical redistribution. Apparently leaders in all three nations conceive of distribution and redistribution as quite different policies. This split is consistent with the differences among the nations in the patterns of consensus and disagreement outlined above: in each nation the pattern of attitudes on radical redistribution differs from that on the welfare state.

In addition, the issue dimension of quotas is differentiated from that of attitudes on gender equality and on equality for ascriptive groups such as American blacks and the buraku people. Although the issue of quotas may arise in connection with such groups—indeed, our questions were about quotas for such groups—a quota policy apparently has a special character in people's eyes and stands apart from the attitudes toward the groups for whom the quotas would be applied.

Income equality. We found that Sweden differed from the other two countries in attitudes toward income equality. In Japan and the United States, all leadership groups believe that the income gap between the highest and lowest earners should be narrowed by cutting income at the top and raising it at the bottom. In Sweden, however, a number of groups propose raising incomes across the board. There is division as to whether the executive's salary—that is, the salary of the highest wage earner—should decrease or increase. Unlike the situation in the other two nations, only the more left groups in Sweden would cut an executive's salary, and many others would raise it.

Sweden thus presents an anomaly in relation to income equality. At first glance it appears that Sweden is least supportive of income equality: many groups are willing to see the difference between top and bottom earners increased. But when we looked at the actual equality achieved in Sweden, we found that Swedes have a much more egalitarian attitude toward income differentiation. They are reacting to a much more egalitarian reality. Even those who want the present gap to increase opt for a much narrower income disparity than that desired by the most egalitarian groups in the other nations.

Indeed, attitudes toward the appropriate size of the income gap vary widely within nations and even more widely among nations. Among the three nations the sharpest contrast is between Sweden and the United States. Although the more and less egalitarian groups accept substantially different earnings gaps, the ranges among the groups within each nation do not overlap: the most egalitarian group in the United States favors a wider income gap than that favored by the most conservative group in Sweden. The boundaries of what would be acceptable public policy are drawn quite differently in the two nations.

The data on income equality highlight an important feature of equality attitudes. The views that individuals hold on appropriate income disparity vary substantially across groups within each nation and across the nations as well. Yet there is a compelling uniformity in their pattern: individuals appear to take as a given the existing income differentials in each nation. These of course vary substantially, but within the framework set by the local pattern individuals use similar standards to evaluate those differentials. For instance, we found that leadership groups all tend to take the same position on the proper ratio of their own income to that of the executive at the top of the income hierarchy and to that of the lowest-paid worker at the bottom. Groups at various places on the income hierarchy want executives to have the same *relative* income to their own, although this implies wide differences in the *absolute* income of executives. The ratio that leaders desire between their own incomes and those of executives differs from nation to nation in a manner consistent with the actual differentiation in each case—somewhat less than 4:1 in the United States, a little less than 2:1 in Sweden, and a somewhat more varied figure in Japan that falls between the other two. In all nations leaders tended to prefer a ratio of their own earnings to those of workers at the bottom of the hierarchy that closely resembles the status quo. The highest-paid and lowest-paid among the leaders, the most conservative and radical, believe that their income advantage over the lowest-paying occupation is about right. They want to raise the earnings of the lowest-paid worker, but they would also raise their own earnings enough to maintain the same proportionality. In short, they apply a common standard of evaluation to a very different set of national contexts.

Another illustration of the way in which attitudes on equality are adjusted to context—in this case to differing national policy contexts—is found in attitudes regarding who is to blame for income inequality. We found a striking similarity across the nations in the positions of counterpart groups. In each country right groups differ in a similar manner from left groups in assigning blame for poverty to individuals rather than to the social and political system. Moreover, we found this despite the vast differences in the patterns of policy in each nation (the U.S. system allows much more room for individual failure than does the Swedish), as well as differences in the general cultural norms of individualism versus social responsibility. Within these differing contexts the leaders array themselves along a similar spectrum. Their views are relatively as far apart within the different contexts established by local policy.

Political equality. The analysis of attitudes on the equality of political influence revealed several important cross-national patterns. First, we found that groups generally overrate the influence of their opponents and underrate that of their allies. The strongest pattern is for groups to deny their own influence, especially among those groups that are the most firmly established. Groups with the most established and routinized channels of political influence are the least likely to acknowledge that they are in fact exercising such influence. In all three countries the main such group is business. Labor unions are also included in Sweden and the United States, but not in Japan where labor is less connected to the regime. An established group's denial of its influence implies that the conflict about influence is often about perceptions rather than about norms— about who has rather than about who should have political influence.

A second finding is the uniformly high position assigned to the media's influence by respondents in all three nations. The media are ranked at or very near the top of the influence hierarchy by most groups in all three nations. Yet unlike other groups, leaders in the media do not deny their high position. They are also unique in wanting to see their influence reduced.

Political and economic equality. Although there was variation among the nations in the amount of equality leaders want, we found substantial similarity across nations in the way that political and economic equality are viewed. In general, leaders tolerate a wider income than influence gap between those at the top and those at the bottom. Leaders from across the ideological spectrum would lower the position of the people at the top of each hierarchy and raise that of those at the bottom, thereby narrowing the disparity in income and influence. But in the case of influence the change would be much greater; they would usually overturn the hierarchical order of the groups. In relation to income they would keep the order of differences as it has been.

There are apparently two reasons for this. First, the conflict over influence is a constant-sum conflict where relative position counts; for income, the other person's high position does not necessarily redound to one's disadvantage. Second, the absence of a clear metric for influence means that groups have widely disparate perceptions as to who is in fact most influential; they have disagreements about reality that are as great or greater than their disagreements over who should have influence. The result of this is, we suggest, that egalitarian political norms are not likely to lead to egalitarian outcomes because groups will disagree substantially as to what kind of change in the influence structure will lead to more political equality. Moreover, we conclude that conflict over political influence, because of the disparities in perception and because of its constant-sum characteristic, will be more intense than conflicts over economic position.

Gender equality. Our analysis of attitudes toward gender equality uncovered a wide difference among the nations in the extent to which gender issues have become salient and in the degree to which equality between women and men is a high value. In addition, we found a variation among the nations in the role of the major political parties. In Sweden, the issue of gender equality has been incorporated by the ruling Social Democratic party into a more general egalitarian policy orientation. In Japan, although the political parties did not take as explicit a position on such issues, the coincidence between the new gender issues and the issues of traditional values that separate the main parties has led to a closer articulation of the gender issues with traditional party differences. By contrast, in the United States, the issue of gender equality grew up largely outside of the party system—although in the 1980s greater partisan differences have emerged.

Values and Equality

Values are, we believe, an important and somewhat neglected reason that these nations differ in the degree of inequality. Basic beliefs about social justice, passed on through processes of socialization that begin early in life and continue through the life cycle, play an important role in determining public and private decisions relating to inequality. We do not argue that such values are immutable; as our chapter on the history of inequality in the three nations made clear, values do not change easily but they do change. Nor do we argue that a society inevitably reaches consensus on such values; our data have shown some of the contours of value conflict over inequality among elite groups in each nation. Instead, we contend that values are not merely dependent or intervening variables but autonomous forces.

They are, however, only part of the story. Economists stress the importance of market factors in determining levels of inequality, and we would not deny their relevance. The differences across the nations in income inequality reflect changing labor markets in each country as well as the changing position of the nations in the international economy. Nor are the noneconomic aspects of equality unaffected by market forces: the rise of a gender-equality issue in each of the nations is in part a response to changing economies that have drawn women into the labor market.

In addition to values and market forces, the political and social structures that exist in the nations play an important role. Examples of the way in which such structures channel the equality issues are found in each of the nations. In Sweden, the strong political party system channeled the demands for gender equality into the political system as part of the more general struggle between the political parties. The Social Democrats, by defining gender equality as a component of a broad party program for equality, inhibited the emergence of an autonomous feminist movement such as that in the United States. This had significant effects on the nature of the equality debate in Sweden. An even clearer example of a structural feature that is not itself a reflection of either values or market forces is found in Japan. The extension of the franchise to women, the legalization of labor unions, and land reform all are the result of decisions made under the American occupation, and these features, in turn, affect the nature of the equality issue. Of course, these reforms from outside could not work alone. The structural reforms were not totally incongruent with the group-cohesion emphasis in traditional Japanese values. Furthermore, the changes were reinforced and finally consolidated by the growing power of groups such as labor unions, women, and the buraku people who were the beneficiaries of the structural reforms. In addition, the high rate of economic growth in Japan helped to strengthen and stabilize the reforms.

Values, market forces, and political and social structures all combine to influence the shape of public policies on inequality. These combinations help to explain why generalizations about such policies are often whittled away by exceptions when one looks closely at any particular policy. Values do not lead to policies, nor do market forces. And particular structures do not entail particular outcomes. Rather the three components interact, creating at best tendencies rather than determinate solutions. Furthermore, the resulting policies reciprocally influence the three components that shape them. Public policies often lead to the creation of social and political structures that have a life of their own. Similarly public policies affect the working of the market. From our own perspective the most important effect of policies is on values. The Swedish elites, who almost unanimously support a level of equality beyond that supported by the most radical egalitarians in the other two nations, are clearly responding to a social consensus formed by decades of public policy. And, of course, those policies were influenced at their origin and have been influenced in their further evolution by values, market forces, and social and political structures.

The domains of equality are linked, for values in one domain have an impact on the values in another. As we have shown, people are more likely to be radical egalitarians in political matters than in economic. Part of this depends on a belief that political equalization will benefit them, but part appears based on a genuine belief that political rights ought to be equal in a democracy. Equality of political rights, in turn, may call into question inequality in other domains. Political rights challenge caste when universal political rights are juxtaposed against inequalities based on race or ethnic group membership. Political rights challenge class when the scope of citizenship expands to encompass social and economic well-being.[1] These examples suggest a potential strain toward congruence: equality in one place leading to equality elsewhere; inequality here fostering inequality there.

The challenge of equality in one domain to inequality in another appears manifested as a clash of values: if we believe in political equality for all as expressed in our political ideology, our constitution, and our schools, how can we deny economic equality to those less well off? But the challenge also works through institutional means. The extension of the vote to those previously denied it does not create full political equality, but it certainly creates a more equal polity than one in which the vote is limited to one gender, or one class, or one race. The franchise helped create the welfare state—whether it be the thorough welfare state created by the Social Democrats in Sweden or the more limited welfare state created by the New Deal Democrats in the United States. In each case the party that instituted the welfare-state programs acted in accord with the needs and preferences of its electoral constituency. The support coalition is different for Japan's governing conservative party, the LDP, but it also has had to cater to electorally powerful groups such as farmers and small merchants. It has raised the level of national health insurance, and in the 1960s it created a national pension scheme covering the self-employed and their families in addition to the already existing program for wage earners. The enfranchisement of an economically disadvantaged group is neither necessary nor sufficient for the development of policies beneficial to it. In fact, some welfare measures preceded universal suffrage (Bismarck instituted some of the earliest), and many welfare measures have had their origins in bureaucracies rather than in party politics and pressures from the electorate. Nor is the vote equivalent to control over policy. But the exercise of the franchise certainly helps a group to receive positive attention from the government.

The equality domains, however, are not joined in lockstep. As the history of the evolution of equality in the three nations indicates, periods of great change in one domain may or may not coincide with change in other domains. In the United States, commitment to political equality far exceeds the commitment to economic. Periods of egalitarian fervor often stressed political rather than economic leveling. Most historical controversies over equality have ended with increased political but hardly changed economic equality. In Sweden today there is continuing debate over whether economic leveling has gone too far, but political democracy and the equality of political rights it entails are not called into question. And, in Japan and Sweden, there have been long periods of political inequality—periods of hierarchical dominance supported by deference values—that facilitated state intervention in reducing economic and social hierarchy.

The partial linkage between political and economic equality embodied in the above historical examples and explicated in a more general way in Chapter 9 helps to explain why political democracy does not automatically lead to economic leveling. Even when formal political rights have been equalized and are generally accepted as appropriate, economic inequality can remain and be accepted as well.

Economic and Political Equality: The Disjunction

There are a number of reasons why political equality, even when accepted, does not translate into economic equality. That excessive economic equality would be costly in terms of overall economic performance appears to be recognized by our respondents. Although they clearly differ on how much economic inequality is excessive, they agree in rejecting an absolute leveling of income at the expense of the ability to reward effort and talent. All but the most radical leaders—and in the United States all, including the most radical, leaders—support substantial income differentiation among occupations.

Another reason involves the gap between formal political rights and their actual use. Equal political rights represent a formal guarantee but such rights are differentially used. Hierarchy in the social and economic sphere—that is, the fact that some have more educational and economic resources—may "subvert" the equality in the political sphere as those resources are deployed for political goals. Much depends, however, on the structure of political competition. If the disadvantaged members of society are not only active, but active in ways that reflect that disadvantage—in working-class-based organizations and parties, for instance—their political activity is more likely to be translated into policies that deal with their economic circumstances.[2] What appears to determine whether a nation will adopt egalitarian policies is not whether the working class is given the franchise or whether they vote, but whether they vote for and elect a Socialist government.[3] That fact, of course, does not diminish the importance of the exercise of the franchise. Disadvantaged groups cannot vote for parties that will try to reverse that disadvantage unless they have the right to the franchise and exercise that right. But whom they vote for is also significant.

A third reason that political equality does not easily translate into economic equality lies in the relationship between values and perceptions. As suggested above, one would expect the general acceptance of political equality to create a strain toward equality in the economic sphere. For the economically disadvantaged, political equality provides a rhetoric to justify demands for equality in income and opportunity. It creates, as well, the expectation that they deserve a better deal in the economy. For those at the top of the economic hierarchy, the acceptance of political equality might create, at minimum, a need to justify the incongruity between the presence of equality in one domain and its absence elsewhere. But it need not work that way. People tolerate a good deal of inconsistency among values: no logical necessity that the same standards apply in the political and economic realms and no psychological necessity either, especially if the incongruity is to one's own advantage.

Furthermore, values about equality create pressures for change when there is a gap between ideal and reality. But that gap depends on the perception of reality. As we have seen, perceptions are often quite disparate—especially in relation to political equality. In the United States, more than in the other nations, a strong ideology of political equality coexists with accepted economic inequality and public policies that maintain this inequality. Such a situation might put those at the top of the economic hierarchy in an uncomfortable position. They consider economic inequality justified, but might they not be undone by their commitment to equality of political rights? First, they would have a harder time justifying wide disparities in economic position if these disparities were among people otherwise equal in political rights. Second, they could not easily oppose measures that gave actual political equality to all, but such political equality might result in a weakening of their economic position. It is here that the perceptions of political influence play a role. Those at the top in economic terms might be in an uncomfortable position, were it not for the fact that they believe themselves to be disadvantaged in political terms. Rather than focusing on the inconsistency between the political and the economic rights of the disadvantaged, they focus on their own perceived political disadvantage. They see no reason to extend more political rights to the disadvantaged because they believe them to have a superfluity already. Their position—and the view of American business is a perfect example—is: "Of course, we believe in equal political rights. Give us ours!"

Lastly, we can point to a paradox revealed by our analysis of the history of governmental intervention to foster equality in each of the nations. Egalitarian values in politics may increase the political potential of the disadvantaged by giving them the franchise and by calling into question the legitimacy of a concentration of political influence in the established sectors of society. They also create a norm of equality that can spill over into the economic sphere (subject to the problems of perception mentioned above). But those same egalitarian political values can undercut the ability of the government to carry out programs of redistribution. The norms of political equality can challenge and limit the authority of the government itself.

Our consideration of the history of equality in the three nations indicates that political inequality may foster economic equality. In Japan and Sweden, hierarchical political relations paradoxically helped create economic equality. Their citizens' deference to authority legitimated, and still legitimates, strong government. In Sweden, this fostered the acceptance of the redistributionist policies of the Social Democratic party during its four decades in office. Without a strong state—a hierarchical state—less would have been accomplished toward such redistribution.[4] In Japan, the state has not been as active in fostering egalitarian policies, but the bureaucracy—the hierarchical political institution par excellence—has established programs for deprived groups such as the buraku people and women. Similarly, as we have argued, the relatively equal structure of earnings in postwar Japan is in part the result of guidance by the Japanese bureaucracy in setting model-wage standards. The contrast of Japan and Sweden makes clear that a strong government can introduce egalitarian policies, but it does not necessarily do so. The government's values and ideology make all—or most of—the difference. If there had been a different government in Japan—perhaps a Social Democratic government—

instead of the LDP, the shape of policy might be quite different. In any case, such a government would have had the means to carry out alternative policies.

By contrast, in the United States the tradition of political equality—a tradition closely connected with an individualistic ethos and opposition to strong state power—has inhibited the development of policies of state intervention to create equality of result. It takes a strong government to introduce redistributive policies, and one central thread in the almost universal American opposition to redistributive policies as well as in the widespread opposition to traditional welfare-state policies is opposition to the powerful government such policies require.

The Future of Equality

Distribution is easier than redistribution. If the economic pie is growing, all can receive more; or, at least, some can receive more without forcing others to receive less. Thus a strong economy makes equalizing income distributions less painful but still far from inevitable. The data are in dispute, but it does appear that the enormous increase in income since World War II has not been universally accompanied by an equivalent change in the distribution of income: in Sweden, there has been substantial leveling of the income distribution; in Japan, the change has been more limited; in the United States, the income distribution has remained remarkably steady despite a massive change in the overall standard of living.

Despite these differences, each nation has experienced an era in which equality has been high on the political agenda. Although income redistribution has not been a main issue in Japan and the United States, equality demands by blacks in the United States, by the buraku people in Japan, and by women in both countries have come to the fore.

In recent years the forward motion of equality has slowed. The economic pie no longer expands as it once did. Overextended economies, caught in the squeeze of inflationary pressures and the demands for greater welfare benefits, have cut back on social programs and held the line on wage increases. Both conservative and social democratic regimes have done so, the former happily and the latter reluctantly. Labor unions, a major force for equality, have weakened; their membership has declined and their bargaining power has diminished because of unemployment. This decline has taken place in all three countries, although they differ substantially in the initial strength of egalitarian parties and unions. In addition, structural changes associated with roller-coaster energy costs, shifts in the relative strengths of old and new industries within nations, and changes in the relative international competitiveness of industries among nations influence distributional policies and outcomes in each nation.

The challenges to egalitarian policies may derive from similar economic strains but they take place in different settings and have different consequences. Normative beliefs as to the appropriate level of income inequality set limits on the variation that economic forces or political decisions can introduce. We have seen this in each of the three nations. In the first chapter we argued that, although our data were collected at one point in time, we believe that they have long-term validity—that they reflect patterns of values about equality which, although not immutable, do not swiftly change. Our studies were conducted in the latter half of the 1970s. Each of the nations we study has undergone political and economic changes since then, but in each case the nature of these changes bears the stamp of the value patterns we have discussed.

United States. The election of Ronald Reagan in 1980 has been described as revolutionary, representing a fundamental change in the approach of the American government to issues of welfare and equality. The major feature of Reaganism is a strong, ideological commitment to restore the autonomy of the market by limiting the role of government. This strategy involves policies of reducing (or, at least, not increasing) taxes, simplifying the tax code, and decreasing government regulations, and at the same time reducing welfare programs for the poor and disadvantaged. The Reagan years represent a movement of political influence away from disadvantaged challenging groups—blacks and other minorities and women—and toward business and the affluent. In addition, the long dominance of the Democratic party in the electorate has been seriously threatened, if not shattered.

There is no doubt that the Reagan years represent a major change in America. The balance of political power between the two political parties and between the haves and the have-nots has changed in significant ways. On the economic side, there has been significant change as well. A gradual redistribution appears to have taken place in the 1970s, a result of the income-transfer effect of government welfare policies as well as inflation-driven "bracket creep" that made income taxes more redistributive. But this trend has reversed under the Reagan administration because of limits on welfare policies as well as changes in tax policy.[5] The changes are significant and represent a major reversal of the thrust of four decades of social policy.

Yet this change has fallen well within the normative boundaries set by values about equality in America. The free market ideology that President Reagan invokes reflects a continuous and dominant belief in equality of opportunity, a belief expressed across the full spectrum of groups in America. His application of that ideology is more controversial, but even that controversy is consistent with American values, in particular with what we have shown to be disagreement among groups as to the scope and legitimacy of the welfare state. Although it has cut back welfare services, the Reagan administration has maintained a commitment to some, albeit minimal, governmental welfare functions. Thus the values that the Reagan administration invokes are in no way revolutionary; they are deeply embedded in the American tradition of equality of opportunity in an uncontrolled market, little or no redistribution, but some responsibility for the welfare of the "deserving poor." Indeed, even the reversal of the modest redistributive effects of the Great Society programs fits into the historical pattern of American conflicts over equality. Periods of egalitarian surge in America have generally resulted in little economic redistribution. The egalitarian result of the Great Society, for example, was somewhat anomalous. Furthermore, as with earlier egalitarian periods, the enduring result of the Great Society may be its effect on the equality of political influence.[6] The Voting Rights Act of the 1960s made black Americans full participants in the electoral process which, in turn, has had a major effect on the political transformation of the American South. Although the Reagan administration has dragged its feet in enforcing those rights, there is no sign of a reversal of the enfranchisement of southern blacks.[7] As at previous points in American history, the stronger commitment of the American people to political over economic equality is manifest.

Sweden. In Sweden, as in the United States, the reaction to the economic difficulties of the 1970s was conditioned by the underlying structure of values about equality. As noted earlier, some Swedes argued that the welfare state had gone too far and that Sweden needed more market-oriented policies. And the climate of Swedish society has changed during the past decade; there is more talk of entrepreneurship and less of equality. The Social Democrats now openly state that wages cannot rise until the economy is in order, that there is little room for new social reforms, and that social benefits are not sacrosanct. Sweden in 1986 is a chastened nation, trying to discover whether it can continue to combine high growth with high aspirations to equalize people's conditions.

A fascinating illustration of the changes in Swedish society over the past decade is the fate of a proposal to use company profits to buy public shares in Swedish companies. First proposed in 1976 by the blue-collar union LO, the project was called the Meidner Plan after the union official who authored it, or, more generally in Sweden, *löntagarfonder* or wage-earner funds. Originally, the proposal called for gradually socializing much of Swedish industry by having a worker-controlled fund acquire a majority share of company stock. Government-passed laws, the argument went, had proved insufficient to equalize power in the workplace. The time had come to address the ownership question.

But wage-earner funds became a major political millstone for the Social Democrats, and in the course of the debate the party changed its arguments. As the political climate shifted, all talk of wage-earner funds as a revolutionary change in Swedish society disappeared. Instead, the Social Democrats argued that the funds would be a way to ensure that profits were reinvested and to dampen worker wage demands by countering the impression that high profits were going into the pockets of the rich. Thus in line with the temper of the times, the party presented wage-earner funds not so much as a social reform but rather as an aid to economic growth.

Nonetheless, there has been no Reaganism in Sweden. The period of non–Social Democratic rule from 1976 through 1982 saw little real effort to roll back the welfare state or to change in any dramatic way existing equality-promoting programs. Although questions about equality going too far have become serious subjects of political discussion, they have not led to dramatic government action. In 1982 the Social Democrats returned to power, pledging to restore Swedish economic growth while maintaining an egalitarian society. In the 1985 elections, when the Social Democrats were reelected, they used nationalistic arguments, claiming that calls by the Conservative party for policies like those of Reagan and Thatcher represented imports of foreign ideologies inconsistent with Swedish traditions of social solidarity. The pickup in economic growth in the mid-1980s, which strengthened Reaganism in the United States, has in Sweden blunted calls for major changes in a less egalitarian, more market-oriented direction. Economic growth has buttressed the incumbent regime, Republican in the United States and Social Democrat in Sweden.

Japan. As we have seen, Japan achieved a good deal of equality—particularly of income—with relatively little government intervention. The tax system and social welfare policies more closely resembled those in the United States than those in Sweden whereas the resulting income distribution more closely resembled that in the latter country than the former. In part, this resulted from egalitarian norms in the private sector that may have limited the salary claims of higher-level employees and from government subsidies to agriculture that kept farm income on a par with wage-earner income during the rapid economic growth in the 1960s. Both causes are consistent with the communitarian norms in Japanese society.

In Japan, under the continuous rule of the conservative Liberal Democratic party since 1955, building a welfare society rather than a welfare state has been the preferred political goal. A welfare society implies a combination of governmental intervention and welfare functions performed by nongovernmental institutions such as the family, the community, and enterprises.[8] In the 1970s, however, governmental expenditure for social security expanded considerably. The impetus for this change came from the emerging demographic pressures of an aging society and the weakening of family ties that accompanied urbanization. The growth was supported by a growing economy.

In the 1980s the LDP responded to a lower rate of economic growth and an increasing governmental deficit by limiting the size of government—that is, by administrative reform. Thus far, the government has succeeded in restraining increases in agricultural subsidies and social security expenditures. And the idea of a Japanese-type welfare society combining governmental and nongovernmental functions has been given more emphasis as the means of coping with an aging society and its inevitable increased need for social security services in the future. Whether such nongovernmental institutions and traditional institutions such as the family and community can in the future continue to perform welfare functions adequately without massive governmental help remains to be seen.

Increases have been suspended for the agricultural subsidies that had contributed to narrowing income inequality between the urban and rural sectors, but drastic cuts would be very difficult for the LDP government. The rural sector is and will remain one of the most important sources of voting support. There has been mounting pressure on LDP agricultural policies from foreign countries, however, who want import restrictions and eventually agricultural subsidies abolished. If that were to happen, Japan might face the emergence of a new rural-urban difference in income or income inequality between larger entrepreneur farmers and the declining number of small farming households.

Other income-equalizing factors among wage earners in Japan—an employment system with lifelong employment, a seniority wage system, and enterprise unions—are facing adjustments that result from the pressures of the prolongation of retirement age, the internationalization of the economy, and technological advancement.

In sum, although the LDP, with its commitment to small government and its emphasis on traditional values, seems to be securely in power, we can expect the emergence of new demands for equality measures on the part of the government as existing equalizing forces weaken.

Values about equality will not by themselves determine how much equality one will find in these three nations in the future. Market forces (domestic and international), political decisions, and evolving social structures all play a role. But values about equality help set the boundaries of the debate.

Appendix

Notes

Index

Overview of Sampling

The leadership samples were drawn on a nation-by-nation basis, but in a manner to maximize their comparability. The following describes the samples in each nation. Table A.1 gives the response rate for each of the sampled groups.

Japan

Many of the Japanese groups were divided into a national and a local sample. The latter depended on the selection of localities. The first step in this process consisted of choosing thirteen prefectures within seven blocs. Then, one hundred cities and districts were chosen from these prefectures—with the stipulation that each had to have a local Chamber of Commerce.

Business. The national sample was drawn from the individual membership of the Federation of Economic Organizations. An approximately equal sample was drawn at the local level by taking the president, vice-president, and managing director of each local Chamber of Commerce.

Labor. The national sample consisted (proportional to membership) of officers of the large union federations: General Council of Trade Unions of Japan (*Sohyo*); Japanese Confederation of Labor (*Dōmei*); New National Federation of Industrial Organizations; and the Federation of Independent Unions of Japan. At the local level, one representative was taken from the local council of the two largest federations above (*Sohyo* and *Dōmei*) and a third person was taken from the largest local unit union in the specified cities.

Farmers. The national sample was drawn from the officers of the various national organizations of Agricultural Cooperatives and the Agricultural Chamber. The local sample consisted of presidents of local unit agricultural cooperatives, drawn from thirteen prefectures proportional to the number of persons engaged in agriculture.

Bureaucrats. The national sample consisted of a selection of persons

Table A.1.   Rates of return for mail questionnaires

Country and group	No. questionnaires sent out	No. returned	Percent returned
Japan			
National business	1059	195	18
Local business	300	104	35
National labor	300	109	36
Local labor	451	91	22
National farm	401	133	33
Local farm	300	104	35
National bureaucrats	305	120	39
Local bureaucrats	300	129	43
National intellectuals	451	188	42
Local intellectuals	149	45	30
National media	310	128	41
Local media	311	133	43
National parties	876	116	13
Local parties	300	110	37
Citizens' movement	432	127	29
Women's movement	329	136	41
Buraku Liberation League	308	113	37
Students	600	583	97
Sweden			
National business	1162	732	63
Local business	383	180	47
Farm	284	197	69
Blue-collar union	817	578	71
White-collar union	489	195	40
Professional union	254	168	66
Television/radio	200	88	44
Professors	525	247	47
Feminists	198	135	68
Social Democrats	400	276	69
Center	346	212	61
Liberals	296	210	71
Conservatives	299	221	74
United States			
National business	281	145	52
Local business	291	167	57
National labor	265	141	52
Local labor	240	125	52

Table A.1 (continued)

United States	No. questionnaires sent out	No. returned	Percent returned
National farm	222	114	52
Local farm	284	152	54
Intellectuals	519	296	57
National media	282	163	57
Local media	296	155	52
National parties	286	149	52
Local parties	287	158	55
National blacks	178	92	52
Local blacks	333	174	52
Feminists	551	367	67
Youth	576	364	63

occupying positions of section chief or higher in a variety of ministries of the national government. The local sample was made up of persons in executive positions in general affairs, financial affairs, and social welfare from each of the sampled localities.

Intellectuals. Three-quarters of this sample were drawn at random from teaching staff at colleges and universities. One-quarter were drawn from a directory of novelists, critics, painters, and musicians.

Media. The national sample consisted equally of department heads or higher from the five major newspapers, two news agencies and five broadcasting networks—one public (NHK) and four commercial networks. The local sample for the print media consisted of department heads or higher from bloc or prefectural newspapers; for the electronic media, heads of NHK local stations and department heads of local broadcasting companies were taken.

Political parties. The national "sample" consisted of all members of the Diet. The local sample was drawn by choosing three members of the municipal assembly for each of the hundred localities.

Feminists. The single national sample consisted of female leaders of protest groups (listed in a directory of citizens' movements) and officers of thirty-eight feminist groups involved in the protest meeting held in 1975 against the delay of governmental action toward gender equality.

Buraku Liberation League. The single sample was drawn from lists of prefectural committee members in thirty prefectures provided by this organization. Unlike members of all the other groups with whom contact was made individually, the questionnaires for this group were distributed through their organization.

Civic groups. The single national sample was drawn from the *male* leaders listed in two directories of protest organizations. Women were excluded from this sample because they were eligible for inclusion in the feminist sample.

Students. Students were selected from among those majoring in specific fields at a variety of institutions in order to produce a good mix on location, public/private support, sex, and major. The schools and majors were law and engineering majors at Tokyo University; politics and economics majors at Waseda University; engineering majors at Keio University; sociology and mathematics majors at Tokyo Women's College; law and engineering majors at Kyoto University; law and engineering majors at Doshisha University; and humanities and natural sciences majors at Nara Women's College. Questionnaires for this group were handed out in class rather than mailed.

United States

As in Japan, sampling for a number of groups in the United States took account of a national/local (or "cosmopolitan/parochial") distinction. One hundred fifty localities were randomly selected. Where possible, the same localities were used to identify local leaders within each of the groups for which this distinction was drawn.

Business. At the national level, the president or chairman of the board of a sample of the Fortune 500 corporations and two hundred largest banks was taken. At the local level, the chief executive officer of the local Chamber of Commerce as well as the CEO of the largest local bank not already sampled at the national level was chosen.

Farmers. The national sample was drawn from the officers of the three largest national membership federations (the American Farm Bureau Federation, the National Farmer's Organization, and the Farmer's Union) as well as national commodity organizations. The local sample came from the county organizations—using the counties in which our localities lay—for those national federations.

Labor. The national sample was drawn from the national officers of international unions with memberships of more than twenty-five thousand. The local sample was done on the basis of a rotation scheme using these same unions and the 150 localities in the locality sample described above.

Intellectuals. Entries from *Who's Who*–type directories in a variety of fields were randomly sampled. This group was not sampled along the national/local distinction.

Media. The national samples were randomly drawn from the congressional radio/television and press galleries. The local samples consisted of the news director of the largest television station and the managing editor of the newspaper with the largest circulation serving each of the localities.

Political parties. At the national level, three persons from the national committee of each party for each state were sampled for each of the two political parties. The local samples consisted of the local (county or city as appropriate) chairperson of each party.

Blacks. The local sample consisted of a local official of the NAACP and/or Urban League for the localities in our sample where those organizations had local chapters plus the highest-ranking black elected official in the locality. The national sample consisted of the entire congressional Black Caucus as well as a random sample of higher black elected officials who were not in the local sample.

Feminists. This sample was locally based and consisted of local leaders of the National Organization for Women, Federally Employed Women, Coalition of Labor Union Women, Women's Equity Action League, National Women's Political Caucus, and state commissions on the status of women.

Youth. Equal numbers of men and women seniors chosen at random from student lists of ten major universities from around the country: Harvard, Yale, Princeton, Chicago, Wisconsin, Indiana, Stanford, Berkeley, Rice, and Duke.

Sweden

Sweden, unlike the United States and Japan, did not depend on a single sample of localities to make up local components of various groups.

Business. The national business group was drawn from a variety of sources: members of the boards of the Swedish Confederation of Employers (SAF), the Swedish Confederation of Industry (IF), and the Swedish Federation of Small Businessmen (SHIO) and their affiliates; the professional staffs of SAF, IF, SHIO, and their affiliates; and the CEOs of commercial and savings banks and the largest industrial corporations in the country. The local sample consisted of a sample of member firms of SAF, with the questionnaire mailed to the firm's owner or CEO.

Labor. In Sweden there were three different labor samples, each drawn from the board and professional staff of one of the three labor federations and its affiliates: the Swedish Confederation of Labor (LO)—the blue-collar federation; the Federation of Salaried Employees (TCO)—the white-collar federation; and the Swedish Federation of Professional Employees (SACO)—the professional federation.

Farmers. This sample consisted of members of the board of the National Federation of Farmers' Cooperatives and its affiliates as well as directors of regional-level cooperative organizations.

Political party leaders. In keeping with the nature of the party system in Sweden, this group was drawn from a number of different sources. Once the data were gathered, cases were subdivided on the basis of parties into Social Democrats, Liberals, Center adherents, and Conservatives. The first source was all members of the Swedish Parliament (divided as noted). Other parts of the sample were drawn from the provincial boards of the four parties, the national and provincial boards of the women's federations of the parties, and the editors of newspapers. This last group was assigned to a party in accordance with the party affiliation of the paper.[1]

TV journalists. This truncated media sample consisted of professional staff of Swedish Television and Radio (SR). Because this is a government enterprise and because all the print journalists have already been grouped with the parties, this group is not fully comparable to similar groups in the United States and Japan.

Professors. This single sample was drawn from a list of full professors on university faculties (excluding medicine) in Sweden.

Feminists. This sample was drawn from the national and provincial boards of the Swedish feminist organization, the Frederika Bremer-förbundet.

Demographic Profiles

The groups in each of the countries are overwhelmingly male, as shown in Table A.2. In the United States, with the obvious exception of the feminists and the students who were deliberately sampled to balance female and male representation, all groups are one-sidedly male. The groups with the highest proportion of women after these two groups are the political party leaders, reflecting policies regarding the makeup of the national committees. Of those groups for which the inclusion of women is a result neither of deliberate policy nor of our sampling design, women make up the largest proportion among intellectuals and among black leaders. Even there, however, barely one in six of those in our sample is a woman. Men almost completely dominate the business sample, and at

Table A.2. Percentage of leaders of each sex[a]

Country and group	Males	Females
Japan		
Business	100	0
Farm	99	1
Labor	99	1
Bureaucrats	100	[b]
Intellectuals	95	5
Media	99	1
Liberal Democrats	100	0
Center parties	92	8
Left parties	95	5
Civic movements	100	0
Feminist movements	0	100
Buraku Liberation League	97	3
Students	67	33
Sweden		
National business	97	3
Local business	93	7
Farm	97	3
Blue-collar union	92	8
White-collar union	79	21
Professional union	82	18
Professors	97	3
Media—television reporters	81	20
Social Democrats	69	31
Center	72	28
Liberals	63	37
Conservatives	65	36
Feminists	1	99
United States		
Business	98	2
Farm	94	6
Labor	95	5
Intellectuals	85	15
Media	90	10
Republicans	75	25
Democrats	67	33
Blacks	86	14
Feminists	1	99
Youth	54	46

a. Percentages do not always add to 100 because of rounding.
b. Less than 1 percent.

least 90 percent of the remaining groups—and often substantially more than that—are men.

The Japanese samples are even more male dominated. Once again, the student sample deliberately included women, and feminist leaders are female. Other groups, however, are overwhelmingly male. Compare, for example, the media: in the United States, this group is 90 percent male; in Japan, it is 99 percent male. Some 85 percent of the intellectuals in the United States are men; the comparable figure for Japan is 95 percent. Female representation in the Buraku Liberation League, corresponding in some sense to the black sample in the United States, is virtually nil. The civic and protest groups are artificially male, because any women located in the sampling were automatically grouped with the feminists. Even if this had not been done, there would be little representation of women.

Sweden seems to be somewhat more egalitarian in relation to gender. To be sure, the business and farm groups have male proportions roughly comparable to those in the United States, and the percentage of women among faculty in Sweden is lower than that among intellectuals in the United States. Representation of women among party leaders is high, however. Moreover, even though this reflects the presence of separate women's party organizations, that in itself speaks to the representation of women. It is among the union groups, however, that the greater degree of female representation in Sweden is most obvious. Blue-collar union leaders are not as predominantly male in Sweden as are union leaders (taken as a group) in the United States and Japan. The representation of women is much stronger in the white-collar and professional unions, approximately one in five. Nonetheless, this comparison should not obscure the fact that most groups in Sweden, as in all three countries, are strongly male.

The fact that women leaders are found largely at the head of women's organizations and rarely in other positions deserves special note. Leadership of a major organization—whether it be an economic organization or another kind—is the main way in which individuals develop power and influence in a society. Such leadership is also often a training ground for national leadership. Women's organizations, this suggests, may provide a special resource for women, a resource that is especially useful in the absence of the multiplicity of organizational leadership opportunities available to men.[2]

Table A.3 shows the age distribution for the samples in the three countries. The first four columns present the percentages for four broad age groups. Columns five and six give, for ease of comparison, the proportions of each group under and over forty-five years of age. In the United States, with the obvious exception of the students, most groups are relatively old. Only among the media leaders and feminists is more than one in ten under thirty, and these two groups are also the only ones where a majority is less than forty-five. Leaders in the established sector tend to be somewhat older than leaders in the other sectors. Business leaders are older than others. The mediating sector is younger. Republicans with two-thirds over forty-five are the oldest of this sector, older than the Democrats, but even they are younger than any of the established groups. Groups in the challenging sector are youngest. Nearly half of the black leaders are under forty-five. The relative youth of the feminists is also noteworthy.

Overall, leadership groups in Japan tend to be older than those in the United States. Virtually all of the business leaders are over forty-five, and eight in ten are at least sixty years old. In contrast to the United States, labor leaders are younger than other established Japanese groups, although the age profile of this group is not markedly younger than that of its counterpart in the United States. Although members of the Buraku Liberation League are the youngest group overall—omitting, of course, students—only one in three is under forty-five. One noteworthy finding is that members of the feminist group in Japan are not especially young, either absolutely or in comparison with other groups.

In Sweden, the groups are relatively more homogeneous in age than in the United States and tend, overall, to be younger than in Japan. The age homogeneity, especially looking at the last two columns, is most striking. Groups in the established sector are at least as young as in America, and business and white-collar and professional labor leaders are somewhat younger. The media leaders are the youngest group in Sweden. (They were close to that position in the United States, although markedly older in Japan.) Feminists in Sweden seem generally typical of other groups in terms of age, presenting thus a contrast both to Japan (where they as a group are relatively old) and to the United States (where they are markedly young).

The leaders are also highly educated. The data on the respondents' education are presented in Table A.4, along with data on the education level of the respondents' fathers. In the United States, at least some exposure to a college education is very common. The only groups in which fewer than nine in ten report at least some college education are labor, farm, and black leaders. Two-thirds of those in the first two groups have this much education and black leaders fall just under the nine-in-ten threshold. There

Table A.3.   Percentage of leaders in various age categories[a]

Country and group	Under 30	30–44	45–60	Over 60	Under 45	Over 45
Japan						
Business	[b]	2	18	79	3	98
Farm	1	6	21	72	8	93
Labor	1	26	67	7	27	73
Bureaucrats	0	13	74	13	13	87
Intellectuals	0	24	52	24	24	76
Media	0	10	88	3	10	90
Liberal Democrats	0	12	36	53	12	88
Center parties	2	12	53	33	14	86
Left parties	0	11	59	30	11	89
Civic movements	4	16	42	39	20	80
Feminists	2	10	42	46	12	88
Buraku Liberation League	10	24	47	19	35	65
Students	100	0	0	0	100	0
Sweden						
National business	1	30	46	23	31	69
Local business	2	29	48	22	31	69
Farm	1	28	42	29	29	71
Blue-collar union	1	34	50	16	34	66
White-collar union	2	51	37	11	53	47
Professional union	7	44	40	9	51	49
Professors	0	11	53	37	11	89
Media—television reporters	0	64	31	5	64	36
Social Democrats	2	26	52	20	28	72
Center	1	23	49	27	24	76
Liberals	2	25	49	25	27	73
Conservatives	3	20	52	26	23	77
Feminists	1	34	43	22	35	65
United States						
Business	1	14	54	32	15	86
Farm	5	24	46	24	29	71
Labor	3	22	54	21	25	75
Intellectuals	2	27	47	24	29	71
Media	11	47	34	8	58	42
Republicans	1	30	50	19	31	69
Democrats	5	36	50	9	41	59

Table A.3 (continued)

United States	Under 30	30–44	45–60	Over 60	Under 45	Over 45
Blacks	5	39	39	17	45	56
Feminists	16	51	29	5	66	34
Youth	98	2	b	0	100	b

a. Percentages do not always add to 100 because of rounding.
b. Less than 1 percent.

is rather more differentiation when it comes to having graduated from college. Almost all the intellectuals have a college degree (many, but by no means all, are faculty members), as do three in four of all groups save labor and farmers. A graduate degree is a good deal less common, attained by fewer than half of those in any group except for intellectuals. It is striking that business leaders are among the most educated in the American study and that a relatively high proportion of political party leaders *and* leaders of the two challenging groups, feminists and blacks, have graduate degrees.[3]

The educational systems in the other countries are not directly comparable to those in the United States. On the one hand, college (or university) education is much more common among the population in the United States than it is in most countries of the world, Japan and Sweden included. On the other hand, subuniversity levels of education are often more selective and more status conferring than is the American high school.

In Japan one finds a low level of education for members of the Buraku Liberation League, half of whom attended only compulsory education (or less). The highest level of education recorded for Japan is the university. Members of the media have almost the same proportion of university education as do intellectuals. Business is next, which places this group relatively higher in the Japanese education hierarchy than their counterparts in the United States. Leaders of civic organizations and feminists, however, are (relatively) less educated than are black leaders and feminists in the United States. Among political leaders, members of the governing bloc have about the same amount of education as the bureaucrats; members of the other two blocs of parties have somewhat less educational attainment.

In Sweden, similar patterns appear. Business leaders—at least at the national level—once again occupy a high rung on the educational ladder.

Table A.4.   Percentage of respondents and their fathers at given levels of education[a]

Country and group	Respondent			Father		
Japan	Compulsory only	Beyond, no university	University degree	Compulsory only	Beyond, no university	Universi degree
Business	7	18	76	41	29	31
Farm	22	57	22	68	26	5
Labor	18	58	24	65	29	6
Bureaucrats	4	35	61	45	31	24
Intellectuals	0	4	96	36	25	39
Media	1	7	92	37	31	33
Liberal Democrats	12	29	59	58	19	23
Center partie	13	46	42	54	33	13
Left parties	18	43	39	60	25	15
Civic movements	9	41	50	59	28	14
Feminists	5	55	40	30	36	34
Buraku Liberation League	51	44	6	89	6	5
Students	0	0	100	15	34	52

Sweden	Realskole or less	Gymnasium	University	Realskole or less	Gymnasium	Universit
National business	20	24	56	69	12	20
Local business	60	20	21	86	6	8
Farm	48	14	39	87	5	8
Blue-collar union	83	3	14	96	2	2
White-collar union	22	19	59	76	9	15
Professional union	0	6	94	57	15	28
Professors	0	0	100	49	9	42
Television reporters	9	22	69	58	7	35
Social Democrats	68	9	23	95	2	3
Center	73	11	16	96	2	3
Liberals	38	18	45	81	6	13
Conservatives	38	19	43	64	11	25
Feminists	28	17	55	66	15	19

United States	No college diploma	College graduate	Graduate degree	No college diploma	College graduate	Graduate degree
Business	19	51	30	79	16	5
Farm	56	32	12	89	9	2

ble A.4   (*continued*)

United States	No college diploma	College graduate	Graduate degree	No college diploma	College graduate	Graduate degree
abor	69	20	12	89	8	3
ntellectuals	6	7	87	71	17	12
Media	26	59	15	68	21	11
Republicans	26	36	38	72	14	14
Democrats	27	29	44	75	12	13
Blacks	30	36	34	87	8	5
Feminists	28	34	38	72	18	10
Youth	15	81	4	33	33	35

a. Percentages do not always add to 100 because of rounding.

Leaders of women's groups, although well educated, are lower than their U.S. counterparts, and the media (TV reporters) are relatively higher compared with other groups. As in Japan, there are strong differences among the parties. The Liberal and Conservative parties show higher educational status consistent with their class bases; the Social Democrats and Center partisans are lower. The distinctly Swedish pattern, however, is to be seen in the unions where a great deal depends on the type of union. Those representing blue-collar workers have the lowest level of educational attainment, those representing white-collar workers come next, and leaders of the professional unions have the highest proportion of university graduates of all groups save the intellectuals.

Table A.4 also shows the educational attainment for respondents' fathers, measured on the same scales as those of their offspring.[4] Across all three countries, respondents tend to have a good deal more education than their fathers. This is a consistent pattern. Feminists in Japan, whose fathers tend to be among the most educated, are an exception in that they are only slightly more likely to have been to university than their fathers were, clearly a result of a stronger gender difference in education compared with generational differences. Reflecting both age (their fathers are younger) and education's heritability, students in both the United States and Japan tend to have more educated fathers than do other groups. This pattern is especially striking in Japan, where more than half of students' fathers have a university education, sharply more than any other group. Status heritability is seen in the fact that businessmen in Japan, and to a lesser extent in Sweden, tend to have relatively educated fathers (a trend

Table A.5.   Percentage of groups supporting various parties[a]

Japan	Liberal Democrats	Democratic Socialists	Clean government	Socialists	Communists	None (independent)
Business	75	15	[b]	[b]	[b]	8
Farm	70	8	[b]	4	1	17
Labor	[b]	35	2	52	4	7
Bureaucrats	54	10	[b]	5	1	29
Intellectuals	13	12	[b]	14	7	50
Media	21	7	[b]	10	4	55
Civic movements	9	5	2	26	13	43
Feminist movements	8	8	2	23	14	42
Buraku Liberation League	3	[b]	1	85	1	9
Students	16	4	1	11	6	57

Sweden	Communist	Social Democrat	Center	Liberal	Conservative
National business	[b]	5	6	17	72
Local business	2	3	11	19	65
Farm	1	2	67	5	25
Blue-collar union	[b]	98	1	[b]	[b]
White-collar union	6	64	3	14	13
Professional union	5	22	6	15	52
Professors	3	17	9	28	44
Feminists	1	13	16	41	30

United States	Republican	Independent	Democratic
Business	80	4	16
Farm	54	7	39
Labor	4	7	90
Intellectuals	28	13	59
Media	21	20	59
Blacks	8	9	84
Feminists	10	9	80
Youth	22	22	55

a. Percentages do not always add to 100 because of rounding.
b. Less than 1 percent.

that seems even stronger when one recalls that business leaders tend to be relatively older and hence have fathers who came through the education system earlier). This pattern is evident in the United States, where business leaders' fathers are less well educated than the fathers of leaders from other groups, probably reflecting the fact that our business sample is older.

In general, our leaders are not representative of the population as a whole or of the groups they lead in educational terms; they tend to be better educated. Nevertheless, there is differentiation among the leaders and the differentiations parallel differences in the groups from which they come. The leaders of disadvantaged groups are less well educated, as are labor leaders. The leaders may not match the others in their sector in educational attainment, but they tend in the direction of the others in their group.

Lastly we see, in Table A.5, the party affiliation of the leaders in the various categories. The data allow no easy summary nor do they offer major surprises. They do indicate that the leadership groups vary on the issue of party affiliation and that the differences among the groups are quite sharp. In some cases the linkage of a group to a party is almost complete; the linkage of the blue-collar union leaders in Sweden to the Social Democratic party is an example. In other cases leadership groups do not demonstrate a very distinctive pattern.

Notes

1. Equality and the Welfare State

1. On this distinction see Marc F. Plattner, "The Welfare State vs. the Redistributive State," *Public Interest,* 55 (1979), 28–48.

2. Samuel P. Huntington, *American Politics: The Promise of Disharmony* (Cambridge, Mass.: Harvard University Press, 1981), stresses the gap between ideals and results.

3. On this general issue see Sidney Verba, Norman H. Nie, and Jae-on Kim, *Participation and Political Equality: A Seven-Nation Comparison* (New York: Cambridge University Press, 1979).

4. This dilemma affects the issue of the desirability of limiting the use of private funds in political campaigns in the United States. See, for instance, the Supreme Court's decision in Buckley v. Valleo, U.S. 1 (1976).

5. See Robert Dahl, *Dilemmas of Pluralist Democracy* (New Haven: Yale University Press, 1982), chap. 8.

6. The political difference between Sweden and the United States—the former with strong unions and a long period of Social Democratic rule, the latter with neither—probably explains much of the difference between the countries, but, as one might expect, the historical origins of their policies are more complex. Early Swedish redistribution policies date from well before the Social Democratic government and received support from a strong state and bureaucracy in collaboration with other social groups. Conversely, in the United States unions opposed many social insurance schemes until the New Deal era. See Arnold Heidenheimer, Hugh Heclo, and Carolyn T. Adams, *Comparative Public Policy* (New York: St. Martin's Press, 1983), chap. 7.

7. This categorization of nations is consistent with that in J. Corina M. Van Arnhem and Geurt J. Schotsman, "Do Parties Affect the Distribution of Income? The Case of Advanced Capitalist Democracies," in Francis G. Castles, ed., *The Impact of Parties: Politics and Policies in Democratic Capitalist States* (Beverly Hills: Sage Publications, 1982), pp. 283–364. They classify democratic nations into four categories. One group contains five nations—France, Italy, the United States, Canada, and Japan. All have strong right parties, weak left parties, and a weak union movement. All but Japan have relatively high income inequality. Sweden falls in the category along with Israel and Norway. See also Walter Korpi

and Michael Shalev, "Strikes, Power, and Politics in Western Nations: 1900–1976," in Maurice Zeitlin, ed., *Political Power and Social Theory*, vol. 1 (Greenwich, Conn.: JAI Press, 1981), pp. 299–332; and Korpi and Shalev, "Strikes, Industrial Relations, and Class Conflict in Capitalist Societies," *British Journal of Sociology*, 30 (1979), 164–187.

Harold Wilensky puts Sweden, Japan, and the United States into separate categories. Sweden is a corporatist democracy where social policy is made by a strong government in cooperation with peak business, agriculture, and labor organizations. Japan has corporatism without labor—corporatist bargaining takes place among peak groups, but labor is kept in a weaker position. The United States is an example of a noncorporatist fragmented system. See Harold L. Wilensky, "Political Legitimacy and Consensus: Missing Variables in the Assessment of Social Policy," in S. E. Spiro and E. Yachtman-Yaar, eds., *Evaluating the Welfare State: Social and Political Perspectives* (New York: Academic Press, 1983), pp. 51–74. The distinction is valid and not inconsistent with the one drawn by Van Arnhem and Schotsman and by Korpi and Shalev. See also T. J. Pempel and Keiichi Tsunekawa, "Corporatism without Labor? The Japanese Anomaly," in Philippe Schmitter and Gerhard Lehmbruch, eds., *Trends toward Corporatist Intermediation* (Beverly Hills: Sage Publications, 1979), chap. 9. That Japan has corporatism without labor while the United States is a fragmented noncorporatist system does not quite explain the difference in income equality. The other nation in the corporatist-without-labor category with Japan is France, where income inequality exceeds even that in the United States. See Malcolm Sawyer, "Income Distribution in OECD Countries," OECD Economic Outlook, *Occasional Papers* (Paris: OECD, 1976).

8. The two most influential exponents of this position are Harold Wilensky, *The Welfare State and Equality* (Berkeley: University of California Press, 1975); and Robert Jackman, *Politics and Social Equality* (New York: Wiley, 1975), and "Socialist Parties and Income Equality in Western Industrial Societies," *Journal of Politics*, 42 (1980), 135–149.

9. Key works are Christopher Hewitt, "The Effect of Political Democracy and Social Democracy on Equality in Industrial Nations: A Cross-National Comparison," *American Sociological Review*, 71 (1977), 467–487; David Cameron, "Politics, Public Policy, and Economic Equality: A Comparative Analysis," unpublished paper, 1981; Douglas A. Hibbs, Jr., "Political Parties and Macro-Economic Policy," *American Political Science Review*, 71 (1977), 1467–87; and Alexander Hicks and Duane H. Swank, "Governmental Redistribution in Rich Capitalist Democracies," *Policy Studies Journal*, 13 (December 1984), 265–286. The data on the impact of voter turnout are in Stephen Stack, "The Effects of Political Participation and Socialist Party Strength on the Degree of Income Inequality," *American Sociological Review*, 44 (1979), 168–171.

10. The data reported in Table 1.1 come from the well-known 1976 study by Sawyer using OECD data from 1966 to 1973. Gini index: Sawyer, "Income Dis-

tribution in OECD Countries," p. 19. When standardized for household size, the United States ranks 9 out of 11 and Japan and Sweden rank 5 and 2 respectively (ibid.); for quintile income equality see Cameron, "Politics, Public Policy, and Economic Inequality" (based on OECD data in Sawyer, "Income Distribution in OECD Countries"). The data have the advantage of comparing all three nations in which we are interested. Furthermore, Sawyer's work is based on data gathered several years before our survey and may, therefore, represent the perceived state of income inequality when we conducted our research. There are, however, some limitations in Sawyer's work that have been addressed in the newer Luxembourg Income Study (Michael O'Higgins, Gunther Schmaus, and Geoffrey Stephenson, "Income Distribution and Redistribution: A Microdata Analysis for Seven Countries," Luxembourg Income Study, Centre d'Etudes de Populations, de Pauvreté et de Politiques Socio-Economiques, June 1985). But this study has no data on Japan. Its comparison of the United States and Sweden resembles Sawyer's; Sweden ranks as the most equal nation and the United States as one of the two least equal (depending on the measure used) of the seven nations covered.

11. Japanese wages are quite heavily a function of age. Data on the "model wage" presented by the Statistics Bureau of the Prime Minister's Office show that age differentiation is greater than differentiation on the basis of education. The model wage is both descriptive (based on objective data) and normative (many private enterprises follow it). If one considered income differentiation in Japan across the life cycle when age differences cancel out, the result might be more equal than the data in Table 1.1 indicate. On the model wage data, see *Japan Statistical Yearbook,* Statistics Bureau, Prime Minister's Office, 1980, pp. 404, 405.

12. Joseph A. Pechman and Benjamin A. Ochner, *Who Bears the Tax Burden?* (Washington: Brookings Institution, 1974), p. 61, find that for most assumptions about the incidence of taxes across income groups, the distribution of income before and after taxes is quite similar. Comparable results are found in Japan. See Keizai Kikaku Cho (Economic Planning Agency), *Shotoku shisan bunpai no jittai to mondaiten* (Status and problems of income and wealth distribution) (Tokyo: Okurasho Insatsukyoku, 1975), pp. 316–317. For a further discussion see Chapter 6, esp. notes 8 and 9. Sources for Table 1.2: for progressivity of tax: OECD, National Accounts of OECD Countries, 1975, vol. 2 (Paris: OECD, 1978); for income transfer expenditures as percent of GNP: OECD Economic Outlook, July, 1982. Japanese and Swedish figures for 1979, U.S. figures for 1978.

13. See International Labor Organization, *The Cost of Social Security (1975–1977)* (Geneva: 1981).

14. Sources for Table 1.3: For Gini index: Hicks and Swank, "Governmental Redistribution in Rich Capitalist Democracies." Based on OECD data. See similar calculations in Sawyer, "Income Distribution in OECD Countries," pp. 34–35, and in van Arnhem and Schotsman, "Do Parties Affect the Distribution of Income?," pp. 283–364. For quintile income share: Sweden and United States,

see Cameron, "Politics, Public Policy, and Economic Inequality"; for Japan, see Keizai Kikaku Cho, *Shotoku shisan bunpai no jittai to mondaiten*, p. 148. Based on 1972 data.

15. Hicks and Swank, "Governmental Redistribution in Rich Capitalist Democracies."

16. Van Arnhem and Schotsman suggest that the high pregovernment income inequality in Sweden may be the result of wage bargains that anticipate the heavy redistributive role of taxes ("Do Parties Affect the Distribution of Income?" pp. 322–323).

17. The Luxembourg Income Study (LIS) finds less difference between the United States and Sweden in terms of the impact of governmental intervention on inequality than is reported in Table 1.3, which is based on the 1976 OECD data set (O'Higgins et al., "Income Distribution and Redistribution"). The authors find that direct taxes have a relatively large impact on inequality in Sweden and in the United States. The United States, nevertheless, remains one of the least equal nations after this impact, whereas Sweden remains the most equal. The difference between the OECD data and the Luxembourg Income Study data may have several sources. The LIS study focuses on direct taxes, whereas indirect taxes play a larger role in the United States and counterbalance the progressive aspects of the direct taxes. Second, the LIS study deals with taxes rather than taxes and transfers. As its authors point out, the distributional effect of taxes can only be understood "by also examining the distributional impact of the manner in which they are spent" (p. 19). Last, the time period between the OECD and the LIS studies was one in which inflation had caused a good deal of "bracket creep" in the United States, leading a large number of Americans to face higher marginal tax rates.

18. The data may understate the redistributive aspects of Japanese tax policy, which has traditionally favored agriculture and small business. This may have a redistributive effect even though there is little redistribution in the industrial sector of the economy; see Hiromitsu Ishi, *Sozei seisaku no kōka* (Effects of tax policy) (Tokyo: Tōyō Keizai Shinpōsha, 1979), and Hiroshi Sato and Hiroshi Miyajima, *Sengo zeisei shi* (A history of the postwar taxation system) (Tokyo: Zeimukeiri Kyokai, 1979). The impact of taxes on income takes a somewhat different form in Japan from that in the United States, although the overall impact on income distribution is similar. In Japan the tax structure is relatively nonprogressive up to the very top brackets, where it begins to slope upward more sharply than in the United States; see Okurasho (Ministry of Finance), *Zaisei kinyū tōkei geppō* (Monthly report of fiscal and monetary statistics), August 1979, p. 328.

19. The data come from a period of transition in the Japanese welfare state. During the 1970s social welfare expenditure increased dramatically in Japan with increased pension and medical expenditures for the elderly. The income equality reflected in the data in Table 1.1, however, predates the introduction of these changes. On the expansion of the welfare state in the 1970s, see Takashi Inoguchi, "The Political Economy of Conservative Resurgence under Recession: Public

Policies and Political Support in Japan, 1977–1983," unpublished paper, Center for International Studies, Harvard University, 1984.

20. See Charles L. Taylor and Michael C. Hudson, *World Handbook of Political and Social Indicators,* 2nd ed. (New Haven: Yale University Press, 1972), p. 23.

21. In dealing with the stratification of political participation, we take a somewhat different approach from that used in relation to economic stratification. In terms of income, we use a measure of dispersion among individuals, the Gini index, that indicates how concentrated is income in the hands of various strata of wage earners. In relation to political participation, we do not ask how concentrated is participation in the hands of various strata of participators. Instead we use a criterion other than participation itself to stratify the population, and ask how concentrated is participation among those in the upper strata of the hierarchy defined by this other criterion—in particular, how concentrated is participation in the hands of the more affluent. The reasons are methodological and substantive. From a methodological point of view, the absence of a divisible metric for participation makes it difficult to apply measures such as the Gini index to political variables. For an explication of this problem as well as an attempt to apply a measure similar to the Gini index—the Thiel index of inequality—to participatory data, see Jae-on Kim, Norman H. Nie, and Sidney Verba, "The Amount and Concentration of Political Participation," *Political Methodology,* 1 (Spring 1974), 105–132. From a substantive point of view, a measure that reveals the disproportion of political participation held by particular categories of citizens identified by their socioeconomic position rather than the disproportion held by the top participators—as would a Gini or Thiel index of the concentration of participation—is more in accord with the group nature of political influence. For a fuller discussion of the methodological and substantive issues associated with political stratification, see Chapter 8.

22. On this general theme see Sidney Verba and Norman Nie, *Participation in America* (New York: Harper and Row, 1972), and Verba, Nie, and Kim, *Participation and Political Equality.*

23. Sources for Figure 1.1: for Japan, Akarui Senkyo Suishin Kyokai (Society for the Promotion of Clean Elections), *Dai 35 kai syūgiingiin sōsenkyo no jittai— genshiryō* (Survey of the thirty-fifth general election) (Tokyo: 1980), p. 46; for Sweden, Olof Petersson, *Väljarna och valet, 1976* (Voters and the election, 1976) (Stockholm: Statistiska Centralbyrån, 1977), p. 202; for the United States, Samuel P. Huntington and Joan M. Nelson, *No Easy Choice* (Cambridge, Mass.: Harvard University Press, 1976), p. 88. One can also compare Japan and the United States in terms of the dispersion of political activity across citizens. On this measure the United States has a greater equality of political activity than does Japan: that is, whatever political activity there is in the United States is carried on by more citizens than is the case in Japan (see Kim, Nie, and Verba, "The Amount and Concentration of Political Participation"). This means that Japan is more

clearly divided into activist and nonactivist citizens than is the case in the United States, but the activist citizens are more representative of the socioeconomic hierarchy. As indicated above, the greater dispersion of political activity across socioeconomic levels in Japan represents a form of political equality with greater substantive implication than does the dispersion of political activity across levels of political activists in the United States; see Chapter 8.

24. Sources for Figure 1.2: for Finland, France, Italy, Norway, Sweden, United Kingdom, United States, and West Germany, see "Dollar Politics," *Congressional Quarterly,* vol. 2, October 1974, pp. 55–60; for Austria and Canada, see *Government Financing of National Elections,* vol. 1, Library of Congress; for Australia, Denmark, Ireland, Japan, The Netherlands, and Switzerland, see David Butler, Howard R. Penniman, and Austin Ranney, eds., *Democracy at the Polls: A Comparative Study of Competitive National Elections* (Washington: American Enterprise Institute for Public Policy Research, 1981).

25. See Gerald L. Curtis, *Election Campaigning Japanese Style* (New York: Columbia University Press, 1971), pp. 230–243.

26. See Van Arnhem and Schotsman, "Do Parties Affect the Distribution of Income?" and Korpi and Shalev, "Strikes, Power, and Politics" and "Strikes, Industrial Relations, and Class Conflict."

27. On this general issue see Ikuo Kabashima, "Supportive Participation with Economic Growth: The Case of Japan," *World Politics,* 36 (1984), pp. 309–338; and Verba, Nie, and Kim, *Participation and Political Equality.* The farm/nonfarm incomes were handled in part by price adjustments. See Tsunehiko Watanabe, "Income Inequality and Economic Development: A Case Study of Japan," in OECD, *Education, Equality, and Life Chances* (Paris: OECD, 1975).

28. See Inoguchi, "The Political Economy of Conservative Resurgence," pp. 16–20, for a discussion of this exchange of tax benefits and subsidies for political support.

29. The following table shows the Gini index of income inequality within the wage-earning private sector in the United States and Japan. As one can see, both before and after taxes there is less income differential in Japan than in the United States.

	Gini before taxes	Gini after taxes
U.S. (1966)	.368	.347
Japan (1970)	.317	.303

The data are from Keizai Kikaku Cho, *Shotoku shisan bunpai no jittai to mondaiten,* p. 118.

30. The boom in the Japanese economy in the early 1960s, accompanied as it was by a shortage of new labor, led to a diminution of wage differentials in Japan as firms competed for new workers. The diminution of differential was not only within enterprises—between permanent and temporary workers and new and older workers—but also between large and small firms between which there had

been a large difference. Furthermore, the tendency set then became institutional-ized as expectations and union tactics adjusted to the new situation; see Tatsuro Uchino, *Japan's Postwar Economy: An Insider's View of Its History and Future* (Tokyo, New York, and San Francisco: Kodansha International, 1983).

2. The Historical Context of Equality

1. Saburo Yasuda, *Shakai idō no kenkyū* (Studies in social mobility) (Tokyo: University of Tokyo Press, 1971), pp. 450–463. Yasuda has pointed to the exis-tence of these two principles to explain Japanese society. He calls one the "status principle" and the other the "village principle." The latter involves several activ-ities: reducing the emphasis on individualism, enhancing emotional amalgama-tion, covering up stratification, keeping the peace within groups, and encouraging struggle between groups.

2. Edwin O. Reischauer, *The Japanese* (Cambridge, Mass.: Harvard Univer-sity Press, 1977), pp. 82–83.

3. *Buraku* means "village" in Japanese. Here the term refers to districts that have been subject to discrimination and administrative negligence. The people of the buraku still experience inferior living conditions owing to the accumulated effects of this discrimination.

4. Reischauer, *The Japanese*, p. 129.

5. Takeshi Ishida, *Japanese Political Culture* (New Brunswick, N.J.: Trans-action Books, 1983), p. 6.

6. In prewar factories the use of different toilets and lunchrooms for staff and workers was common.

7. Ishida, *Japanese Political Culture*, p. 12.

8. Ibid., p. 13.

9. Reischauer, *The Japanese*, p. 157.

10. Nevertheless, this emphasis on status ranking often has greater symbolic than actual meaning. And even when real, leaders are expected to be sensitive to group needs, rather than forceful or domineering. "Consensus through consulta-tion is the norm." Reischauer, *The Japanese*, p. 165.

11. Ibid., p. 132.

12. There had been two streams of prewar established political parties in the House of Representatives. Despite frequent splits and mergers and changes of name, *Seiyū-kai* and *Minsei-tō* were the party labels identifying those two streams. Although *Seiyū-kai* was slightly more locally oriented and *Minsei-tō* more city oriented, they differed little in terms of their programs and policies. After World War II those two streams revived as two or more conservative parties and eventually merged as the Liberal Democratic party in 1955.

13. Tomohiko Harada, *Hisabetsu buraku no rekishi* (A history of discrimi-nated-against buraku) (Tokyo: Asahi Shimbun sha, 1975), p. 277.

14. See Mitsu Kono, *Nihon shakai seitō shi* (A history of socialist parties in Japan) (Tokyo: Chūo Kōron sha, 1960), pp. 21–23.

15. Kazuo Koike, *Nihon no Jukuren* (Skills in Japan) (Tokyo: Yūhikaku, 1981), pp. 4–12, 71–86. Using Japanese, United States, and OECD statistics, Koike has shown that the wage differential between blue-collar and white-collar workers in Japan is the least among advanced industrialized countries.

16. The turnout rate in the 1946 general election was 78.52 percent for men and 66.97 percent for women. The gender gap in the turnout rate has continuously decreased in successive elections, and since the 1972 general election the turnout rate for women has surpassed that for men.

17. Yoshiyuki Takayama, *Fubyōdō no keizai bunseki* (Economic analysis of inequality) (Tokyo: Tōyōkeizai Shinpōsha, 1980), chap. 2.

18. Rodosho Fujin Shonen Kyoku (Bureau of Women and Children, Ministry of Labor, Japanese Government), *Shōwa 56-nenban fujin rōdō hakusho* (1981 white paper on women's labor); Naohiro Yashiro, *Gendai Nihon no byōri kyūmei* (Inquiries into the pathology of contemporary Japan) (Tokyo: Tōyōkeizai Shinpōsha, 1980), p. 58.

19. In the Japanese bureaucracy women occupy only 0.6 percent of positions above vice-section chief in central ministries. In elementary schools, where the majority of teachers are women, only 1.1 percent of schoolmasters and 2.7 percent of vice-schoolmasters are female. Only 0.2 percent of full professors and 0.6 percent of associate professors at all national universities in Japan are women, compared with 9.6 percent and 17.8 percent, respectively, in the United States. Female university graduate students face more difficulty finding jobs than do male counterparts, and the insufficiency of day-care centers for children still forces women to break their occupational careers. At least 80 percent of all companies, according to a Japanese government study, have one or more job categories for which women may not apply. At the local governmental level women filled only 796 (1.1 percent) of the 70,084 positions in prefectural, municipal, and village assemblies, based on 1982 government figures. *New York Times,* May 18, 1985, pp. 1, 5.

20. Some claim that the law lacks teeth, because it contains no enforcement penalties. Others argue that the bill's repeal of restrictions on overtime and late-night working hours by women will actually hurt working-class women. Some women's rights activists maintain that this law is a start toward equalization of the sexes, even if an imperfect one. Ibid.

21. Takatoshi Imada, "Shakaiteki fubyōdō to kikai kōzō no sūsei bunseki" (Trend analysis of social inequality and opportunity structure), in Ken' ichi Tominaga, ed., *Nihon no kaisō kōzō* (Strata structure in Japan) (Tokyo: University of Tokyo Press, 1979), pp. 107–114.

22. Imada, "Shakaiteki fubyōdō to kikai kōzō no sūsei bunseki," pp. 121–125.

23. Walfrid Enblom, *Privilegiestriderna vid frihetstidens början* (The battle over privileges at the beginning of the age of freedom) (Uppsala: Almqvist and Wiksell, 1925), p. 5.

24. Sten Carlsson, *Byråkrati och börgarstånd under frihetstiden* (Bureaucracy

and the bourgeoisie during the age of freedom) (Stockholm: Norstedts, 1963), p. 140.

25. Ibid., p. 72.

26. Eli Hecksher, *An Economic History of Sweden* (Cambridge, Mass.: Harvard University Press, 1954), p. 126.

27. The king clearly wanted to appear to be giving the estates completely free rein in this question, while at the same time giving them the commission report as a starting point for their work. In this report those who had worked on and influenced the solution of the question were made coresponsible through their membership in the commission, which produced the hope that the report would be followed in large measure in Parliament. Gunnar Hesslen, *Det svenska kommittéevasendet intill år 1905* (The Swedish commission system through 1905) (Uppsala: Edv. Berlings Nya Boktryckeri, 1927), pp. 186–187, 188.

28. Quoted in ibid., pp. 194, 258.

29. See Alexander Gerschenkron, *Bread and Democracy in Germany* (Berkeley: University of California Press, 1943), and Barrington Moore, *Social Origins of Dictatorship and Democracy* (Boston: Beacon Press, 1966).

30. First, its rapid industrialization was fueled by foreign demand for Swedish timber and iron ore. Because export industries oppose tariffs whereas farmers support them, industry had an incentive to combine with workers against the noble class. During the 1890s, when tariff agitation was heavy, Swedish industry sided with the workers. Second, Swedish craftsmen were not adversely affected by the introduction of machine production. Swedish industrialization concentrated on products that had not yet been marketed, rather than those displaced by new manufacturing methods. As a result the number of artisans increased during Sweden's early decades of industrial growth. Third, because raw-material extractions industries were not particularly capital intensive, the changeover to an industrial-based society exerted less pressure on living standards. See Steven Kelman, "Swedish Social Democracy: Its Roots in the Economic and Social History of the Nation," honors thesis, Harvard University, 1970, chaps. 4 and 5.

31. See Bo Sarlvik, "Sweden: The Social Bases of the Parties in a Developmental Perspective," in Richard Rose, ed., *Electoral Behavior: A Comparative Handbook* (New York: Free Press, 1974), p. 398.

32. Sten Carlsson, *Svensk historia II* (Swedish history II), 2nd ed. (Stockholm: Bonniers, 1961), p. 592.

33. Ibid., pp. 605, 643–647.

34. Ibid., p. 601.

35. A similar effort at social egalitarianism occurred in government circles, when the practice of submitting proposals to the cabinet formally addressed to the king and signed "your most humble and obedient servant" was abolished. Now government leaders ride subways to work and appear on television. Equality has also entered the educational system: teachers no longer sit on raised platforms, and students no longer stand up when the teacher enters the room.

36. Steven Kelman, *Regulating America, Regulating Sweden: A Comparative Study of Occupational Safety and Health Policies* (Cambridge, Mass.: MIT Press, 1981), pp. 19–21.

37. Carlsson, *Svensk historia II*, p. 593.

38. Ibid., p. 513.

39. Ibid., pp. 603–605.

40. For a somewhat outdated but generally good description, see Albert H. Rosenthal, *The Social Programs of Sweden: A Search for Security in a Free Society* (Minneapolis: University of Minnesota Press, 1967).

41. The Liberals first proposed the establishment of a commission to investigate accident and old-age insurance for workers and also raised and pursued the issue of unemployment compensation, although no bill was passed before World War I. Hugh Heclo, *Modern Social Politics in Britain and Sweden* (New Haven: Yale University Press, 1974), pp. 71, 75, 180–184.

42. Ibid., pp. 192–193.

43. Ibid., pp. 217–219.

44. *Översikt över Riksdagen 1947* (Parliamentary overview 1947) (Stockholm: Norstedts, 1948), pp. 122–124.

45. *Översikt över Riksdagen 1946* (Parliamentary overview 1946) (Stockholm: Norstedts, 1947), p. 69.

46. Björn Molin, *Tjänstepensionsfrågan* (The supplementary pensions question) (Gotheborg: Akademiförlaget, 1965).

47. Unemployment, the Social Democrats note, is one of the most significant elements of inequality in a society. As the leading Swedish trade economists Anna Hedborg and Rudolf Meidner note in a recent book on the "Swedish model": "Full employment is the biggest pro-equality reform. It counteracts traditional sex roles in the labor market by easing the ability of women to exchange work in the home for paid work. It makes it easier for disadvantaged people such as the poorly educated and the handicapped to find jobs. It increases workers' freedom to choose and hence contributes to increased demands for the quality of the workplace environment." Anna Hedborg and Rudolf Meidner, *Folkhemsmodellen* (The "people's home" model) (Stockholm: Rabén and Sjögren, 1984), pp. 45–46.

48. See Carlsson, *Svensk historia II*, pp. 677–681, and Leif Lewin, *Planhushållningsdebatten* (The debate over a planned economy) (Stockholm: Almqvist and Wiksell, 1967).

49. On the active labor market policies see Hedborg and Meidner, *Folkhemsmodellen*, chap. 6.

50. *Arbetsmarknadspolitik* (Labor market policy) (Stockholm: SOU 1965:9).

51. 1936 Års Skattekommitté, *Betänkande med förslag till omläggningen av den direkta statsbeskattningen* (Report on changes in the system of direct taxation) (Stockholm: SOU 1937:42), p. 70. That commission also recommended replacing the existing progressive taxation system at the local level with a proportional system and suggested lowering tax rates for poorer people. The rates for all

others were kept the same, except for the rich, whose rates went up slightly. The commission also called for increases in corporate taxation. (Ibid., p. 267.)

52. Nils Elvander, *Svensk skattepolitik 1945–1970* (Swedish tax policy 1945–1970) (Stockholm: Rabén and Sjögren, 1972), p. 322.

53. Ibid., chap. 4.

54. Ibid., pp. 148, 151.

55. Lewin, *Planhushållningsdebatten,* chaps. 3–4.

56. See Berndt Öhman, *Fonder i en marknadsekonomi* (Wage-earner funds in a market economy) (Stockholm: Studieförbundet Näringsliv och samhälle, 1982). The joint Social Democratic-LO report on wage-earner funds is *Arbetarrörelsen och löntagarfonder* (The labor movement and wage-earner funds) (Stockholm: Tiden, 1981). For the perspective of a business leader involved in opposition to the funds, see Erland Waldenström, *Spelet om fonderna* (The wage-earner fund game) (Stockholm: Norstedts, 1982).

57. Bengt Lundberg, *Jämlikhet: Socialdemokratin och jämlikhetsbegreppet* (Equality: social democracy and the concept of equality) (Lund: Bokförlaget Dialog, 1979), p. 71.

58. Walter Korpi, "Socialpolitiken: hundraåring i snålblåst" (Social policy: hundred-year-old in difficult times) Occasional Paper 112, Institut för social-forskning, Stockholm, 1903, p. 108.

59. Ibid. Also see Hedborg and Meidner, *Folkhemsmodellen,* pp. 184–186.

60. Gunnar Myrdal, *An American Dilemma: The Negro Problem and Modern Democracy,* 20th anniversary ed. (New York: Harper and Row, 1962).

61. James Bryce, *The American Commonwealth,* 3rd ed. (New York: Macmillan, 1899).

62. Alexis de Tocqueville, *Democracy in America,* vols. 1 and 2 (New York: Knopf, 1945).

63. Gabriel A. Almond and Sidney Verba, *The Civic Culture* (Boston: Little, Brown, 1966), pp. 64–65.

64. Samuel Huntington, *American Politics: The Promise of Disharmony* (Cambridge, Mass.: Harvard University Press, 1981), p. 4.

65. J. R. Pole, *The Pursuit of Equality in American History* (Berkeley: University of California Press, 1978), p. 50.

66. Huntington, *American Politics,* p. 33.

67. Ibid., p. 15.

68. Sidney Verba and Gary R. Orren, *Equality in America: The View from the Top* (Cambridge, Mass.: Harvard University Press, 1985), p. 12.

69. Ibid., p. 4.

70. Seymour Martin Lipset, *The First New Nation,* 2nd ed. (New York: Norton, 1979), p. 341.

71. Huntington, *American Politics,* p. 197.

72. Louis Hartz, *The Liberal Tradition in America* (New York: Harcourt Brace Jovanovich, 1955), p. 6.

73. Huntington, *American Politics,* p. 19.

74. Ibid.

75. Ibid., p. 20.

76. Richard Hofstadter, *The Age of Reform* (New York: Knopf, 1956), p. 91. See also Edward Banfield and James Q. Wilson, *City Politics* (New York: Vintage Books, 1963), pp. 329–330.

77. Verba and Orren, *Equality in America,* chaps. 1, 11.

78. Huntington, *American Politics,* p. 24.

79. See Peter Blau and Otis Dudley Duncan, *The American Occupational Structure* (New York: Wiley, 1967); Seymour Martin Lipset, *Social Mobility in Industrial Society* (Berkeley: University of California Press, 1959).

80. This section, which briefly traces the history of the equality issue in the United States, draws heavily on the more extended discussion in Verba and Orren, *Equality in America,* chap. 2.

81. Pole, *The Pursuit of Equality,* p. 48; Verba and Orren, *Equality in America,* pp. 27–28.

82. Quoted in Pole, *The Pursuit of Equality,* p. 144.

83. Verba and Orren, *Equality in America,* p. 37.

84. The Populists declared that "the forces of reform this day organized will never cease to move forward until every wrong is remedied, with equal rights and equal privileges securely established for all the men and women in this country." Pole, *The Pursuit of Equality,* p. 209.

85. On the other hand, some of the Progressives' reforms actually undercut the increasing democratization of politics. Intentionally or not, certain Progressive proposals such as voter registration rules and various procedures that took power from political parties may have sharpened the economic bias against the political participation of lower-class citizens and given a greater voice to the upper strata. See Verba and Orren, *Equality in America,* pp. 40–41.

86. William E. Leuchtenburg, *Franklin D. Roosevelt and the New Deal* (New York: Harper and Row, 1963), p. 347.

87. Verba and Orren, *Equality in America,* pp. 41–44.

88. See John Kenneth Galbraith, *American Capitalism: The Concept of Countervailing Power* (Boston: Houghton Mifflin, 1952).

89. See Verba and Orren, *Equality in America,* chap. 7.

90. Jeffrey G. Williamson and Peter H. Lindert, *American Inequality: A Macroeconomic History* (New York: Academic Press, 1980), esp. pp. 3–31, 33–53.

91. Joseph A. Pechman and Benjamin A. Okner, *Who Bears the Tax Burden?* (Washington: Brookings Institution, 1974).

92. Lipset, *The First New Nation,* p. 327.

93. See Verba and Orren, *Equality in America,* chaps. 1, 11.

94. See Sidney Verba, Norman Nie, and Jae-on Kim, *Participation and Political Equality: A Seven-Nation Comparison* (New York: Cambridge University Press, 1979).

95. Verba and Orren, *Equality in America,* pp. 16–17.

96. Ibid., pp. 9–11.

97. Theodore H. White, "New Powers, New Politics," *New York Times Magazine,* Feb. 5, 1984, p. 22.

98. Speech by Lyndon Johnson, Howard University, June 4, 1965.

99. Peter Steinfels, *The Neoconservatives: The Men Who Are Changing America's Politics* (New York: Simon and Schuster, 1979), pp. 214–215.

100. Thomas Edsall, *The New Politics of Inequality: How Political Power Shapes Economic Policy* (New York: Norton, 1984).

101. *New York Times,* May 10, 1983, p. A19.

102. Michael J. Boskin, "Reaganomics and Income Distribution: A Longer-Term Perspective," *Journal of Contemporary Studies,* 5 (Summer 1982), pp. 31–44.

103. White, "New Powers, New Politics," p. 51.

3. Who Are the Leaders?

1. The literature on political elites and leadership is vast. For a general overview see Robert D. Putnam, *The Comparative Study of Political Elites* (Englewood Cliffs, N.J.: Prentice-Hall, 1976). Recent examples of elite research are in Moshe M. Czudnowski, ed., *Does Who Governs Matter?* (Dekalb: Northern Illinois University Press, 1982), and Moshe M. Czudnowski, ed., *Political Elites and Social Change* (Dekalb: Northern Illinois University Press, 1983). The definition of what is an elite varies substantially from study to study. Our definition is very broad, encompassing those who hold a wide range of positions of influence in various sectors of society. Our study differs from many of the traditional elite studies in that we deal neither with the recruitment or the circulation of political elites nor with the processes by which elites take part in decision making; rather we focus on the variations among leadership groups in their perceptions and values. Our study is, nevertheless, related to other elite studies. Although we do not study this directly, we assume that the values and perceptions of the groups with which we deal are of significance because these groups of leaders play important roles in decision making about issues of equality.

2. The Japanese elite sample includes bureaucrats, a group that does not fit into the study's approach of sampling nongovernmental elites. Our decision to limit the sample to nongovernmental elites was more practical than intellectual; we had limited resources and had to draw the line somewhere. The Japanese research group was particularly interested in bureaucrats and managed to mobilize sufficient resources to study this interesting and significant group. Because we analyze the various groups separately, the inclusion of bureaucrats in Japan enriches the analysis there without detracting from the comparative aspects of the study.

3. Occasionally, as will be evident in subsequent chapters, a similar differen-

tiation will be made in other countries. The local and national groups are distinct at a more basic level in Sweden than elsewhere, however, in terms of how they were selected and the questions asked.

4. In Sweden these questions were not asked of all leadership groups but there are enough data for comparison. Those in the local business, television reporters, and party samples were not asked the questions about acquaintanceships.

5. See T. J. Pempel and Keiichi Tsunekawa, "Corporatism without Labor? The Japanese Anomaly," in Philippe Schmitter and Gerhard Lehmbruch, eds., *Trends towards Corporatist Intermediation* (Beverly Hills: Sage Publications, 1979), chap. 9.

6. The need for certain political actors to expand the scope of a political contest by mobilizing bystanders is one of the main themes of E. E. Schattschneider's classic, *The Semi-Sovereign People* (New York: Holt, Rinehart and Winston, 1960). It is a key component of the strategy required of protest groups who lack the full panoply of political resources enjoyed by their opponents. See Michael Lipsky, *Protest in City Politics: Rent Strikes, Housing, and the Power of the Poor* (Chicago: Rand McNally, 1970).

7. In Sweden we did not ask specifically about speaking to an official but about contacting one. The question format was also substantially different. We inquired about the success of leaders' contacts with officials. Those leaders listed as contacting officials are those who reported either successful or unsuccessful contact with officials. The question is not directly comparable with that in the other nations, although the within-nation comparison among groups is valid. In the United States we also asked one question about writing to a member of Congress. Contacting an official is not the same as being successful in that contact. We shall present some data on that subject in Chapter 7.

4. Equality Demands and the Political System

1. Note that the trade-union leaders presented here are leaders of the blue-collar union federation. Leaders of the white-collar and professional union federations were also surveyed, and results for them will be presented in other chapters.

2. The mean scale scores for all Swedish party leaders surveyed are as follows:

	All but old/ handicapped	Government provide jobs	Government redistribute	Fair to tax rich
Social Democrat	3.9	1.5	1.1	1.3
Liberal	3.6	2.8	1.8	3.0
Central	3.4	2.8	1.7	2.8
Conservative	3.1	3.7	2.4	4.4

3. The question on aid to the old and handicapped may not be a very useful one for tapping the attitudes toward the welfare state in Japan in that Japanese views tend to be quite negative about dependence on others—see note 6 below.

4. Swedes do not typically use the expression "the poor" to refer to any group in contemporary Sweden, although the term is often used with regard to the Sweden of a hundred years ago, to the situation in Third World countries, and to poor people in the United States. Swedes would tend to use expressions such as "low-income earners" or "disadvantaged groups" instead. This created a dilemma for translations of these questions, because using the expression "the poor" would tend to change the respondent's frame of reference from Sweden toward societies in general. After consulting Swedish colleagues, we decided to retain the starker word "poor" (*fattig*) in the question about government's reducing the income gap. This was at the cost of universalizing it (and perhaps abstracting it from a strictly Swedish context) by changing the wording to "The government should work to substantially reduce the income gap between rich and poor in a country." On the second question about progressive taxation, we used the expression "disadvantaged groups" rather than "poor."

5. Ezra F. Vogel, *Japan as Number 1* (Cambridge, Mass.: Harvard University Press, 1979), pp. 201, 203. The specific nature of the question on the old and handicapped is highlighted in the following comments by Miyake et al. in their book on the Japanese part of the elite survey. "First, if we ask about the necessity of 'social welfare' without adding the phrase 'except for the old and handicapped,' or if we ask about the necessity of 'social security' which is conceptually broader than 'social welfare,' it is highly probable that a high degree of consensus in terms of both position and distance would emerge. We did not include such a question in the Elite Survey. However, we did so in the 1983 Japanese Election Survey. To the sample of Japanese citizens at large, i.e., national eligible voters, we posed two questions: one is the same one we asked in the Elite Survey, and the other is the question with the phrase '(social welfare) such as pension and medical care for the old.' The results were two quite different distributions of responses. Regarding the latter question, a great majority or more than seventy percent of respondents support the promotion of social welfare [while only half were supportive on the first]." Ichiro Miyake et al., *Byōdō o meguru erīto to taikō-erīto* (Elites and counterelites on equality) (Tokyo: Sobunsha, 1985), pp. 68–69.

6. See Chapter 6 for a closer analysis of attitudes on fair income distribution, an analysis that confirms this one.

7. For a presentation of the main arguments, see the contributions in John H. M. Laslett and Seymour Martin Lipset, eds., *Failure of a Dream? Essays in the History of American Socialism* (New York: Doubleday, 1974).

8. There are immigrant groups in Sweden whose economic status is generally lower than that of the average Swede, but they are not well organized nor do they raise any significant political demands, perhaps because most do not expect to

stay in Sweden. Fraternal organizations of immigrants do exist, but they raise few political demands. Many immigrant workers are union members, and the blue-collar unions sometimes raise demands of special interest to immigrants. Sweden has no significant native ethnic minorities; Lapps, for example, number only several thousand and make few complaints about their situation. Although the country has environmental and antinuclear groups somewhat comparable to the Japanese civic movements, we did not include them in our survey because they are not particularly associated with the equality issue. They tend to challenge the system on the growth-antigrowth issue.

9. Note that we did not survey bureaucrats in the United States or Sweden. The Swedish media sample consists of television and radio journalists only; print journalists appear in the party samples because of the party ties of Swedish news-papers. Note also that the sample of intellectuals in Sweden consists only of uni-versity professors; the American sample includes other intellectual leaders (considerably more than half are professors); and the Japanese sample includes both professors and independent intellectuals and cultural figures.

10. Sten Lindroth, *A History of Uppsala University, 1477–1977* (Stockholm: Almqvist & Wiksell, 1976) conveys the Swedish situation. On the American side see Seymour Martin Lipset, "American Intellectuals: Their Politics and Status," in *Political Man* (New York: Doubleday Anchor Books, 1960) and Seymour Mar-tin Lipset and Everett Carll Ladd, Jr., *The Divided Academy* (New York: Mc-Graw-Hill, 1975).

5. The Dimensions of Equality

1. Douglas Rae deliberately entitled his recent analysis of equality with the plural noun to emphasize the fact that there are many equalities and they are by no means always—or often—compatible with one another. See *Equalities* (Cam-bridge, Mass.: Harvard University Press, 1981).

2. For some of the vast literature see Philip E. Converse, "Attitudes and Non-Attitudes: Continuation of a Dialogue," in Edward Tufte, ed., *The Quantitative Study of Politics* (New York: Addison-Wesley, 1971); Philip E. Converse, "The Nature of Belief Systems in Mass Publics," in David E. Apter, ed., *Ideology and Discontent* (New York: Free Press, 1964); Norman Nie and Kristi Andersen, "Mass Belief Systems Revisited: Political Change and Attitude Structure," *Jour-nal of Politics,* 36 (August 1974), 540–587; John C. Pierce and Douglas D. Rose, "Non-Attitudes and American Public Opinion: The Examination of a Thesis," *American Political Science Review,* 68 (June 1974), 626–649; Norman H. Nie, Sidney Verba, and John R. Petrocik, *The Changing American Voter* (Cambridge, Mass.: Harvard University Press, 1980), chap. 8, epilogue; George Bishop, Alfred J. Tuchfarber, and Robert W. Oldendick, "Change in the Structure of American Political Attitudes: The Nagging Question of Question Wording," *American Journal of Political Science,* 22 (May 1978), 250–269; John L. Sulli-

van, James E. Piereson, and George E. Marcus, "Ideological Constraint in the Mass Public: A Methodological Critique and Some New Findings," *American Journal of Political Science,* 22 (May 1978), 233–249; Norman Nie and James N. Rabjohn, "Revisiting Mass Belief Systems Revisited: Or, Why Doing Research Is Like Watching a Tennis Match," *American Journal of Political Science,* 23 (February 1979), 139–175; John Petrocik, "The Changeable American Voter: Some Revisions of the Revision," in John C. Pierce and John L. Sullivan, eds., *The Electorate Reconsidered* (Beverly Hills: Sage Publications, 1980).

3. See Norman R. Luttbeg, "The Structure of Beliefs among Leaders and the Public," *Public Opinion Quarterly,* 32 (Fall 1968), 388–409; George F. Bishop, "The Effect of Education on Ideological Consistency," *Public Opinion Quarterly,* 40 (Fall 1976), 337–348.

4. For a description of the factor analytical technique used see G. Donald Ferree, Jr., "Appendix B: Factor Analysis and Methods," in Sidney Verba and Gary R. Orren, *Equality in America: The View from the Top* (Cambridge, Mass.: Harvard University Press, 1985).

5. We list the factors in each nation in the order in which they emerged from the factor rotation.

6. The Inequality of Income

1. Most economists argue that earnings are determined by marginal productivity on the demand side and in proportion to the scarcity of the skill in question or a worker's worry and responsibility on the supply side. See Albert Rees, *Economics of Work and Pay* (New York: Harper and Row, 1973), chaps. 4, 5; and Harold F. Lydell, *The Structure of Earnings* (Oxford: Clarendon Press, 1968), pp. 125–127. Those who have argued that economic characteristics such as level of affluence or structure of the economy affect the degree of income inequality include Harold Wilensky, *The Welfare State and Equality* (Berkeley: University of California Press, 1975) and Robert W. Jackman, *Politics and Social Equality: A Comparative Analysis* (New York: Wiley, 1975).

2. See, among others, Christopher Hewitt, "The Effect of Political Democracy and Social Democracy on Equality in Industrial Democracies: A Cross-National Analysis," *American Sociological Review,* 42 (1977), pp. 450–463; Douglas A. Hibbs, Jr., "Political Parties and Macro-Economic Policy," *American Political Science Review,* 71 (1977), pp. 1467–87; and Steven Sack, "The Effects of Political Participation and Socialist Party Strength on the Degree of Income Inequality," *American Sociological Review,* 44 (1979), pp. 168–172.

3. Some economists argue that wage differentials also reflect people's values. See, for example, Harry Phelps Brown, *The Inequality of Pay* (Berkeley and Los Angeles: University of California Press, 1977); Jan Pen, *Income Distribution* (London: Allen Tate, Penguin Press, 1971); and Derek L. Phillips, *Equality, Justice, and Rectification* (London: Academic Press, 1979).

4. See Steven Kelman, "Limited Government: An Incoherent Concept," *Journal of Policy Analysis and Management,* 3 (Fall 1983), pp. 31–44.

5. See Lester Thurow, *Generating Inequality* (New York: Basic Books, 1975). This notion also plays an important role in theories of job ladders and within-firm labor markets and in the origin of the downward stickiness of wages in macroeconomic theory. See, for example, Arthur Okun, *Prices and Quantities: A Macroeconomic Analysis* (Washington: Brookings Institution, 1981).

6. Isaiah Berlin, "Equality," *Proceedings of the Aristotelian Society,* 56 (1955–56), pp. 301–326.

7. See Joel Feinberg, *Social Philosophy* (Englewood Cliffs, N.J.: Prentice-Hall, 1973), chap. 7.

8. John Rawls, *A Theory of Justice* (Cambridge, Mass.: Harvard University Press, 1971).

9. Ibid., pp. 100–104.

10. On this issue see Lester Thurow, "The Pursuit of Equity," *Dissent,* Summer 1976, pp. 253–259.

11. For the United States see Joseph A. Pechman and Benjamin A. Okner, *Who Bears the Tax Burden?* (Washington: Brookings Institution, 1974), p. 61. They find that, for most assumptions about the incidence of taxes across income groups, the distribution of income before and after taxes is quite similar. Similar analyses of the before and after tax distribution in Japan show a parallel result. See Keizai Kikakucho (Economic Planning Agency), *Shotoku shisan bunpu no jiitai to mondaiten* (Status and problems of income and wealth distribution) (Tokyo: Okurasho Insadtsukyoku, 1975), pp. 316–317.

In an analysis of the impact of government taxes and transfers in a number of countries, Hicks and Swank find that the percentage change in the Gini index of income inequality owing to governmental intervention is fairly low in the United States and Japan compared with other nations. The United States ranked ninth and Japan tenth out of thirteen nations in the degree to which government actions reduced the Gini index; the reductions were 14 and 13 percent respectively. Hicks and Swank find that Sweden ranks first among the thirteen countries in the percentage change in the Gini index due to governmental intervention via taxes and transfers; the reduction was 36 percent in Sweden. See Alexander Hicks and Duane H. Swank, "Governmental Redistribution in Rich Capitalist Democracies," paper presented at the Annual Meeting of the American Political Science Association, Chicago, September 1983. They base their estimates on Malcolm Sawyer, "Income Distribution in the OECD Nations" (Paris: OECD, 1960). See also J. Corina van Arnhem and Geurt J. Schotsman, "Do Parties Affect the Distribution of Income? The Case of Advanced Capitalist Democracies," in Francis Castles, ed., *The Impact of Parties* (Beverly Hills: Sage Publications, 1982). An alternative estimate of the Gini index finds even less change in Japan due to national income tax: a change from a pretax Gini index of 0.189 to a posttax Gini of 0.182. Keizai Kikakucho, *Shotoku shishan bunpu no jiitai to mondaiten,* pp. 316–317. Such comparisons are difficult because of differences in the income concept used and in the assumptions chosen with regard to taxes and expenditures. But the difference appears robust even if alternative assumptions are used. See the comparison between Sweden and the United States in Thomas Franzen, Kirsten Lovgren, and Irma Rosenberg, "Redistributional Effects of Taxes and Public Expenditures in Sweden," *Swedish Journal of Economics,* 177 (1975), 31–55.

The Luxembourg Income Study reports relatively little difference between Sweden and the United States in terms of the effects of direct taxes on income inequality. The authors find a substantial reduction in inequality in both nations due to direct taxes. As they point out, the study does not take into account the impact of transfers on which Sweden and the United States differ substantially or the phenomenon of "bracket creep" that took place in the United States in the few years preceding the LIS study. (See Michael O'Higgins, Gunther Schmaus, and Geoffrey Stephenson, "Income Distribution and Redistribution: A Microdata Analysis for Seven Countries," Luxembourg Income Study, Centre d'Etudes de Populations, de Pauvreté et de Politiques Socio-Economiques, June 1985, pp. 16–20.)

The impact of taxes on the distribution of income is somewhat different in the United States and Japan. In Japan, the tax structure is relatively nonprogressive up to the very highest incomes, where it begins to slope upward more sharply. See Ōkurashō (Ministry of Finance), *Zaisei kinyū tōkei geppō* (Monthly report of fiscal and monetary statistics), August 1979, pp. 32–33. For examples of how the data analyzed in this chapter would differ if one used posttax measures, see Sidney Verba and Gary R. Orren, *Equality in America: The View from the Top* (Cambridge, Mass.: Harvard University Press, 1985), chap. 7. The use of a question about income after taxes and transfers takes into account the major impact of the government on income differentiation. It does not take into account the full impact, however, because it does not cover the possible redistributive impact of government spending on social services and collective consumption.

12. Phelps Brown, *The Inequality of Pay,* uses quite precisely defined categories in his work on the subject. See also Harold L. Wilensky, "The Political Economy of Income Distribution," in J. Milton Yinger and Stephen J. Cutler, eds., *Major Social Issues: A Multidisciplinary View* (New York: Free Press, 1978), pp. 87–108; and Erik O. Wright and Luca Perrone, "Marxist Class Categories and Income Inequality," *American Sociological Review,* 42 (1977), pp. 32–55.

13. The sources for the objective measures of earnings for occupations are as follows.

For Japan, the figure for doctors was kindly provided by Kcizo Takemi based on a national random sample of doctors with more than 5.1 beds in 1979 (*n* = 1,500); top executive: *Sandē Mainichi,* May 24, 1979; airline captain: interview with an airline captain with ten years' experience; professor, schoolteacher, and policeman: Nihon Jinji Gyosei Kenkyusho, *Kyūyo shō-roppō* (The wage laws of government employees) (Gakuyo Shobo, 1980); carpenter and auto worker: Jinji-in (National Personnel Authority), "Minkan kyūyo no jitti" (The status of wages in the private sector), 1980; bank teller and unskilled manual worker: data based on a model wage by Kansai Kei-ei-sha Kyokai (Kansai Employers Association).

For Sweden, unless otherwise noted, data are from *Arbetsmarknadsstatistisk Årsbok 1978* (Workingman's statistical yearbook 1978) (Stockholm: Statistiska Centralbyrån, 1978); the SAF; Volvo; and Byggnadsarbetareförbundet (Construction Workers Union). All posttax figures are estimates, calculated according to the following official taxes: 50,000 to 60,000 crowns per year—25 to 30 percent tax; 60,000 to 100,000 crowns per year—50 to 60 percent tax; 100,000 crowns and more per year—85 percent tax.

For the United States, executive: *Business Week,* May 23, 1977; star center and professor: "A Random Sample of Pay," *Time,* June 13, 1977; doctor, aeronautical engineer, and plumber: Bureau of Labor Statistics, "Occupational Outlook Handbook," 1978; cabinet secretary: *World Almanac and Book of Facts,* 1976; auto worker and elevator operator: 1970 U.S. Census extrapolated to 1976; policeman: Bureau of Labor Statistics, "Current Wage Developments," February 1979, extrapolated to 1976; elementary-school teacher and bank teller: Bureau of Labor Statistics, "Current Wage Developments," February 1977.

14. The estimates of the differences in earnings between various levels seem to be of the correct order of magnitude among the three nations. Assar Lindbeck indicates that the wage differential between skilled and unskilled workers in Sweden is about half that in other advanced industrial nations. How well our data conform to his estimates depends on the specific occupations involved, but they are close to that order of difference. Lindbeck also compares factor income (earnings before taxes and transfers) with disposable income after government intervention. Several of the occupational categories for which he reports data are similar to those about which we questioned our respondents. The estimates by our respondents of earnings before and after government intervention are quite close to the figures he presents (in thousands of Swedish crowns per year):

	Lindbeck data		Respondent estimates	
	Factor income	Disposable income	Pretax income	Disposable income
Auto worker	60	38	59.6	38.9
Bank teller	70	40	70.0	42.7
Dishwasher	40	30	41.4	30.4
Engineer	100	50	116.9	57.2

See Assar Lindbeck, "Inequality and Redistribution Policy Issues: Principles and Swedish Experience," in *Education, Inequality, and Life Chances,* vol. 2 (Paris: OECD, 1975), pp. 282, 312.

15. There are two possible reasons why the leaders in Japan would cut doctors' incomes so substantially. First, the respondents overestimate doctors' earnings substantially and thus would tend to cut their incomes more than the incomes of others. The overestimation of doctors' earnings probably reflects a social stereotype based on frequent reports about the high earnings of doctors, often in relation to reputed tax evasion, on television and in newspapers. The second reason may derive from a mismatch between the social standing of doctors and their ranking in the earnings hierarchy. In Japan, doctors are considered to be lower in general social standing than top executives and professors, but they are perceived to earn more than individuals in these two occupations. The leaders may want to cut the earnings of doctors so that their rank in earnings will correspond more closely with their general social standing. See Kenichi Tominaga, ed., *Nihon no kaisō kōzō* (Social structure in Japan) (Tokyo: University of Tokyo Press, 1975), p. 446, for the general social standing of doctors in relation to other occupations.

16. The data presented in this chapter and in Chapters 7 and 9 are based on calculations of logged income estimates. We use logged estimates for several reasons. For one thing, this procedure reduces the impact on group means of estimates that are extreme. Furthermore, it more accurately reflects the way individuals think about income differences—in ratio terms rather than in absolute terms (an income of $10,000 is to an income of $20,000 as $100,000 is to $200,000, rather than as $100,000 is to $110,000). This is reflected in logged income quite effectively. To compute logged income estimates for a group, we first log the estimate (of either perceived or fair earnings) for each individual leader, compute the mean for the leaders in a particular group, and then take the antilog of the mean to convert back to the original scale. To calculate income ratios, we first compute the ratios on the raw estimates for each individual, log them, compute the group means, and take the antilog. For a fuller discussion see Verba and Orren, *Equality in America,* chap. 7.

For a discussion of conceptual differences among various popular measures of intergroup income equality, see Mark Fossett and Scott J. South, "The Measurement of Intergroup Income Inequality: A Conceptual Review," *Social Forces,* 61 (1983), 655–671. The authors find various measures to be flawed in one way or another and recommend a measure of inequality based on the means of the logarithm of income, a measure quite similar to that used here.

17. In the unlikely case that one half of a leadership group want to double earnings and the other half want to cut them in half, the resulting ratio would be 1.

18. The similarity between the United States and Japan may be somewhat misleading. In Japan the lowest-paying occupation that anchors the bottom of our scale is a "young, newly hired manual worker." Because earnings in Japan are heavily affected by age and experience, this provides a lower base in Japan than in the United States. The Japanese income gap, as we shall see, is not as wide as in the United States—either in terms of the perceptions of the respondents or

in terms of their values of what is appropriate. We shall return to this point in the next section when we consider the income gap among several pairs of occupations.

19. The ratios are calculated in the same manner as are those discussed previously between what the income for an occupation is perceived to be and what it ought to be. See text and note 13.

20. The difference between Japan and the United States would be greater if the Japanese lowest income earner were not designated a *young* worker.

21. Psychological experiments suggest that people's judgments in uncertain situations are influenced by the cognitive world with which they are familiar, phenomena referred to in the literature as "anchoring" and "availability." See Daniel Kahneman et al., eds., *Judgment under Uncertainty: Heuristics and Biases* (Cambridge: Cambridge University Press, 1981), pp. 14–16, chap. 11.

7. Has Equality Gone Too Far?

1. Although the theme of the welfare state and equality going too far is relevant in Japan and the United States as well, we pursue it only in Sweden, taking advantage of questions asked there but not in other nations—especially questions on income before and after taxes and government transfers. In the United States, Charles Murray's book *Losing Ground: American Social Policy 1950–1980* (New York: Basic Books, 1984) was but the latest salvo in the debate on the impact of welfare measures—especially income support measures. The issue was whether income support programs create rather than alleviate poverty by reducing work incentives. For criticism of Murray, see David T. Ellwood and Lawrence H. Summers, "Is Welfare Really the Problem?" *Public Interest* (Spring 1986), pp. 57–78; and Christopher Jencks, "How Poor Are the Poor?" *New York Review of Books,* 32 (May 9, 1985).

2. The word used in Swedish for welfare in the last item was *socialhjälp,* which is the closest to the American concept of being on welfare. The previous question used the expression *bidrag,* which includes social-welfare benefits available not only to the poorest citizens.

3. The first two questions were asked of members of Parliament and the mass public in surveys appearing in Soren Holmberg, *"Riksdagen representerar svenska folket"* ("Parliament represents the Swedish people") (Lund: Studentlitteratur, 1974). The second question appears for a mass public sample in Olof Petersson, *Väljarna och valet 1976* (Voters and the election 1976) (Stockholm: Statistiska centralbyran, 1977). The third question appears for a blue-collar trade union leadership and membership sample in Leif Lewin, *Hur styrs facket?* (How are unions governed?) (Stockholm: Rabén and Sjögren, 1976). The wording of Lewin's question is very slightly different.

4. Mean responses for the questions in 1969 are on a five-point scale, where "ambivalent" was coded as 3, "disagree somewhat" as 4, and "strongly disagree"

as 5. Our 1978 survey responses have, for purposes of this comparison, been coded similarly, with "don't know/no opinion" coded as 3. Thus the numbers for 1978 are slightly different from the data in Figure 7.1. The percentage of respondents giving this response was very small in both surveys. The 1969 data are discussed in Holmberg, *"Riksdagen representerar svenska folket,"* p. 43.

5. See also Steven Kelman, *Regulating America, Regulating Sweden: A Comparative Study of Occupational Safety and Health Policy* (Cambridge, Mass.: MIT Press, 1981), chap. 7.

6. For a discussion of the Swedish economy, see the report of the 1980 Long-Term Planning Commission, *Tillväxt eller stagnation?* (Growth or stagnation?) (Stockholm: SOU 1982:14), and Bengt-Arne Vedin, *Innovationsklimatet i Sverige* (The innovation climate in Sweden) (Stockholm: Studieförbundet näringsliv och samhälle, 1982). For two views arguing for various limitations of the welfare state, see Staffan Burenstam Linder, *Den hjärtlösa välfärdsstaten* (The heartless welfare state) (Stockholm: Timbro, 1983), and Klas Eklund, *Den bistra sanningen* (The bitter truth) (Stockholm: Tiden, 1982).

8. Political Equality

1. For a general statement of the position of the media, see Stanley Rothman, "The Mass Media in Post-Industrial Society," in S. M. Lipset, ed., *The Third Century* (Stanford: Hoover Institution Press, 1979).

2. For a closer analysis of the materials in the United States, see Sidney Verba and Gary R. Orren, *Equality in America: The View from the Top* (Cambridge, Mass.: Harvard University Press, 1985), esp. chap. 10. For further data on Japan see Ikuo Kabashima and Jeffrey Broadbent, "Referent Pluralism: Mass Media and Politics in Japan," *Journal of Japanese Studies,* 12 (1986), 329–361.

3. The one exception is that business leaders rank themselves fairly low in the hierarchy. This is an example of a phenomenon known as influence denial to which we shall return.

4. For a further discussion see Robert A. Scalapino and Junnosuke Masumi, *Parties and Politics in Contemporary Japan* (Berkeley: University of California Press, 1962), and Taketsugu Tsurutani, *Political Change in Japan* (New York: Longman, 1977), pp. 70–115. See also Haruhiro Fukui, "Studies in Policymaking: A Review of the Literature," in T. J. Pempel, ed., *Policymaking in Contemporary Japan* (Ithaca: Cornell University Press, 1977), pp. 22–58.

5. Chitoshi Yanaga, *Big Business in Japanese Politics* (New Haven: Yale University Press, 1969), argues for the dominant role of big business in Japanese politics. See also Fukuji Taguchi, *Shakai shūdan no seiji kinō* (The political functions of social groups) (Tokyo: Miraisha, 1969).

6. For a perceptive discussion of these changes, see Takashi Inoguchi, "Politicians, Bureaucrats and Interest Groups in the Legislative Process," paper delivered at the Workshop on One-Party Dominance, Ithaca, April 1984. Inoguchi

draws on Muramatsu Michio, *Sengo Nihon no kanryōsei* (Postwar Japanese bureaucracy) (Tokyo: Tōyōkeizai Shinpōsha, 1981).

7. See T. J. Pempel and Keiichi Tsunekawa, "Corporatism without Labor? The Japanese Anomaly," in Philippe Schmitter and Gerhard Lehmbruch, *Trends towards Corporatist Intermediation* (Beverly Hills: Sage Publications, 1979), chap. 9.

8. Marvin Olsen's study of the influence ratings that leaders of various organizations gave their own organizations found that, before the switch in government, the LO rated themselves as much more influential than other groups. As we shall see, our data are consistent with this: LO leaders, when asked in our study about influence before the change in government, place themselves at the top. See Marvin Olsen, *Participatory Pluralism: Political Participation and Influence in the United States and Sweden* (Chicago: Nelson-Hall, 1982), p. 224. Olsen has a very good description of the various influence channels used in Sweden and leader ratings of their relative importance.

9. An example of the structuralist argument, phrased in terms of the privileged position of business, is found in Charles E. Lindblom, *Politics and Markets: The World's Political-Economic Systems* (New York: Basic Books, 1977), esp. chap. 13.

10. On this issue see Charles Tilly, "Revolutions and Collective Violence," in Fred I. Greenstein and Nelson Polsby, eds., *Handbook of Political Science* (Reading, Mass.: Addison-Wesley, 1975), III, 506–509.

11. In the 1980s labor may also have become a liability to Democratic candidates who appear too closely connected to special interests. That labor unions would be such a liability because of their perceived influence is, of course, consistent with the argument in this chapter.

12. This is not an artifact of a tendency in Sweden to use the rating scale in a restrictive way. In relation to other groups the magnitude of desired changes in Sweden is similar to elsewhere.

13. The leaders of the Japanese Communist party in the left party category would cut the BLL from an influence level of 4.8 to 2.9, the lowest level given them by any group. In contrast the Japanese Socialist party leaders would raise them from 4.1 to 4.8, the highest rank given them by any group save the BLL leaders themselves.

9. Political and Economic Equality

1. The presentation of material in this chapter parallels and draws on the analysis of data for the United States in Sidney Verba and Gary R. Orren, *Equality in America: The View from the Top* (Cambridge, Mass.: Harvard University Press, 1985), chap. 10.

2. See Talcott Parsons, "The Distribution of Power in American Society," in *Structure and Process in Modern Societies* (Glencoe, Ill.: Free Press, 1960), pp.

199–225, and James S. Coleman, "Political Money," *American Political Science Review,* 44 (1970), 1074–87.

3. Lester C. Thurow, *The Zero-Sum Society* (New York: Basic Books, 1980).

4. See Richard Easterlin, "Does Money Buy Happiness?" *Public Interest,* 30 (Winter 1973), 3; and Thurow, *The Zero-Sum Society,* p. 18. Also see Lee Rainwater, *What Money Buys* (New York: Basic Books, 1974), chap. 3.

5. This discussion is somewhat oversimplified. The situation is more complex. Someone else's gain in influence might increase my own, if the person or group who gains were my ally. I necessarily lose influence only when the influence gainer is active in the same policy arena as I am and has different preferences. A gain by my ally can be my gain as well. It is possible, however, that a gain by my ally may strengthen the position I prefer in the policy arena but reduce my own influence within the alliance. Indeed, political leaders are often more wary of their positions vis-à-vis their closest collaborators than they are of the positions of their antagonists.

6. Talcott Parsons in his review of C. Wright Mills's *Power Elite* stressed that power and influence can be thought of as resources that can expand to the benefit of all society. See Parsons, "Distribution of Power." Arnold Tannenbaum makes a similar point in relation to organizations: the amount of influence in an organization can vary. In some industries more influence is exerted over the behavior of the participants than in others—exerted not necessarily by management but by all participants. See Arnold Tannenbaum et al., *Hierarchy in Organizations* (San Francisco: Jossey-Bass, 1974), p. 220. For the contrary position—that influence is a fixed quantity—see Ralf Dahrendorf, *Class and Class Conflict in Industrial Societies* (Stanford: Stanford University Press, 1968).

7. Sweden, as discussed in Chapter 6, differs from the other two countries in that respondents do not uniformly want to see the earnings of the top earner reduced. In some cases groups would prefer to see the top earners receive more after-tax income. But this difference between Sweden and the other two nations does not change the overall point to be made about Figure 9.1, which is that all changes leave an earnings gap between the top and bottom earners.

8. The sharpness of the cut is obscured on the graph because of the log scale used, but it is apparent on close inspection.

9. There are, of course, differences among these groups which would be revealed by regression slopes rather than correlations. The slopes would all be positive but the steepness would vary because the groups differ in how steep an income hierarchy they desire. For our purposes, however, the order of the hierarchy is what counts.

10. See Dan Usher, *The Economic Prerequisite to Democracy* (New York: Columbia University Press, 1981), pp. 28–31, for an interesting discussion of the greater conflict associated with the change of rankings in a hierarchy compared with a change in the distribution of rewards that maintain current positions.

11. An interesting discussion of the general view that normative consensus is

consistent with high levels of political conflict appears in Samuel Huntington, *American Politics: The Promise of Disharmony* (Cambridge, Mass.: Harvard University Press, 1981).

10. Gender Equality

1. See Steven Kelman, "Party Strength and System Governability in the Face of New Political Demands: The Case of Feminism" (manuscript).

2. Eva Moberg, "Kvinnans villkorliga frigivning," in Hans Hederberg, ed., *Unga liberaler* (Young liberals) (Stockholm: Almqvist and Wiksell, 1961).

3. *Familjen i framtiden: en socialistisk familjpolitik* (The family of the future: a socialist family policy) (Stockholm: Sveriges Socialdemokratiska Kvinnoförbund, 1972).

4. Ibid., p. 5.

5. Ibid., p. 63.

6. Ibid., p. 5.

7. These features are noted in Karin Widerberg, *Kvinnor, klasser, och lagar, 1750–1980* (Women, classes, and laws, 1750–1980) (Stockholm: Liber, 1980), p. 104.

8. Ibid., p. 105. A report on these activities appears in Rita Liljestrom et al., *Roller i omvandling* (Roles in transition) (Stockholm: SOU 1976:11).

9. Much of the history of women's suffrage in the United States revolves around the relation of votes for women to votes for blacks. Suffragists often formed political alliances with white supremacists, seeking women's suffrage at the expense of universal suffrage. See Aileen Kraditor, *The Ideas of the Woman Suffrage Movement* (New York: Columbia University Press, 1963).

10. Betty Friedan, *The Feminine Mystique* (New York: Norton, 1963); Kate Millett, *Sexual Politics* (New York: Doubleday, 1970).

11. On the early history of NOW see Barbara Deckard, *The Women's Movement* (New York: Harper and Row, 1975), chap. 2.

12. Jo Freeman, *The Politics of Women's Liberation* (New York: McKay, 1975), p. 85; and Betty Friedan, *It Changed My Life: Writings on the Women's Movement* (New York: Norton, 1985), pp. 107–108, 147–157.

13. Quoted from Maren Lockwood Carden, *The New Feminist Movement* (New York: Russell Sage, 1974), p. 117.

14. See Jeremy Rabkin, "Office of Federal Contract Compliance," in James Q. Wilson, ed., *The Politics of Regulation* (New York: Basic Books, 1980).

15. On the initial passage of the ERA in Congress see Janet K. Boles, *The Politics of the Equal Rights Amendment* (New York: Longman, 1979).

16. For the votes see *Congressional Quarterly,* October 16, 1971, and March 25, 1972, pp. 2145, 692.

17. Boles, *The Politics of the Equal Rights Amendment,* p. 64.

18. Janet K. Boles, "Systemic Factors Underlying Legislative Responses to

Women Suffrage and the Equal Rights Amendment," *Women and Politics*, 2 (Spring 1982), 5–22.

19. See Raymond Tatalovich and Byron Daynes, *The Politics of Abortion: A Study of Community Conflict in Public Policymaking* (New York: Praeger, 1981).

20. For the history of movements for women's suffrage in Japan see Fusae Ichikawa, ed., *Nihon fujin mondai shiryō shūsei* (Data on feminist issues in Japan) (Tokyo: Domesu Shuppan, 1977), and Katsuko Kodama, *Fujin sanseiken undō shōshi* (A history of the women's suffrage movements) (Tokyo: Domesu Shuppan, 1981). In English see Susan J. Pharr, *Political Women in Japan* (Berkeley: University of California Press, 1981).

21. Pharr, *Political Women in Japan*, p. 15.

22. Ichikawa, *Nihon fujin mondai shiryō shūsei*, p. 72, and Kiyoko Nishi, ed., *Senryōka no Nihon fujinseisaku* (Feminist policies in Japan under the occupation) (Tokyo: Domesu Shuppan, 1985), pp. 23–24.

23. Our sample of feminist leaders in Japan included leaders of those civic movements.

24. Hanako Nuita, "Kokuren fujin no jūnen o furikaette" (Looking back at the United Nations' decade for women), *Jurist Zokkan Sōgō Tokushū*, No. 39, 1985.

25. Ichikawa, *Nihon fujin mondai shiryō shūsei*, p. 74.

26. Our sample of feminist leaders included leaders of thirty-eight women's associations who joined in a 1975 meeting to criticize governmental plans as lukewarm. This included the Federation of Women Voters.

27. See Appendix Table A.1.

28. For the 1975 results see Ministry of Foreign Affairs, *Status of Women in Modern Japan* (Tokyo, 1975), p. 21. For 1982 see Prime Minister's Office, *Comparison of Results of Surveys on Women's Problems in Selected Nations* (Tokyo, 1983), p. 7.

29. Ministry of Foreign Affairs, *Status of Women*, p. 22.

30. We also sampled leaders of the women's federations of the different political parties. Their attitudes more closely resembled those of their male counterparts in their respective parties than the attitudes of women in other parties.

31. The actual wording of questions about the role of women involved two statements on either end of a seven-point scale.

32. This pattern is less clear for Sweden on the question regarding whether the responsibility for women not advancing lies with discrimination against them or with women themselves. As can be seen in Figure 10.1, responses of all Swedish respondents to this question differed rather dramatically from those of respondents in the United States and Japan. Responses bunched together, indicating a high degree of consensus, and they were generally quite conservative, in the sense that respondents were relatively reticent about giving a proequality response of attributing blame to social discrimination, compared with the general run of answers to other equality questions in the survey, involving economic as well as gender equality, where Swedish responses tended generally to be to the left of those

typical in Japan and in the United States. We suggest that this anomaly results from actual differences in Swedish as compared with American and Japanese society, where there is probably less discrimination against women. This question about the causes of the inequality of women did not load on the feminism factor in Sweden, although it did do so in the United States and Japan. If we look at the other question that loaded on the feminism factor in Sweden—whether women with husbands should be laid off before men—we see a pattern of partisan differences similar to the one on the question reported here about whether women should stay at home. (The question regarding layoffs is not reported here because, although it was asked in the American survey, it was not posed in the Japanese one.)

33. See Chapter 5 for a discussion of these scales.

34. On this issue and on the general issue of the cleavage between traditional values and westernization in the Japanese party system, see Joji Watanuki, *Politics in Postwar Japanese Society* (Tokyo: University of Tokyo Press, 1977), chap. 5.

11. Conclusion

1. The classic account of the extension of the meaning of citizenship is T. H. Marshall, *Class, Citizenship, and Social Development* (Garden City, N.Y.: Doubleday, 1964). Gunnar Myrdal's *An American Dilemma* (New York: Harper, 1944) is one of many books that have traced the conflict between political democracy and racial inequality in the United States and elsewhere.

2. This is the main theme of Sidney Verba, Norman H. Nie, and Jae-on Kim, *Participation and Political Equality: A Seven-Nation Comparison* (New York: Cambridge University Press, 1979).

3. See Douglas A. Hibbs, Jr., "Political Parties and Macro Economic Policy," *American Political Science Review,* 71 (December 1977), 1467–87; David T. Cameron, "The Expansion of the Public Economy: A Comparative Analysis," *American Political Science Review,* 72 (December 1978); Alexander Hicks and Duane H. Swank, "Governmental Redistribution in Rich Capitalist Democracies," paper presented at the annual meeting of the American Political Science Association, Chicago, September 1983; and Hicks and Swank, "On the Political Economy of Welfare Expansion: A Comparative Analysis of Eighteen Advanced Capitalist Democracies, 1966–1971," *Comparative Political Studies,* 17 (April 1984). The relationship between citizen participation and the level of government activity is complex. Some "public choice" theorists argue that there is a dynamic leading to governments that are too big—though not necessarily in a direction that fosters equality. A critical essay on this subject is Richard A. Musgrave, "Leviathan Cometh—Or Does He?" in Helen F. Ladd and T. Nicholaus Tideman, eds., *Tax and Expenditure Limitations* (Washington: Urban Institute, 1981).

4. On this general theme see Steven Kelman, *Regulating America, Regulating Sweden* (Cambridge, Mass.: MIT Press, 1981), chap. 4 and pp. 235–236.

5. See John L. Palmer and Isabel V. Sawhill, eds., *The Reagan Record* (Cambridge, Mass.: Ballinger, 1984).

6. See Chapter 2. For a fuller exposition of this point see Sidney Verba and Gary R. Orren, *Equality in America: The View from the Top* (Cambridge, Mass.: Harvard University Press, 1985), chap. 3.

7. It is ironic, however, that the entry of black voters into the politics of the American South has been accompanied by a general transformation of southern politics: although blacks now have an important voice, it is in a Democratic party that is growing continuously weaker.

8. On the Japanese-type welfare society see Joji Watanuki, "Is There a Japanese-type Welfare Society?" *International Sociology,* 1 (1986), 259–269.

Appendix

1. It is also worth noting that—in contradistinction to both the United States and Japan—the strength of the party system in Sweden is such that party dominates other groups. Thus, even though editors are classified as journalists in both the United States and Japan, they are grouped with party leaders in Sweden—according to the party affiliation of their papers. Similarly, leaders of women's organizations associated with particular parties are categorized as party leaders, not feminist leaders.

2. Leaders in the United States are also predominantly white. Aside from the leaders of black organizations, blacks are underrepresented in all other leadership categories. The percentage of blacks in our U.S. sample ranges from less than 1 percent among business leaders to 8 percent among leaders of feminist organizations. For a fuller discussion see Verba and Orren, *Equality in America,* pp. 62–64.

3. For U.S. feminists this finding relates to their youth and elite status. For the blacks it is, at least in part, a reflection of the traditionally important role of the black church and its leadership. Many of the black leaders in the sample were members of the clergy and had theological degrees.

4. Particularly for the Japanese, one needs to take into account the major shift in the educational pattern that accompanied the end of World War II. Almost all the respondents' fathers—with the possible exception of those of the students—would have gone through the pre-occupation education system, in which many had very little formal schooling.

Index